Neighborhoods, Communities, and Urban Marginality

Series Editors
Carol Camp Yeakey
Washington University in St. Louis
St. Louis, MO, USA

Walter R. Allen
University of California
Los Angeles, CA, USA

This series examines the ecology of neighborhoods and communities in not only twenty-first century America, but across the globe. By taking an ecological approach, the study of neighborhoods takes into account not just structures, buildings and geographical boundaries, but also the relationship and adjustment of humans to highly dense urban environments in a particular area or vicinity. As the violent events of the past year in marginalized urban neighborhoods and communities across the country have demonstrated, "place matters." The series contain original research about the power of place, that is, the importance of where one lives, how public policies have transformed the shape and geography of inequality and disparity in our metropolitan areas, and, the ways in which residents impacted by perceived inequality are trying to confront the problem.

More information about this series at
http://www.palgrave.com/gp/series/15097

Enikő Vincze • Norbert Petrovici
Cristina Raț • Giovanni Picker
Editors

Racialized Labour in Romania

Spaces of Marginality at the Periphery of Global Capitalism

Editors
Enikő Vincze
Faculty of European Studies
Babeș-Bolyai University
Cluj-Napoca, Romania

Norbert Petrovici
Department of Sociology
Babeș-Bolyai University
Cluj-Napoca, Romania

Cristina Raț
Department of Sociology
Babeș-Bolyai University
Cluj-Napoca, Romania

Giovanni Picker
School of Social Policy
University of Birmingham
Birmingham, UK

Neighborhoods, Communities, and Urban Marginality
ISBN 978-3-319-76272-2   ISBN 978-3-319-76273-9 (eBook)
https://doi.org/10.1007/978-3-319-76273-9

Library of Congress Control Number: 2018939164

© The Editor(s) (if applicable) and The Author(s) 2019
This work is subject to copyright. All rights are solely and exclusively licensed by the Publisher, whether the whole or part of the material is concerned, specifically the rights of translation, reprinting, reuse of illustrations, recitation, broadcasting, reproduction on microfilms or in any other physical way, and transmission or information storage and retrieval, electronic adaptation, computer software, or by similar or dissimilar methodology now known or hereafter developed.
The use of general descriptive names, registered names, trademarks, service marks, etc. in this publication does not imply, even in the absence of a specific statement, that such names are exempt from the relevant protective laws and regulations and therefore free for general use.
The publisher, the authors, and the editors are safe to assume that the advice and information in this book are believed to be true and accurate at the date of publication. Neither the publisher nor the authors or the editors give a warranty, express or implied, with respect to the material contained herein or for any errors or omissions that may have been made. The publisher remains neutral with regard to jurisdictional claims in published maps and institutional affiliations.

Cover illustration: Photograph by Adrian Nemeti © Taken at the activist event "SOS: Scoateți-ne din Pata Rât" (Take us out from Pata Rât), 17 December 2013

Printed on acid-free paper

This Palgrave Macmillan imprint is published by the registered company Springer International Publishing AG part of Springer Nature.
The registered company address is: Gewerbestrasse 11, 6330 Cham, Switzerland

Preface

We are pleased to welcome *Racialized Labour in Romania. Spaces of Marginality at the Peripheries of Global Capitalism* to our series Neighborhoods, Communities and Urban Marginality. The intent of our series is to examine original research which investigates urban marginality and social inequality in communities across the globe. In so doing, we take into account not only structures and geographical boundaries but also the relationship and adjustment of humans to dense urban environments and the evolving social, political, economic and cultural patterns that result from the sufficiency or insufficiency of material resources. *Racialized Labour in Romania* richly captures and furthers the intent of our series with their ethnographic journey through five cities located in various regions of urban Romania. The authors explore the shadows of uneven development to reveal a category of racialized labourers, many ethnic Roma, within stigmatized spaces of marginality. Far from seeing insular communities, this volume acknowledges the social, political and economic processes in cities dynamically tied to global capital. While the lens of *Racialized Labour in Romania* is on marginalized populations in cities in Romania, its implications for low-wage workers throughout the globe are most timely.

As we witness growing class and racial/ethnic divisions across the globe due to urbanization and globalization, *Racialized Labour in Romania* represents a welcome addition to the rich body of work that shows the human side of worker exploitation, stigmatization and marginalization. Read it, reflect on it, and become informed.

Series Editors: Carol Camp Yeakey, The Marshall S. Snow Professor of Arts and Sciences, Washington University in St. Louis, and
Walter R. Allen, Distinguished Professor of Education, Sociology and African American Studies, The Allan Murray Cartter Professor of Higher Education, University of California at Los Angeles

Acknowledgements

This volume emerged from joint research undertaken within the project "Spatialization and racialization of social exclusion. The social and cultural formation of 'Gypsy ghettos' in Romania in a European context" (www.sparex-ro.eu), which was supported by a grant of the Romanian National Authority for Scientific Research, CNCS—UEFISCDI, project number PN-II-ID-PCE-2011-3-0354, director Enikő Vincze.

The 2011 Census Data used for some of our analyses was made available through the PN-II-TU-TE-2014-4-1377 grant financed by National Research Council of Romania, awarded to principal investigator Mihaela Hărăguș, with the contract number: 252/01.10.2015.

The work of Giovanni Picker for the current volume received funding from the European Union's Horizon 2020 research and innovation programme under the Marie Sklodowska-Curie grant agreement No. 661646.

Interviews quoted from 2016 in the chapter of Enikő Vincze were recorded within the two programmes of Foundation Desire (www.desire-ro.eu) run in that year with the support of Open Society Foundations' Human Rights Initiative and Roma Initiative Office ("Justice for Roma through the legal enforcement of housing rights", and "Consult us! Roma are not garbage").

We are grateful to our colleagues Michal Buchowski, Adrian Dohotaru, Iuliu Kozák, László Fosztó, Hajnalka Harbula, Camelia Moraru, Tibor Schneider, and Michael Stewart for their collaboration during fieldwork in segregated and impoverished areas, as well as in collecting data on their media representations, and in writing up the initial SPAREX research reports that offered valuable resources for the present volume.

Two anonymous reviewers of the publishing house generously provided feedback on earlier chapter summaries and the Introduction, and their valuable input is hereby acknowledged. The initial draft of the volume received insightful comments from Călin Cotoi and Florin Poenaru, discussants at our book presentation at the University of Bucharest in September 2016, Bogdan Suditu, and other colleagues from within and outside of the academia.

Heidi Samuelson provided a careful and competent proofreading for the manuscript.

We benefited from open-handedly provided interviews and local-level data from various key actors in the five researched cities, such as representatives of welfare and employment agencies, urban planners, the police, non-governmental organizations involved in social interventions, Roma health and school mediators, teachers, journalists, and so on, and the persons living in deprived and segregated areas themselves. Nicu Arsene, Balog Péter, Mihaela Berki, Ernest Creta, Mihai Ciorba, Gelu Czuli, Ioan Doghi, Lucian Găman, Linda Greta, Kurkuj Elek, Leontina Lingurar, Marosi László, Ion Micuță, Gabriela Petre, Daniel Stancu, and many others helped us navigate through the five cities and their marginalized places.

While life in the visited segregated and severely impoverished areas rolls on busy with work and family duties, their Roma and non-Roma dwellers kindly shared with us their experiences of precarious labour and subsistence at the spatial and symbolic margins of the cities. We hope that this book, which we have promised them to write, reflects some of their contentions and contributes to the critical understanding of systemic processes that marginalize and racialize them and deceitfully exploit their labour.

Contents

1 Introduction: Racialized Labour of the Dispossessed
  as an Endemic Feature of Capitalism   1
  *Norbert Petrovici, Cristina Raț, Anca Simionca,
  and Enikő Vincze*

2 Working Status in Deprived Urban Areas
  and Their Greater Economic Role   39
  Norbert Petrovici

3 Ghettoization: The Production of Marginal Spaces
  of Housing and the Reproduction of Racialized Labour   63
  Enikő Vincze

4 Social Citizenship at the Margins   97
  Cristina Raț

5 Framing the "Unproductive": A Case Study of High-Level
  Visions of Economic Progress and Racialized Exclusion   123
  Anca Simionca

6 Segregated Housing Areas and the Discursive
   Construction of Segregation in the News   145
   Hanna Orsolya Vincze

7 How Many Ghettos Can We Count? Identifying
   Roma Neighbourhoods in Romanian Municipalities 179
   Cătălin Berescu

8 Conclusion: (Re)centring Labour, Class, and Race 207
   Giovanni Picker

Index   227

List of Figures

Fig. 2.1　Localities with exports in Romania in 2011. (Source: Author's graph is generated in ArcGIS. Data courtesy to the Romanian National Institute of Statistics and the project Competitive Cities (2013) of the World Bank – Romania Regional Development Program, project coordinator: Marcel Ionescu-Heroiu　46

Fig. 3.1　The share of the Roma living in the marginalized areas as compared to the share of the total population in the case of five Romanian cities. (Source: Romanian National Institute of Statistics, 2011 Census. Author's calculations and graph)　66

Fig. 4.1　The evolution of ILO unemployment and the number of families receiving means-tested welfare benefits 2008–2016. (Source: The Statistical Bulletin of the Ministry of Labour and INS 2016. Author's graphs)　103

List of Maps

Map 3.1	Municipality of Călărași, Călărași County, South Development Region	87
Map 3.2	Municipality of Cluj-Napoca, Cluj County, North-West Development Region	88
Map 3.3	Municipality of Miercurea-Ciuc, Harghita County, Central Development Region	89
Map 3.4	Municipality of Ploiești, Prahova County, South-East Development Region	90
Map 3.5	Municipality of Târgu-Mureș, Mureș County, Central Development Region	91
Map 3.6	Romania, counties and county centres	92

List of Tables

Table 1.1	The occupational status of the Roma population in the researched areas	22
Table 2.1	Occupational positions held in 2011 by those who emigrated from the cities of Călăraşi, Cluj-Napoca, Miercurea Ciuc, Ploieşti, Târgu Mureş	44
Table 2.2	Occupational structure of the cities in 2011	47
Table 2.3	Stable city population and emigrants from the five cities between 1991 and 2011	51
Table 2.4	The occupations in 2011 of Roma migrants after 1990 and Roma inhabitants in the five cities of Călăraşi, Cluj-Napoca, Miercurea Ciuc, Ploieşti, Târgu Mureş	52
Table 2.5	Distribution of occupied persons by economic sector in 2002 in the five cities of Călăraşi, Cluj-Napoca, Miercurea Ciuc, Ploieşti, Târgu Mureş	55
Table 6.1	Coding scheme	157
Table 7.1	Typology of disadvantaged urban areas in the *Atlas of marginalized urban zones* issued by the World Bank and the Romanian government	200

1

Introduction: Racialized Labour of the Dispossessed as an Endemic Feature of Capitalism

Norbert Petrovici, Cristina Raț, Anca Simionca, and Enikő Vincze

Introduction[1]

The current landscape of Romania is striking due to its unevenness. Once you drive off a main road, recently repaired with European money, typically amidst two corruption scandals, or you step out from the cubicle of a transnational corporation, eagerly swallowing the cosmopolitan graduates who duly report their numerous unpaid internships as "work experience," or you exit the backdoor of the greenest homemade cafeteria, you may rapidly lose your way on the unpaved lanes running through a hectic mixture of shacks that accommodate the precariat. In the passionate postsocialist quests to praise or condemn global capitalism, service sector

---

N. Petrovici (✉) • C. Raț • A. Simionca
Sociology Department, Babeș-Bolyai University, Cluj-Napoca, Romania
e-mail: crat@socasis.ubbcluj.ro

E. Vincze
Faculty of European Studies, Babeș-Bolyai University,
Cluj-Napoca, Romania
e-mail: eniko.vincze@ubbcluj.ro

© The Author(s) 2019
E. Vincze et al. (eds.), *Racialized Labour in Romania*, Neighborhoods, Communities, and Urban Marginality, https://doi.org/10.1007/978-3-319-76273-9_1

"growth" and gentrification were often in the spotlight, while the decomposition of the former working class, the emergence of a racialized stratum of the dispossessed, and its violent expulsion to the margins remained sidelined as a geopolitically contingent issue of "backwardness."

Usually, deprivation and marginalization are explained in terms of insufficient development of (human) capital, historically persistent ethno-racial prejudice, public policy failure, or the relentless culture of informal economy. We propose a different approach: our focus lies in how processes of precarization and social-spatial polarization constitute endemic features of capitalism. Embracing expanded definitions of "dispossession" (Kasmir and Carbonella 2014) and "class" (Kalb 1998, 2015), we explore the shadows of "uneven development" (Harvey 2003, 2011) in order to reveal how a category of racialized labourers, the majority of them (self-)identified ethnic Roma, was produced and confined within stigmatized spaces of marginality and drawn into the engines of capitalism Thus, our analysis entangles class divisions in a Marxist tradition with racialization and spatialization, while addressing how these phenomena are mutually producing each other.

The ethnographic journey goes through five cities located in various regions of Romania, a country at the periphery of global capitalism, and it visits twenty urban areas recorded in local narratives as no-go areas of "Țigănie."[2] While we acknowledge their spatial marginality, deep deprivation, and stigma, we do not see these settlements as insular communities governed by their own historically embedded cultural norms (as some scholars of Romani studies might do), but as emergent places dynamically tied to the social, political, and economic processes crossing through the city in its connectedness to global capital. Thus, we join voices with those claiming that inner-city development cannot be understood unless we also look at what happens at the peripheries or in the spaces of marginality, as both are connected to the current regime of capitalist accumulation.

In doing this, we situate our research in a particular place and time, that of urban Romania in the mid-2010s, a country marked by a history of peripheral status in the global economy, that made it particularly vulnerable to changing capital flows and markets, even under the more regulated and domestically oriented economic order of state socialism (1947–1989). We explain the relevance and timeliness of this choice in the first section of this introductory chapter. We acknowledge that the ethnicization or racialization of precarious workers, far from constituting a historical contingency, provides an enduring means for the subordination, dispossession, and productive exploitation of those rendered to belong to dispossessed groups in a given political order. For a better understanding of how these processes play out in the case of the Roma, an ethnic group with a well-documented history of slavery, dispossession, and persecution, we connect to the literature on postcolonialism. On the one hand, we take inspiration from the South Asian subaltern group studies in showing how the de-proletarization of legally freed former slaves brought about new forms of *unfree labour*, in our case provided disproportionately more by the Roma. On the other hand, we follow the Latin American decolonial studies tradition in asserting that *unfree labour* is quintessential for capital accumulation, and furthermore, cultural classifications (race, ethnicity, gender, religion, etc.) are embedded in the division of labour. In the case of Central and Eastern Europe, as elsewhere, racialization occurs entangled with spatial marginalization and segregation in severely deprived areas, a process that further strengthens ethno-racial borders already entwined with class boundaries, constrains participation in unfair and ultimately unfree labour, and, at the same time, perversely devaluates the financial costs of labour force reproduction. Thus, in building our theoretical lenses, we take a step forward from a mere description of the spatial dimension of social and economic inequalities and scrutinize the entangling between global capitalism, racialized labour, and spatial marginalization.

Relevance and Timeliness of Our Study

We are not the first to make the point that global capitalism has made its ascent by incorporating various types of labours to produce commodities for the global markets, while simultaneously disqualifying that very labour. A major Central and Eastern European theme, at the turn of the nineteenth century, was exactly that the modernization process, which includes industrialization, was strongly hindered by the ways in which local economies were incorporated in global capitalism. The second serfdom at the

East of Elba in Central Europe (Kochanowicz 1989; Janos 2000) and rural peonage and debt bondage in Eastern Europe (Stahl 1980; Mateescu 2012) were far from being feudal residues of a still traditional society but, rather, particular ways in which labour was reconfigured in the nineteenth century as part of an agriculture that served the need of Western capital (Brenner 1989; Boatcă 2007; Guga 2015). The dismantling of communal property, the increasingly severe deprivation faced by the majority of the population, the harsh work conditions, the new forms of unfree labour, and the persistency of slavery of the Roma population in the Romanian provinces until 1856 are no accidents. In the radical interpretation of nineteenth-century socialists, these are effects of the "law" by which "undeveloped" economies become satellites of "developed economies" (Dobrogeanu-Gherea 2010 [1910]), and consequently they maintain a cheap and politically oppressed labour force. However, much of this critical thinking with Marxist roots was phrased in the nationalist frame of the time, and collective dignity claims were amended in the local intellectual endeavour to create national communities and build independent states (Boatcă 2003; Costinescu 2014). The ethnicist undertones and sometimes blunt racism against the urban bourgeoisie, mostly composed of ethnic minorities such as the Jews, Armenians, Albanians, and Greeks, are finely ingrained in these theories (Chirot and Reid 1997). This is mirrored, at the other edge of the economic assets spectrum, by the inferiorization of the Roma and the creation of dual-labour markets, which render them under-proletarianized. Finally, even if labour relations are conceptualized as asymmetrical exchanges, they fail to observe the way in which ethnicity and race are justificatory categories used in the attempts to control economic life, property relations, and labour.

These debates received a new life in the 1970s as part of their incorporation in the compelling language of dependency theories and world system theories. Especially with the work of Wallerstein (1974), Chirot (1976), and Stahl (1980), the thesis of the second serfdom in Eastern Europe was brought into dialogue with the emerging efforts to conceptualize slavery and serfdom as an integral part of the primitive accumulation in the periphery (Amin et al. 1982). Yet, the explicit theorization of the link between race and labour is done by heirs to the latter, more specifically the two regional branches of postcolonial studies.

First, the South Asian subaltern studies tradition, with the debate over the de-proletarization (Brass 1999, 2011, 2014) and the agrarian semi-feudalism in India (Akram-Lodhi and Kay 2012; Patnaik and Dingawaney 1985), has shown that the persistency of unfree labour—chattel slavery, peonage, debt bondage, indenture—is far from being a historical accident. The legal abolition of slavery, as part of the complete subsuming in the capitalist logic, does not transform the whole mass of workers from a region into free wage labourers. On the contrary, their faith is an open question, linked with the processes of class composition and decomposition, a contingent issue of class struggle. Free workers possess political, ideological, and economic resources and advantages used as basis for contractual negotiation of wages, work time, and resources, which unfree workers do not have. In the periphery, often it is the case that workers are dispossessed in much more violent and harsher ways of their resources for collective action against capital. Nonetheless, these processes are not contained only in the periphery. As Brass (2014) argues, the neoliberal turn shows that debt bondage and precarious work are becoming more the standard even in the central capitalist spaces. In fact, wage labour is rather an exception, an accomplishment of class formation and resistance. Yet, obscuring these aspects is a major ideological prop to classify the unfree labour force as a traditional, semi-feudal remnant of a distant past, and free labour as the normalcy of advance capitalism. The de-proletarization debate has put forward a very fine conceptual analysis and a very rich empirical documentation on the variety of unfree work conditions, but it addressed rather superficially the constitutive classification of labour as such.

Second, the Latin American decolonial tradition (Mendieta 2003; Moraña et al. 2008) has shown, following the same line of the argument rooted in dependency theories, that different regimes of work control—slavery, serfdom, reciprocity, community-based reproduction work—are far from being successive in historical time. On the contrary, as Quijano (2000) pertinently observes, it was through the simultaneous enforcement of slave work and wage work that the global advent of capitalism gained its success. A great contribution of this corpus of literature, and a point of divergence from the rest of the postcolonial studies, consists of its insistence on the link between classificatory schemes and work regimes. The insistence that racialization, namely, the division of the world population into categories based on the colour of their skin and their geographical origin, was the mechanism by which the naturalization of the inferiority of certain categories of people and contingencies of labour force was institutionalized. The wage labour was the privilege of the "white" people, and in the Eurocentric narratives of history, it is their labour only that has contributed to world "progress." A less visible aspect is that racialized unfree work was central to capital accumulation. While less empirically dense, the Latin American decolonial tradition created a very strong theoretical focus on the very link between racialization, cultural classificatory schemes, and labour processes.

Recently, the division between wage labour and wagelessness has become the object of study of the global labour anthropology research agenda (Carrier and Kalb 2015; Kasmir and Carbonella 2014). In conversation with various dependency and world system theories, this line of thought is keen on restoring the fine-grained ethnographies of labour in the periphery (see the work of Sidney Mintz, Eric Wolf, Max Gluckman, Julian Steward, George Balandier, Godfrey Wilson, and Monica Wilson). Methodologically, these works aim at studying the workings of capitalism from the local to the global. The central contention is that the accumulation by dispossession thesis (Harvey 2003; Jessop 2002) has to be supplemented by an analysis of class formation and class differentiation where the main line of division rests in the production of both wage labour and wagelessness. Gender, race, religion, and other complex cultural artefacts play the role of classificatory devices that construe class and are instrumental in marking "surplus populations," which constitute permanent "outsiders" of capitalism. Yet, the outsiders bear the weight of not being paid even if they are incorporated directly as unfree labour or indirectly as responsible for reproducing wage labourers through domestic work. In addition, the very class solidarity needed for resisting capital is under threat by fragmentation through classificatory schemes. The myriad of class positions that appear in the division of labour is continually enforced by appeal to race/ethnicity or gender.

In the case of the Roma, similar to the case of other oppressed ethnic groups gaining some civil rights after the abolition of slavery, proletarization did not follow straightforwardly after the moment of political liberation in 1856. The variety of Roma groups followed different strategies for economic survival, which had been already documented elsewhere (see Guy 2001; Fosztó 2009; Szalai and Zentai 2014) and falls outside of our purposes to describe. What remains of interest for the argument of this book is that by the beginning of the twentieth century a sizeable segment of the "free" Roma population lacked any form of property, and, in particular, land, that could have empowered them to negotiate over the labour relations they entered. The dual nature of the labour market remained in place, with few, if any, opportunities for the Roma to exit from labour-intensive, underproletarianized positions in a country without any comprehensive welfare and educational institutions before the Second World War. Their genocide under the fascist regimes (Năstasă and Varga 2001) most tragically reveals the political vision that the Roma were "outsiders" and "dangerous" for the "nation," perversely altering the original ideals of those who, a century earlier, championed ethnic emancipation.

The proletarization of the Roma eventually occurred under the communist regime, which incorporated them mostly on low-skilled, labour-intensive positions in agriculture and heavy industry, and provided means for upward social mobility through ethnocultural assimilation. The collapse of the agricultural and industrial state sectors during the 1990s left the Roma, who lacked any nationalized property to claim back, in a position of a seemingly "surplus population," supposedly disconnected from productive labour, who should be somehow retrained and "integrated" in the new capitalist labour market. In contrast to this, and in line with the theories presented in this section, we claim that the Roma and other dispossessed workers labelled as "Tsigane" have been essential after 1990 for the functioning of the most deregulated sectors of manual work, namely, agriculture, recycling industry, constructions, and infrastructural development. All these sectors rely heavily on seasonal labour, often without a contract, and as a rule without social insurance provisions. They use communal or kinship ties in order to recruit workers and lay the bondage of usury as a means to control workers and to expropriate large shares of the value of their work. Moreover, these domains often require temporary or circular migration (national or international) between home and the place of work, and consequently they disrupt family life, at times with severe consequences on the well-being of children.

To summarize, we do not seek to explain the plight of the Roma as merely a problem of inequality along social, economic, and political dimensions, with lengthy roots in history, although we consider these approaches as highly relevant and insightful in their own terms. Instead, we propose to analyse the inequalities faced by the Roma and other precarious workers racialized as "Tsiganes" as emerging from the ways in which global capitalism functions, and how it shapes labour and class in its peripheral regions from Central and Eastern Europe.

Labour and Class in Central and Eastern Europe

Social transformations of the last two and a half decades periodically swayed the epistemic balance between rejection and embracement of a special regime conferred by the status of "post," which came with the fall of actually existing socialism (Stenning and Hörschelmann 2008). Most of the time the "post" is completely devoid of any meaningful concept of capitalism predicated on class and class struggles. More than two decades after the demise of actually existing socialism, much of the contemporary literature produced about Central and Eastern Europe is still organized around a dichotomy between socialism and postsocialism (Gille 2010; Tlostanova and Mignolo 2012). The advent of the "transition debate" placed the central concern on whether the market produced more inequalities than the redistributive system (Szelényi and Kostello 1996; Cao and Nee 2000). The privatization process and the emerging market clearly favoured the well-off, and much of the discussion focused on assessing the inequalities. Within these debates, however, the approach towards urban inequalities was mostly descriptive, and the discussion focused on the size, density, and diversity of the city (Hamilton et al. 2006; Stanilov 2007; Tsenkova and Nedovic-Budic 2006) and, more rarely, on the formation of "Roma ghettos" in Eastern Europe (Kertesi and Kezdi 1997; Sandu 2005). Currently, many contributions simply acknowledge that capitalism produces more inequalities and diversity, and when it comes to explanations of the urbanization process their focus is still on the new middle class and the elite, active in shaping the development of the city, while those dominated and epistemologically dispossessed become the subject of compassion for their marginality, their incapacity to act, their reactionary attitude, and ultimately their "passivity" as subjects who endure the negative "side-effects" of "progress" (Hirt and Kovachev 2006; Ourednicek and Temelova 2009; Ruopilla and Kährik 2003).

As Riabchuk (2009) rightly points out, the discourse on the demobilized, disorganized, and non-adapted workers in the new postsocialist context is just another device that creates and reproduces social inequalities. More and more voices criticize the grand narratives underpinning the transition debate in epistemological terms and plead for a more nuanced analysis of the fluxes of power and resistance (Bodnar 2007; Gille 2007; Haney 2002; Petrovici and Simionca 2011). Aware of the gap between everyday categories of practice and the expectations created by the systemic transition narrative, a more grounded approach is favoured, one that pays attention to particular social processes or relations rather than to entire regimes of inequality patterns. Instead of falling back on facile dualisms, such as powerless versus powerful, market versus redistribution, inequality versus equality, historical and situated accounts of the actual interplay between institutions and agents are preferred (Bodnar 2007; Cucu 2014; Smith et al. 2009; Stenning and Hörschelmann 2008). In addition, a new stream of scholarship has been revaluating the role of workers both in socialism and postsocialism, arguing that far from being simply manhandled workers, they played an important part in reshaping the shop floor, the factory, and everyday politics (Dunn 2004; Heumos 2010; Horváth 2005; Kideckel 2008; Ost 2005; Pittaway 2005).

Ethnicity is systematically rejected as a category that straightforwardly creates inequalities, but its use as a classificatory devise that regulates class composition is acknowledged, driving scholars of the region towards an analytically important convergence point with the emerging global anthropology of labour (Faje 2011; Petrovici 2013; Poenaru 2015; Simionca 2012). As we identify with this theoretical framework, we distance ourselves from mainstream approaches within cultural anthropology and the Romani studies paradigm. Even if anthropologists emphasize that "Tsigane" (at times used interchangeably with "Gypsy") is an "identity constructed and constantly remade in the present in relations with significant others" (Stewart 1997: 28), and even if Romani studies scholars[3] are committed to deconstructing and resisting stereotypical, including romantic, images of "the Roma" (Okely 1996; Stewart 1997; Matras 2002; Hayes and Acton 2006; Tremlett 2009), by talking about the "Gypsy ways of doing everyday activities" (Liégeois 1986; Blasco 1999; Okely 1983), they have been instrumental in building up and sustaining an image of the "authentic Gypsy," an effect that was critically addressed by Willems (1997). Moreover, even when Romani studies scholars address the phenomenon of anti-Gypsism (Stewart 2012) by explaining it in the terms of a cultural politics of difference rooted in "the sense of frustration" of the majority population generated in the Central and East European context of "fragile democracies" or of the insufficient commitment to "structural reforms"—they reinforce the mainstream cultural paradigm of Romani studies.

One attempt to escape from reproducing the fixed notion of "the eternal Roma," who always outsmart the *Gadjo* and find a way of success by their cultural practices, was the endeavour of some sociologists to understand the deprivations that Roma are subjected to from a socio-historical perspective, and, in particular, by using the term of "underclass" in order to define the situation of Roma minorities today in Central and Eastern European countries (Ladányi and Szelényi 2001a, b). At our turn, we acknowledge the risk resulting from the association of "the Roma underclass" approach with the "culture of poverty" perspective (Stewart 2002), but also the analytic weakness of "the underclass" as a concept (Wacquant 2012b: 67) which, in our view, describes a structural rupture in the configuration of classes without explaining its causes in the broader political economy. We are also aware about the dangerous limitations of the "Roma cultural practices" frame, which maintains that these practices are well matched to the opportunities created by "the world-capitalist market for the entrepreneurial initiatives" and that advanced capitalism opens up "spaces for people to lift themselves without constraints of status or background" (Stewart 2002: 149).

Therefore, our proposal is to link these complex socio-economic and cultural processes to the larger issue of the development of a capitalist regime in a postsocialist country embedded in global capitalism and, consequently, to address the political construction of Roma as part of colonization.

During the late 1990s, regardless of the fact that the Roma politics of the day[4] referred to Roma, Travellers, and Sinti, EU integration discourse slightly transferred political attention on Roma onto Eastern Europe, as if "the Roma problem" were an "East European issue" (Vincze 2014). In doing so, it created Roma as one of the objects on which to negotiate the accession of former socialist countries to the EU and through which the distinction between the original EU and the "postcommunist countries" was maintained. This is the legacy that even nowadays fuels, among other factors, racist classifications between the rich and poor countries, or between countries whose citizens should be entitled to enjoy the right to free movement and those undeserving of it, or between "authentic" Europe and the "newcomers."

Under these conditions, as the current political debates around the "free movement of people" show us, the entire anti-Roma-immigration politics and its underlying racism is part of an effort to justify on the side of "old" EU member states why capital may travel freely across the EU, while labour (especially the labour from Eastern and Central Europe) should not. Anti-Roma racism is part of this neoliberal regime promoting, on the one hand, the extension of the "free market" conceived as a product of civilization (in the interests of a handful of more powerful EU countries) and, on the other hand, sustaining austerity measures and marketization processes in the more "peripheral" countries as means to lower the cost of labour, to "attract" capital and generate economic "growth." This current form of anti-Roma racism functions to protect the former states from the "invasion" of the impoverished populations from the latter countries, perceived as carriers of "primitivism" and backwardness.

Parallel with these processes, we may witness how the impoverished populations (mostly from Romania and Bulgaria) are racialized, and how the political category of the Roma is associated with "East European poverty" by those who had a crucial role in creating and sustaining that poverty. Meanwhile, the political decision-makers of the "peripheral countries" (economically benefiting from the system described above) are doing their best to distance themselves from their native population (self-)identified as Roma while blaming the latter for all the failures encountered in their road towards the promised land of the EU (Vincze 2014: 446). This is how, at the end of the day, the stereotype of the

"Tsigane" as an ethnic/racial classificatory device plays similar roles at different scales of global economic and political processes. In the relations between countries, it serves to reinforce Romania's (and more generally Eastern Europe's) peripheral position as supplier of a racialized, cheap labour force. At the local (national) level, it functions as a tool that "legitimizes" the increasing pay gap and dismantles potential class solidarities with the consolidated working class. While in this sense our approach is close to Edna Bonacich's *split labour market* theory, who convincingly argues that ethnic antagonisms as a rule conceal deeply underlying economic and class conflicts between "business or employers," "higher paid labour," and ethnicized "cheaper labour" (Bonacich 1972), we move beyond her theoretical framework in at least two ways. First, we explore more deeply the mechanisms that maintain at a low price the labour of racialized categories (in our case "Tsiganes"), and identify spatial marginalization and segregation in areas with poor infrastructure as one of these mechanisms, which reinforces other processes of economic and political dispossession also mentioned by Bonacich. Second, as described in the previous section, we investigate the dual nature of labour markets and explain how the labour of the racialized group is ultimately *unfree* not because of the individual (ethnic) characteristics of those who supply that labour, neither because of individual discrimination suffered from employers (a point also emphasized by Bonacich), but because of the structural features of capitalism that systematically creates such underproletarianized, precarious, nonetheless productive positions (jobs) that mostly racialized groups end up to fulfil.

Our book demonstrates that these processes are part of the recent history of global capitalism, and the racialization of labour enmeshed with the formation of marginalized spaces, as we depict through our empirical cases, is an endemic feature of the capitalist regime. The situation of the Roma minority in Romania provides a critical case of how racialized labour is spatially confined and marginalized, as it represents the *internal* periphery of a country located, at its turn, at the semi-periphery of global capitalism, marked by the disentanglement of really existing socialism, the global diffusion of neoliberal policies, and also by the recently acquired membership in an increasingly troubled European Union.

In order to construct theoretical lenses aimed at scrutinizing this critical case of racialized labour in Eastern Europe, we have reviewed the most important existing studies from the above-described angle. Our interest is to build a theoretical frame that reveals the entanglements between racialization, precarization, dispossession, and spatial marginalization, on the one hand, and productive inclusion in the long chains of global capitalism, on the other. As the next section explains, our main contention is that the racialization of precarious workers as "Tsiganes," together with the simultaneous diffusion of neoliberal ideas concerning "flexible" labour and workfare, facilitated their postcommunist de-proletarization and the privatization of their labour power reproduction costs. The phasing out of state support, in particular in the domain of housing, and its limited role in mediating class conflict, reinforced a pattern of spatial exclusion that existed long before, on the venues of centuries-old "Tsigane colonies" (*colonii de țigani*), but it also created new pathways of exclusion via evictions from gentrifiable zones. Spatial marginalization in severely deprived settings allowed, on the one hand, the diminishing of the costs of families' daily survival, and, on the other hand, the perpetuation of cultural classificatory schemes that portray the "Tsiganes" as being "dirty," "work-shy," "unreliable," and "welfare dependent," prejudices that constrain them to commodify their work at lower costs, to assume the manifold risks of unregulated labour, or ultimately those of unfree labour.

Building Our Analytic Framework and the Main Thesis of the Book

We turn upside down the concept of "integration," and instead of lamenting over the lack of integration of the deeply impoverished and racialized "Tsiganes" dwelling segregated at the margins, we look at the manifold ways in which they are part and parcel of local and global processes that perversely render invisible their work, habitat, and very identity.

We also aim to move forward from the mere description of how spatial and social segregation are intertwined, and instead investigate the production of "ghettos" (Wacquant 2008, 2012a), at times on the grounds of previous "Tsigane colonies," but not always so, as a historical occurrence tied to the structural power (Wolf 2001) of Eastern-European neoliberalism (Böröcz and Kovács 2001; Bohle and Greskovits 2012). We definitely consider that the communitarian explanations given for the formation of (poor) "Tsigane areas" are not only incomplete but also damaging due to how they culturally essentialize and justify the socio-spatial inequalities produced by political economy and public policies that together dispossess and dislocate precarious labourers and push them towards (physically and/or symbolically) polluted peripheries.

Following Kasmir and Carbonella (2014), we refrain from envisaging the "local" as "a natural political or cultural space in which daily life is lived" (2015: 21), although we try to meaningfully connect to previous ethnographic work on everyday life in the "Tsigane ghetto" (Botonogu 2011; Pulay 2011, 2015; Toma 2009; Stewart 1997). Instead, we unfold how these *loci* were constructed within processes of postsocialist de-proletarianization and gentrification, listening to the painful histories of repeated evictions and enclosures, and scrutinizing the footprints of developmental policies on local administration and public policy documents (Vincze 2015a, b).

In a similar vein, we refuse the theoretical corset of the term "survival strategies" (Stănculescu and Berevoescu 2004), that falsely suggests that the economic activities of marginalized persons only serve *their own* subsistence from one day to the other. On the contrary, we approach the work of the officially unemployed as *labour* that produces surplus value, and analyse how this apparently de-proletarianized category is actually utterly well "integrated" in the global neoliberal economy, characterized by the "multiplication of the proletariat" (Kasmir and Carbonella 2014). Moreover, we explore the entrepreneurial ways in which new forms of being productive are generated precisely by those rendered uncreative and "dependent." We also pay attention to how the privatization of labour force reproduction plays out in severely deprived settings and how state social transfers play (or not) a role in subsidizing the costs of this reproduction.

Critically engaging the work of Sanyal and Bhattacharyya (2009) on the relation between informal work and capital in processes of "accumulation by dispossession" (Harvey 2003), Samson (2010, 2015) convincingly argues that informal work at the peripheries cannot be categorized as linked to the circuit of capital only through subcontracting or as completely detached from capital. She illustrates, with the example of recyclable waste reclaimers in South Africa, how unproletarianized workers in the informal economy act as neoliberal subjects, transforming the waste dump in an entrepreneurial way from "a commodity cemetery into a resource mine" (Samson 2015: 814), organizing themselves into an economic association, gaining subcontracts from middlemen in the emergent recycling business, and actively fighting the state in order to maintain access to the "mine." However, they are not recognized as such, but stigmatized as "scavengers" and constrained to undergo a process of proletarianization, which employs their productive knowledge but deprives them from epistemic agency. Consequently, Samson (2015) concludes that "dispossession" of waste reclaimers concerns not only cutting off their access to the "mine" of the dump (previously a public site commodified by a collective agency) but also linking them to the circuits of capital as proletarians as well as their "epistemic dispossession" (Samson 2015: 24–25) from being knowing subjects of the commodity value of otherwise wasted material.

Extreme urban poverty, characterized by joblessness, social exclusion, and poor living conditions in segregated areas, is often seen as a consequence of insufficient state intervention to temper economic inequalities, redistribute via taxation and welfare, and ensure universal access to public healthcare, education, and child/elderly care services. The Bretton-Woods Convention of 1984 announced a scaling-back of de-commodifying attempts (Esping-Andersen 1990) and the neoliberal turn soon penetrated the end of the welfare state's "golden era" (Pierson 2001; Schwartz 2006). After a short detour of "third way" illusions (Dean 2003), this tendency materialized in the straightforward reframing of "social rights" as "social investment" at the very heart of "social Europe" (Lister 2004). Under this novel regime of "expanded reproduction" (Harvey 2003), which turned away from post-war Keynesianism, large parts of the former working classes were not only made redundant but rendered responsible for their (lack of) "employability," irrespective of the structural causes of their unemployment. Simultaneously, public services scaled back, leaving behind the quest of universalism. Sizeable segments of the middle class, formerly the "double-winners" of capitalist welfare state development, also shrank into the new precariat (Standing 2007, 2011).

One of the symptoms of neoliberal policies is that of transforming citizenship into a merit-based category. The most vulnerable to the untamed market forces are exactly those whose skills have lost exchange value and whose identities have been socially and culturally stigmatized as inferior, dirty, and dangerous—put otherwise, those whose labour power cannot be commodified and whose social identities are seen as "unworthy" (Fraser 1997). These people are described as those left outside as they fail to contribute to economic "progress"; moreover, this "progress" actually no longer requires their input. They are "residuals," "disposable people" in the current workings of the system. In this logic, it is the local welfare state that is not caring enough to develop visions of "inclusive" urban restructuring through coherent social housing policies, vocational training, job mediation, minimum income guarantee, and so on, that would facilitate desegregation and social participation of the poor. From a welfare state perspective, exclusion emerges because the state fails to acknowledge and to properly address the structural condition of the most vulnerable, allowing deprivation and stigma to perpetuate from one generation to the other. The excluded seem to be composed of those whose existence not only lacks commodity value and is detached from capital but is also factually and discursively constructed as lacking both commodificability and legitimacy of redistribution claims. They are the radically uncommodifiables, who can commodify neither their work, nor their needs (Esping-Andersen 1990). We take a step forward from describing such pathways of "disempowering inclusion" (Fraser 1997; Anthias 2001) through which "beneficiaries" of social policies and affirmative action bear public disdain for alleged "welfare-dependency" (Dean and Taylor-Gooby 1992), and analyse the political and administrative actions that limit and distort their citizenship rights, while discursively blaming their uncivility and "reliance" on welfare.

In the context of Central and Eastern Europe, the voluntaristic image of the policymaker is easily translated by public and academic discourses into the malevolent corrupt state-maker or the impotent figure of the cadre in a "young democracy," aided in learning from the elder sibling, the "advanced Western democracy" (Buden 2010). If we were to engage seriously in a voluntaristic reading of the role played by policymakers,

Krippner's (2011) analysis on the US, an "advanced democracy," comes in handy. According to this analysis, policymakers had a central role in the 1980s and 1990s in transforming the distributional conundrums from political dilemmas into technical and economic issues. Thus, they avoided a legitimizing crisis produced by the increasing financial deficit of the core hegemonic state in the 1970s world system configuration (Wallerstein 2004), by transforming it in a matter of individual productivity. Increased commodification, in this account, is the result of a process of trial and error of policymakers in addressing the puzzle of the capitalist state: even if the final beneficiaries of state spending are private industries, the capitalists are not willing to fund state spending with a sustained increase in taxation. The solution, global in its origin, where the dialogue between East and West played a major role (Bockman 2011; Evans and Aligica 2009; Ban 2016; Collier 2011), is to avoid direct class conflict being mediated by the state, and to transform the question of "who gets what" into a question of "who and with what amount one contributes to profit-making." Policymakers in Central and Eastern Europe were all too eager to experiment with radical commodification and privatization in the 1990s, avoiding an all too political debate about redistribution of state-controlled assets (Eyal et al. 2001; Eyal et al. 1998). But this opens a new line of inquiry, or at least calls into doubt the uncommodifiable character of the excluded, in the current conjunction.

A similar, policy-related argument has been made in terms of the development of the city and its economic vision. The prevailing solution in dealing with the 1970s state fiscal crisis in the US, which diffused globally after the 1980s, was to downscale it to the level of local economies. Therefore, contemporary cities entered the logic of maximizing their chances of becoming local and regional hubs, that is, of becoming "competitive cities" in order to fix capital locally, to ensure employment and well-being to their own local citizens. Competitive subjects with merit and creativity in profit-making ideally would be attracted and rewarded by living in competitive cities (Florida 2002). However, as eloquently put by Neil Smith (1996, 1998), the US bourgeoisie resentful of the liberties gained by workers in the redistributive post-war era found a great ally in the disenfranchised middle class, whose members were losing their old welfare and market entitlements in the new competitive cities. Minorities, immigrants, and the increasing strata of the poor and homeless became perfect scapegoats in the emerging narrative of the market, producing a revanchist city against its citizens. Gentrification, redevelopment, and regeneration became instruments at hand to exploit the differential gap between the potential value of land inhabited by the poor and the actual rent they paid, rebuilding a new city free of minorities, underemployed, and unemployed. Conversely, gentrification served capital accumulation and the creation of a capitalist-class, and postsocialist state bucreaucracies had particularly important roles in this process (Chelcea 2006). By the beginning of the 2000s, Smith's thesis was increasingly confirmed as a strategy spreading across Europe (MacLeod 2002; Uitermark and Duyvendak 2008), Latin America (Swanson 2007), South Asia (Whitehead and More 2007), and Africa (Samara 2010), becoming global (Slater 2004; Smith 2002). After the 2008–2009 global financial meltdown, a new wave of empirical and theoretical developments argued that international rent gaps became constitutive for speculative land investments, evictions, and a new geography of urban violence (Harvey 2011; Slater 2015). Revanchist urbanism has not lost its grip as a discursive prop in creating local hegemonic narratives against the excluded; on the contrary, it is still a major tool in the new wave of profiting from global rent gaps (Slater 2015).

While we fully agree with the diagnostics above, we argue that eviction, exclusion, and revanchist narratives are also mechanisms of producing cheap labour pools and not only cheap spaces for investing surplus capital. Cheap labour is produced in at least three ways. First, the city itself devalues its citizens on national and global markets to be attractive for global investments speculating on wage gaps. Those fractions of the labour force who oppose such devaluation are constantly reminded that they may impede the collective well-being with their claims. Second, those who cannot compete on the high end of the formal labour market often end up being evicted in different cycles of gentrification from the city. Nonetheless, they remain important resources for the manufacturing industries moving towards the suburbs or in the nearby rural areas. As labour pools become redundant in the city centre, the public revanchist narrative argues that this eventually occurs for their well-being: they are relocated by the "blind and just" forces of the market into areas that are cheaper, less visible, and less conspicuously expensive. Those who do not qualify to live up to the standards of "personal development" needed for the highly qualified labourers dwelling in the city (Chertkovskaya et al. 2013; Simionca and Gog 2016) deserve to live at some distance. And third, the cheap labour force needed for industries with low technological investment is much easier to exploit if they are forced into instances of extreme vulnerability, for example, into making a living in informal and precarious housing areas, cut off from alternative state provisions, and denied access to commons, often with police intervention. Revanchist discourse in these instances bluntly takes racial tones, attacking the basic possibility of making ontological equivalences between those who are entitled to the city and citizenship and those who are denied such entitlements.

Our work in this volume reports that areas undergoing ghettoization, predominantly inhabited by ethnic Roma, have a high percentage of people employed precariously in labour-intensive industries; barely paid on the free market, they are systematically cut off from state support in the mediation of labour relations and social security. Exclusion from state provisions seems to play a major role in instituting the market whims as the sole link between work productivity and retribution in industries with low technological investments. Exclusion actually can be seen, in this reading, as an ultimate act of policymakers in making a market where bare work can be directly exploited. This was not something unexpected. As Wacquant convincingly argues, neoliberalism as a political project has at its core "an articulation of state, market and citizenship that harnesses the first to impose the stamp of the second on the third" (Wacquant 2012b: 71). Public policies play an active role in creating a cheap, exploitable labour force, precisely in those places that seemingly lack the interference of the state or where public provisions are reduced at a minimum: access to drinkable water at public pipes but no running water or sewage; school buses for children but no regular public transport to reach the city; scarce social assistance benefits conditioned by community work that should be nonetheless compensated with paid labour; no entitlement for proper identity cards, only to temporary identity papers that certify belonging to the suspicious category of the homeless and restrict citizenship rights, and so on. Our predicament with Wacquant is that neoliberal state policies can be straightforwardly depicted in the places he considered Roma "ghettos" in Eastern Europe[5]; therefore, in our view, the criteria of "institutional parallelism" (Wacquant 2012a: 7)[6] and lack of state intervention

(Wacquant 2000: 112–4) are only partially met in these severely deprived, segregated, and racialized (if not ethnically homogeneous) places. If we were to call them "ghettos," we should accept that, nonetheless, neoliberal state policies, through the presence and not the absence of the state, directly contribute to their generation and persistence in time.

To summarize, our contention is that far from a contingency induced by locally emergent power relations and structural violence, and even further away from being a consequence of the cultural features and options of its inhabitants, the marginal spaces hosting racialized labourers have a productive role in the functioning of capitalism. We argue that the ghettoized areas are not only systemic by-products but places marked by the presence of neoliberal state policies, and also resources that fuel capital accumulation and shape the formation of a specific labour. Moreover, we assert that through the formation and maintenance of the open/fluid category of "Tsigane," which essentializes and inferiorizes a large segment of the dispossessed, capitalist political economy easily benefits from the neoliberalization of housing, employment, and social policy.

The Strategic Site of Our Ethnographic Endeavour

The option of addressing the formation of marginal spaces in this volume in relation to the racialization of labour goes beyond the initial framing of our research based on a spatial approach, which proposed to analyse the social and cultural formation of "Tsigane ghettos" in Romania in a European context. In its early phase of planning, the paradigm of social exclusion informed our research, while we sought to address processes that lie behind the formation of precarious housing areas, such as spatialization and racialization of poverty. No surprise, these territories were predominantly inhabited by persons and groups (self-)identified as Roma and labelled as *țigănie*. As we moved forward with deciphering the structural processes behind these situations, it became necessary to expand our explicative frame from the spatial exclusion approach towards a more systemic understanding of ghettoization, which depicts how categories of racialized labourers are produced and confined within the marginalized spaces by the capitalist system.

The sites of our empirical research consist of five Romanian cities, all of them administrative centres of their corresponding counties (Călărași, Cluj-Napoca, Miercurea-Ciuc, Ploiești, and Târgu-Mureș), with diverse histories of urbanization and economic development (as they have been affected differently by deindustrialization), but which share similar patterns of pushing towards the peripheries the impoverished, mostly Roma dwellers who cannot afford housing on the private market. The five cities differ in terms of their ethnic balances between Romanians, Hungarians, and Roma, and also in terms of the diversity of local Roma groups differentiated alongside diverse factors (traditional/*spoitori, căldărari,* or *Gábor* versus assimilated Roma, or Hungarian versus Romanian Roma and Turkish versus Romanian Roma) and relations among them. These cities have different economic and social histories, current revenues and wealth, and political agency (public authorities, local politics, and civil society). They are not regarded as a "representative sample" of Romanian cities but as loci of a set of representative processes of capitalist development in Romania that led to the precarization of the working class and the formation of marginal, severely impoverished residential spaces, with inadequate infrastructure and unclear legal status. The chapters rely on quantitative and qualitative data about the five selected cities, including the socio-demographic characteristics of populations living in the twenty urban areas that we have visited, as compared to the general populations of the cities. Table 1.1 provides a brief presentation of the ethnic composition of these areas and the occupational distribution of the self-identified Roma dwellers.

As Table 1.1 illustrates well, our research sites are not homogeneously inhabited by self-identified Roma, and the occupational distribution of those who consider themselves Roma is considerably heterogeneous as well. Thus, it is important to emphasize that we neither investigated "Roma settlements," nor "concentrations of unemployed population," but urban areas that had been considered by majority populations as being deprived and inhabited mostly by "Tsiganes."

To this end, we conducted interviews with NGO representatives, politicians, local authorities, officials from territorial agencies of national public institutions, social workers, and so on, and, most importantly,

Table 1.1 The occupational status of the Roma population in the researched areas

Locality	Researched site	Total Dwellers	Of which Roma	The occupational status of the Roma population[a]					
				Pre-school & pupils (%)	Home-makers (%)	Employees (%)	Un-employed[b] (%)	Self-employed (%)	Pensioners (%)
Călărași	Cinci Călărași	927	193	30	13	23	12	3	12
	Doi Moldoveni	286	43	19	30	16	7	0	26
	Livada	1807	878	30	13	21	6	2	16
	Obor	1323	765	42	14	19	7	1	6
Cluj-Napoca	Pata Rât	2184	1249	45	7	17	8	0	2
Miercurea Ciuc	Primăverii street[c]	151	151	47	14	9	6	1	1
	Sumuleu	216	32	38	16	3	28	0	6
Ploiești	Bariera București	1007	197	37	12	15	9	3	13
	Bereasca	987	247	41	7	23	9	0	9
	Boldescu	1825	534	31	13	23	7	1	12
	Mimiu and "Nato" block of flats	1112	697	40	13	13	19	1	5
	Radu de Afumați	2499	874	31	15	25	10	1	9
	Rudului street	1058	213	33	12	23	11	1	12
	Teleajăn	1821	476	30	11	22	8	1	12

Târgu-Mureș	"Castel" and barracks near Băneasa street	286	109	40	3	17	8	2	2
	Dealului street	598		44	5	18	10	0	5
	The shore of Mureș river	537		40	14	24	4	1	8
	Remetea	609		41	15	24	5	1	7
	Unirii	998		40	16	8	9	7	11
	Valea Rece	1506		38	13	23	4	2	5
Roma living in the researched sites		8726		38	12	20	8	1	8
Roma living scattered across the five cities		7741		32	13	21	8	2	9
Total Non-Roma in five cities		758,760		23	3	42	3	1	23

Source of data: Census Tracks 2011

[a] Percentages on the distribution by occupational status do not add up at 100%, given that some dwellers had another status than those listed in the table, for example elderly persons no longer working but without being entitled to pensions, young people who abandoned school before reaching the legal age for employment, etc.

[b] The category of "unemployed" includes all those who considered themselves as such, that is, the registered unemployed but also those not registered at the labour force offices

[c] Including the barracks near the wastewater plant in Miercurea Ciuc

Methodological note. For each researched site, the corresponding census tracks have been identified, which contained that particular site at the 2011 Census. For the total of 20 researched sites, there were 58 corresponding census tracks, as their juxtaposition was not perfect. Therefore, the number of dwellers refers to the total population living in the census tracks that contain a given investigated site. We analysed for the 58 census track those dwellers that identified themselves as Roma. The 2011 Census contained an open-ended question on ethnic self-identification, and the results of the Census indicate 19 Roma-related self-identification categories. Based on the data from our 58 census tracks, the following categories of ethnic self-identification were lumped together as "Roma" (ethnic denominators in the Romanian original): *rom, țigan, țigan de mătase, spoitor, pletos, gabor, ursar, căldărar, rudar, lăieș*. In the neighbourhood of Obor from Călărași there were 265 self-identified Turks. Based on our ethnographic material and the area of their residence in the city, they had been indexed as "Roma" for this research.

with the persons living in these areas. Some of our interviewees did not hold positions directly focused on the urban poor or the Roma, but they played important roles in shaping the economic future of the cities. We also undertook content analyses of documents on social and housing policies and, separately, on the media representations of segregated housing areas and their inhabitants.

For each of the five cities, our joint research revealed the existence of several deprived and marginalized areas,[7] characterized by different scales of exclusion and poverty, and different degrees of their juxtaposition with ethnic enclaves and racialized stigmatization, respectively, by diverse grades of connectedness to the rest of the cities or even by various forms of resistance towards marginalization. The most extreme and recent instances of ghettoization related to evictions and homelessness were encountered in the following cases: the four marginalized areas near the landfill of Cluj-Napoca (*Cantonului, Dallas, Coastei,* and *Rampa*); the families relocated in metal barracks near the wastewater plant on *Primăverii/ Tavasz* street in Miercurea Ciuc, the Turkish-Roma community of *Obor* district in Călărași; two severely deprived substandard housing areas in Târgu Mureș (*La Barăci,* with very small container houses and improvised shacks built by the evicted families themselves on the shore of the Mureș river); the small area near the railway lines of the of Ploiești-West railway station, composed of the improvised shacks of a few Roma families (again, called *Dallas*), as well as the container housing zone (inhabited predominantly by poor Romanians), or the deprived co-housing building pejoratively called *the NATO-block* in Ploiești, close to *Mimiu* neighbourhood. However, our research also documented cases in which the current ethnic enclave resulted from the decisions of particular Roma groups to settle on empty fields or in non-residential, low-quality buildings separated from the main city area (for example, the cases of *Valea Rece/Hidegvölgy* and *Dealului/ Domb* streets in Târgu Mureș, *Șumuleu/Somlyó* Street and *Pork City* in Miercurea Ciuc, *Livada* district in Călărași, or *Mimiu, Bereasca,* and *Boldescu* in Ploiești). It must be mentioned that in the case of the latter, too, elements of voluntary separation (and related in-group solidarities sustained in terms of kinship or ancestry and lineage) are interlinked with socio-economic constraints (such as the lack of material or social capital to move out of these areas), which might be also interpreted as factors that impose on these people the "chosen" ethno-social enclosure.

As space is a fundamental dimension of capital and labour accumulation, our methodology was, from the onset, devised to capture the ways in which localities are produced at the intersection of various forces and, simultaneously, to allow us to see different intersections depending on housing, urban development, social policies, and media discourses. However, our volume is not based on a comparative case methodology in the strict sense of the term. We neither intend to draw comparisons and classifications of locations subtracted from a representative sample of marginalized spaces inhabited by racialized labourers, nor to compare the capitalist development of five Romanian cities. Rather, we investigate processes running across the locations of our fieldwork, processes which display similarities and differences, and which carry the localized influence of more general global processes of unequal development, accumulation by dispossession, labour precarization, and spatial segregation based on class position and racial categorization. This does not mean that our five cities were randomly selected. On the contrary, we purposefully selected cities of comparable sizes that function as administrative centres for their corresponding counties from different historical regions of Romania, and which differ along the lines of those historical, political, economic, and social factors that have explanatory power for the emergence of marginalized and racialized areas at urban peripheries. We construct the micro–macro or local–global linkages through social theory, in a way similar with Burawoy's (2009) approach of the extended case method. The "cases" that we refer to in our chapters are not geographically determined territories but issue-oriented cases, dimensions of analysis which highlight different aspects of the economically productive role of the interconnectedness between spatial marginality and racialization of labour for capitalist development.

The Structure of the Volume

The theory that transforms our empirical material into "the case of something" is constructed at the intersection of dependency theories, de-proletarization debates, postcolonial and decolonial studies, global anthropologies of labour, theories of postsocialism, and Romani studies. Following Burawoy's reflexive ethnography, we aim to adapt our chosen theories to explain old issues (such as racialization of labour and spatial marginalization) in new contexts, situated at one of the semi-peripheries of global capitalism marked by the disentanglement of really existing socialism and EU integration.

The different chapters of this book complement each other in offering a substantiation of our arguments on different levels that we touch upon. *The first one* investigates the overall instrumentality of ethnic and racial categories for the functioning of the capitalist system, and more narrowly of its labour regime. While these kinds of ethnographies proliferated in the cases of indigenous nations, African Americans, and ethnicized migrants from the Global South, there are surprisingly few studies which document corresponding processes in the case of the Roma in Central and Eastern Europe. Our ethnographies bring to light forms of bonded labour, underproletarianized but highly necessary and productive, that those racialized as "Tsigane" are constrained to perform.

The second level is that of the actual capitalist actors who directly benefit from the labour of this racialized category, enhancing their profits precisely because of the deregulation of their employment in a dual labour market. On the empirical sites we have visited, these forms of capitalist entrepreneurship and labour management were as a rule made invisible. The most striking case was that of landfills, where clearly impressive quantities of chaotic waste were manually processed in order to select recyclable items, that is, raw material for a next production cycle, while labour relations remained underspecified, weakly regulated and often undocumented, as it was the case of child labour.

The third level is that of the "visible" economic and political actors, such as employers, community "leaders," social workers, policymakers, and, more generally, the local administration of the cities. This is exactly the level on which the reversal of the causality chain is being operated, where the labour and "adverse inclusion" of racialized precarious workers is rendered invisible, and they become labelled as "excluded", unproductive "surplus population". On this level the systemic nature of invisibilization processes can be revealed. For most of these actors, the "Tsiganes" simply exist, and there is no reflection on how "Tsigane" eventually constitutes a classificatory device that inferiorizes a part of the population. Moreover, their preoccupations for the "Tsiganes" (seen an ethnic group in need of better houses, social aid, education, formal employment etc.) restrain either to solve "their" problems or to push them as far away from the area of visibility as possible. In this view, what brought the category of "Tsiganes" into being is not the capitalist system as such, and not even neoliberalism, but the intrinsic negative cultural qualities of the people themselves. They are not useful, but a nuisance that requires active effort on the part of various state and non-state agencies to be tackled.

The fourth level is that of the workers themselves, the ways in which the whole employability paradigm can be implemented because you have this "residual" category that gives plausibility to the way in which the "disciplining eye" sees the role of individual input. On this level we can depict those mechanisms that keep their labour at a low price and look more deeply on their spatial marginalization and racialization as two crucially intertwined mechanisms of this sort.

Correspondingly, our book is divided into two larger parts: the first part deals with the creation of racialized labour and spaces of marginality, while the second part investigates how invisibility is produced.

In the first part, individual chapters identify and describe various dimensions of the racialization of precarious labour and spatial marginalization. Norbert Petrovici analyses the spatiality of capital accumulation and of racialized labour produced by the capitalist political economy, rendered to reside in segregated and relatively homogeneous parts of the cities in terms of ethnicity, education, and occupational status. Enikő Vincze depicts several types of ghettoization or varying patterns of the formation of housing areas that are carved out physically and symbolically from the rest of the built urban environment and within which material destitution overlaps with ethnic seclusion. Cristina Rat explores the pressures to commodify work embedded in "activation" policies, increasingly salient after the neoliberal turn of welfare states and the deregulation of labour.

In the second part, each chapter explores a different dimension on which the invisibilization of racialized labour and spaces of marginality occurs. Anca Simionca reveals the kind of imaginaries guiding the development of the city and the labour market, how these visions largely ignore the spatially and socially marginalized categories, and by that directly contribute to their formation and maintenance. Orsolya Vincze investigates to what degree the ideologies used for justifying inequalities are making appeal to the racialization of marginalized spaces and precarious labour, in other words how the moral problem of inequality is made invisible and "absolved" by portraying the disadvantaged as alien and inferior. Cătălin Berescu critically engages with the ways of making use of the typology of ghettoes by different decision-maker actors in order to naturalize their existence and thus conceal the political agency behind their constitution. Thus, each chapter analyses in detail particular instances and processualities (or "cases") within the broader dynamics of labour racialization and spatial marginalization, and of making them invisible.

We acknowledge that the processes we analyse are not country-specific, and most importantly, not locality-specific, but they are global processes of contemporary capitalism.[8] Accordingly, in the concluding chapter, Giovanni Picker offers a zoom-out from Romania towards other territories across space and time, stretching from the Global North and to the South, and evolving from the colonial history of capitalism towards contemporary neoliberal governance. As such, it highlights similar and divergent patterns of the racialization of labour and the segregation of precarious workers at marginal spaces, and the invisibilization of their lives and labour.

Notes

1. This book is largely based on research conducted within the project "Spatialization and racialization of social exclusion. The social and cultural formation of 'Gypsy ghettos' in Romania in a European context" (abbreviated SPAREX), supported by a grant from the Romanian National Authority for Scientific Research, CNCS—UEFISCDI, project number PN-II-ID-PCE-2011-3-0354. The first set of articles on this subject was published by the research team in a thematic issue of a sociological journal from Romania (Studia Universitatis Babes-Bolyai Sociologia, 58(2), 2013). It included articles on the following topics: neoliberal proletarization along the urban–rural divide in postsocialist Romania (Norbert Petrovici); underdevelopment and impoverished Roma commu-

nities (Anca Simionca); ethnic housing areas of Călărași (Cătălin Berescu); state retrenchment and population profiling in segregated and severely deprived areas in Romania (Cristina Raț); family as a means of survival in a Roma ghetto in Șumuleu (Hajnalka Harbula); performative anthropology through the Case of the Pata-Rât ghetto (Adrian Dohotaru); socio-spatial marginality of Roma as form of intersectional injustice (Enikő Vincze). The research also concluded in the Romanian language volume *Pata* (The Stain) edited by Adrian Dohotaru, Hajnalka Harbula, and Enikő Vincze (Cluj-Napoca: EFES, 2016) and in three documentary films. Two of the films, shot in Călărași and Târgu Mureș, focus on the relationship between labour and housing, while the third briefly tells the story of fight for social justice in Cluj-Napoca. All these products are available on the project website (www.sparex-ro.eu)
2. This pejorative Romanian term connects a supposedly negative human feature/behaviour with an ethnic group (Roma) and a supposedly dangerous territory, and it is used to mark "troubled" spaces regardless of the effective ethnic composition of their population. It might be translated into English as "Gypsyhood" or a "Gypsy colony"; however, these English denominations do not necessarily reflect the local ethnicized/racialized negative connotations attached to the Romanian term *țigănie*. Therefore, wherever possible, we use the term "Tsigane" rather than "Gypsy" for the English translation of the Romanian word "țigan," in order to prevent any misunderstandings around the divergent national significances of these terms.
3. According to the *Romani Studies* international journal, founded in 1888 as the *Journal of the Gypsy Lore Society*, Romani Studies deals with "the cultures of groups traditionally known as Gypsies as well as Travelers and other peripatetic groups," covering subjects of "history, anthropology, sociology, linguistics, art, literature, folklore and music."
4. A concerted European preoccupation for "Roma policies" did not begin right after 1990. Those seeking to advance Roma issues were initially focused on nation-building and the construction of the Roma as "a truly European minority" (see Mirga and Gheorghe 1997). Although we acknowledge that these processes might have influenced how places of marginality racialized as *Țigănii* (Tsigane neighbourhoods) entered the political agenda and ultimately also how various policy interventions changed these places in time, it is beyond our purposes to analyse in detail the European "Roma platform" or how it has been formed.

5. "If there is one category whose experience deviates sharply from this pattern [of the anti-ghetto – n.] to veer toward ghettoization, it is the Roma of eastern Europe" (Wacquant 2012a: 19).
6. In Wacquant's view, there are "four constituent elements of the ghetto, namely, (i) stigma, (ii) constraint, (iii) spatial confinement, and (iv) institutional parallelism" (Wacquant 2012a: 7).
7. For an incomplete, yet more general view on the number, size, ethnic composition, and dimensions of deprivation in marginalized urban areas throughout Romania, see Swinkels et al. (2015).
8. In this sense, our volume subscribes to the *singularity of capitalism* perspective. However, we admit that it was beyond the purposes of this volume to explicitly engage in the debate over the *plurality of capitalisms* versus the *singularity of capitalism*, and we would welcome any follow-up work that would undertake that.

References

Akram-Lodhi, Haroon, and Cristobal Kay, eds. 2012. *Peasants and Globalization: Political Economy, Agrarian Transformation and Development*. New York: Routledge.

Anthias, Floya. 2001. The Concept of 'Social Divisions' and Theorizing Social Stratification: Looking at Ethnicity and Class. *Sociology* 35 (4): 835–854.

Ban, Cornel. 2016. *Ruling Ideas. How Global Neoliberalism Goes Local*. Oxford: Oxford University Press.

Blasco, Paloma Gay. 1999. *Gypsies in Madrid. Sex, Gender and the Performance of Identity*. Oxford: Berg.

Boatcă, Manuela. 2003. *From Neoevolutionism to World Systems Analysis: The Romanian Theory of "Forms Without Substance" in Light of Modern Debates on Social Change*. Opladen: Leske und Budrich.

———. 2007. The Eastern Margins of Empire: Coloniality in 19th Century Romania. *Cultural Studies* 21 (2–3): 368–384.

Bockman, J. 2011. *Markets in the Name of Socialism: The Left-Wing Origins of Neoliberalism*. Stanford: Stanford University Press.

Bodnar, Judit. 2007. Becoming Bourgeois: (Postsocialist) Utopias of Isolation and Civilization. In *Evil Paradises: Dreamworlds of Neoliberalism*, ed. Mike Davis and Daniel Monk, 140–151. New York: The New Press.

Bohle, Dorothee, and Bela Greskovits. 2012. *Capitalist Diversity on Europe's Periphery*. Bloomington: Cornell University Press.

Bonacich, Edna. 1972. A Theory of Ethnic Antagonism: The Split Labor Market. *American Sociological Review* 37 (5): 547–559.

Böröcz, József, and Melinda, Kovács, eds. 2001. *Empire's New Clothes: Unveiling EU-Enlargement*. EBook, a Central Europe Review.

Botonogu, Florin, ed. 2011. *Comunități ascunse. Ferentari [Hidden Communities. Ferentari]*. Bucharest: Expert.

Brass, Tom. 1999. *Towards a Comparative Political Economy of Unfree Labour: Case Studies and Debates*. London/Portland: Frank Cass Publishers.

———. 2011. *Labour Regime Change in the Twenty-First Century: Unfreedom, Capitalism and Primitive Accumulation*. Leiden/Boston: Brill.

———. 2014. Debating Capitalist Dynamics and Unfree Labour: A Missing Link? *Journal of Development Studies* 50 (4): 570–582.

Brenner, Robert. 1989. Economic Backwardness in Eastern Europe in Light of Developments in the West. In *The Origins of Backwardness in Eastern Europe*, ed. Daniel Chirot, 15–52. Berkeley/Los Angeles: University of California Press.

Buden, Boris. 2010. Children of Postcommunism. *Radical Philosophy* 159: 18–25.

Burawoy, Michael. 2009. *The Extended Case Method*. Berkeley: University of California. Press.

Cao, Yang, and Victor G. Nee. 2000. Comment: Controversies and Evidence in the Market Transition Debate. *American Journal of Sociology* 105 (4): 1175–1189.

Carrier, James G., and Don Kalb. 2015. *Anthropologies of Class: Power, Practice, and Inequality*. Cambridge: Cambridge University Press.

Chelcea, Liviu. 2006. Marginal Groups in Central Places: Gentrification, Property Rights and Post-socialist Primitive Accumulation (Bucharest, Romania). In *Social Changes and Social Sustainability in Historical Urban Centres: The Case of Central Europe*, ed. György Enyedi and Zoltán Kovács, 107–126. Pécs: Centre for Regional Studies of Hungarian Academy of Science.

Chertkovskaya, E., P. Watt, S. Tramer, S. Spoelstra, K. Berglund, V. Vesterberg, and H. Elraz. 2013. Giving Notice to Employability. *Ephemera: Theory & Politics in Organization* 13 (4): 701–716.

Chirot, Daniel. 1976. *Social Change in a Peripheral Society: The Creation of a Balkan Colony*. New York/London: Academic.

Chirot, Daniel, and A. Reid, eds. 1997. *Essential Outsiders: Chinese and Jews in the Modern Transformation of Southeast Asia and Central Europe.* Washington, DC: University of Washington Press.

Collier, S.J. 2011. *Post-Soviet Social: Neoliberalism, Social Modernity, Biopolitics.* Princeton: Princeton University Press.

Costinescu, I.M. 2014. Path Dependency, World Systems Analysis, or Alternative Modernity? Research Notes on Interwar Romania and the Bucharest Sociological School. *Romanian Sociology* 12 (1-2): 119–132.

Cucu, Alina-Sandra. 2014. Producing Knowledge in Productive Spaces: Ethnography and Planning in Early Socialist Romania. *Economy and Society* 43 (2): 211–232.

Dean, Hartley. 2003. The Third Way and Social Welfare: The Myth of Post-Emotionalism. *Social Policy and Administration* 37 (7): 695–708.

Dean, Hartley, and Peter Taylor-Gooby. 1992. *Welfare Dependency: The Explosion of a Myth.* Hemel Hempstead: Harvester Wheatsheaf.

Dobrogeanu-Gherea, Constantin. 2010 [1910]. Neo-serfdom. In *Modernism: The Creation of Nation States*, ed. A. Ersoy, Vol. 3, 419–425. Budapest/New York: Central European University Press.

Dunn, Elizabeth. 2004. *Privatizing Poland: Baby Food, Big Business, and the Remaking of Labor.* Ithaca: Cornell University Press.

Esping-Andersen, Gosta. 1990. *The Three World of Welfare Capitalism.* Cambridge: Polity Press.

Evans, Anthony J., and Dragos Aligica. 2009. *The Neoliberal Revolution in Eastern Europe: Economic Ideas in the Transition from Communism.* Cheltenham/Northampton: Edward Elgar Publishing.

Eyal, Gil, Iván Szelényi, and Eleanor Townsley. 1998. *Making Capitalism Without Capitalists: Class Formation and Elite Struggles in Post-Communist Central Europe.* London: Verso.

———. 2001. The Utopia of Postsocialist Theory and the Ironic View of History in Neoclassical Sociology. *American Journal of Sociology* 106 (4): 1121–1128.

Faje, Florin. 2011. Football Fandom in Cluj: Class, Ethno-Nationalism and Cosmopolitanism. In *Headlines of Nation, Subtexts of Class: Working Class Populism and the Return of the Repressed in Neoliberal Europe*, ed. Don Kalb and Gabor Halmai, 78–92. New York: Berghahn Books.

Florida, R.L. 2002. *The Rise of the Creative Class: And How It's Transforming Work, Leisure, Community and Everyday life.* New York: Basic Books.

Fosztó, László, ed. 2009. *Colecție de studii despre romii din România [Collection of Studies About the Romanian Roma].* Cluj-Napoca: Editura ISPMN and Kriterion.

Fraser, Nancy. 1997. *Justice Interruptus: Critical Reflections on the "Postsocialist" Condition*. New York: Routledge.

Gille, Zsuzsa. 2007. *From the Cult of Waste to the Trash Heap of History: The Politics of Waste in Socialist and Postsocialist Hungary*. Bloomington: Indiana University Press.

———. 2010. Actor Networks, Modes of Production, and Waste Regimes: Reassembling the Macro-Social. *Environment and Planning A: Economy and Space* 42 (5): 1049–1064.

Guga, Ștefan. 2015. *Sociologia istorica a lui Henri H. Stahl*. Cluj-Napoca: Tact.

Guy, Will, ed. 2001. *Between Past and Future. The Roma of Central and Eastern Europe*. Hatfield: University of Hertfordshire Press.

Haney, Lynne. 2002. *Inventing the Needy: Gender and Politics of Welfare in Hungary*. Berkeley/Los Angeles: University of California Press.

Harvey, David. 2003. *The New Imperialism*. New York: Oxford University Press.

———. 2011. *The Enigma of Capital: And The Crises of Capitalism*. London: Profile Books.

Hamilton, Ian, Kaliopa Dimitrovska Andrews, and Natasha Pichler-Milanovic, eds. 2006. *Transformation of Cities in Central and Eastern Europe: Towards Globalization*. Tokyo: United Nations University Press.

Hayes, Michael, and Acton Thomas, eds. 2006. *Counter-hegemony and the Postcolonial "Other"*. Newcastle: Cambridge Scholars Press.

Heumos, Peter. 2010. Workers Under Communist Rule: Research in the Former Socialist Countries of Eastern-Central and South-Eastern Europe and in the Federal Republic of Germany. *International Review of Social History* 55: 83–115.

Hirt, Sonia, and Atanas Kovachev. 2006. The Changing Spatial Structure of Post-socialist Sofia. In *The Urban Mosaic of Post-Socialist Eastern Europe*, ed. Sasha Tsenkova, 113–130. Dordrecht: Springer.

Horváth, Sándor. 2005. Everyday Life in the First Hungarian Socialist City. *International Labor and Working-Class History* 68: 24–46.

Janos, A.C. 2000. *East Central Europe in the Modern World: The Politics of the Borderlands from Pre-to Postcommunism*. Stanford: Stanford University Press.

Jessop, Bob. 2002. *The Future of the Capitalist State*. Cambridge: Polity Press.

Kalb, Don. 1998. *Expanding Class: Power and Everyday Politics in Industrial Communities, The Netherlands 1850–1950*. Durham: Duke University Press.

———. 2015. Introduction: Class and the New Anthropological Holism. In *Anthropologies of Class: Power, Practice, and Inequality*, ed. James G. Carrier and Don Kalb, 1–27. Cambridge: Cambridge University Press.

Kasmir, Sharryn, and August Carbonella. 2014. *Blood and Fire: Toward a Global Anthropology of Labor*. London/New York: Berghahn Books.

Kertesi, Gábor, and Gábor Kézdi. 1997. *Cigány etnikai gettók. Az 1990. évi népszámlálás számlálókörzeti adatai alapján készült elemzés [Tsigane Ethnic Ghettos. An Analysis Based on the 1990 Hungarian Population Census]*. Budapest: TARKI.

Kideckel, David. 2008. *Getting by in Postsocialist Romania. Labor, the Body, and Working-Class Culture*. Bloomington: Indiana University Press.

Kochanowicz, J. 1989. The Polish Economy and the Evolution of Dependency. In *The Origins of Backwardness in Eastern Europe*, ed. Daniel Chirot, 92–130. Berkeley/Los Angeles: University of California Press.

Krippner, G.R. 2011. *Capitalizing on Crisis*. Cambridge/London: Harvard University Press.

Ladányi, János és Iván Szelényi. 2001a. *A kirekesztettség változó formái [The Changing Forms of Exclusion]*. Budapest: Napvilág Kiadó.

———. 2001b. The Social Construction of Roma Ethnicity in Bulgaria, Romania and Hungary During Market Transition. *Review of Sociology* 7 (2): 79–34.

Liégeois, Jean-Pierre. 1986. *Gypsies: An Illustrated History*. London: Al Saqi Books.

Lister, Ruth. 2004. *Poverty*. Cambridge: Polity Press.

MacLeod, G. 2002. From Urban Entrepreneurialism to a 'Revanchist City'? On the Spatial Injustices of Glasgow's Renaissance. *Antipode* 34 (3): 602–624.

Mateescu, Oana. 2012. Losing the Phenomenon: Time and Indeterminacy in the Practice of Anthrohistory. In *Anthrohistory: Unsettling Knowledge, Questioning Discipline*, ed. C. Bhimull, D.W. Cohen, F. Coronil, E.L. Murphy, M. Patterson, and J. Skurski. Ann Arbour: University of Michigan Press.

Matras, Yaron. 2002. *Romani. A Linguistic Introduction*. Cambridge: Cambridge University Press.

Mendieta, E. 2003. *Latin American Philosophy: Currents, Issues, Debates*. Bloomington: Indiana University Press.

Mirga, Andrej, and Nicolae Gheorghe. 1997. *The Roma in the Twenty-First Century. A Policy Paper*. Princeton: Project on Ethnic Relations.

Moraña, M., E.D. Dussel, and C.A. Jáuregui. 2008. *Coloniality at Large: Latin America and the Postcolonial Debate*. Durham: Duke University Press.

Năstasă, Lucian, and Diana Varga. 2001. *Mărturii documentare. Țiganii din România 1919–1944. [Testimonials in documents. The Tsiganes in Romania 1919–1944]*. Cluj-Napoca: Centrul pentru Resurse pentru Diversitate Etnoculturală.

Okely, Judith. 1983. *The Traveller-Gypsies*. Cambridge: Cambridge University Press.

———. 1996. *Own or Other Culture*. London/New York: Routledge.
Ost, David. 2005. *Defeat of Solidarity. Anger and Politics in Postcommunist Europe*. Ithaca: Cornell University Press.
Ourednicek, Martin, and Jana Temelova. 2009. Twenty Years After Socialism: Transformation of Prague's Inner Structure. *Studia UBB Sociologia* 53 (2): 9–30.
Patnaik, U., and M. Dingawaney, eds. 1985. *Chains of Servitude: Bondage and Slavery in India*. Madras: Sangam.
Petrovici, Norbert. 2013. Neoliberal Proletarization Along the Urban-Rural Divide in Postsocialist Romania. *Studia Sociologia* 58 (2): 23–54.
Petrovici, Norbert, and Anca Simionca. 2011. Productive Informality and Economic Ties in Emerging Economies: The Case of Cluj Business Networks. In *Transformation and Transition in Central and Eastern Europe & Russia*, ed. T. Bhambry and C. Griffin, 134–144. London: University College London.
Pierson, Paul. 2001. *The New Politics of the Welfare State*. Oxford: Oxford University Press.
Pittaway, Mark. 2005. Introduction: Workers and Socialist States in Postwar Central and Eastern Europe. *International Labor and Working-Class History* 68 (Fall): 1–8.
Poenaru, Florin. 2015. Power at Play. Soccer Stadiums and Popular Culture in 1980s Romania. In *Socialist Escapes: Breaking Away from Ideology and Everyday Routine in Eastern Europe, 1945–1989*, ed. Cathleen M. Giustino, Catherine J. Plum, and Alexander Vari, 232–251. New York: Berghahn Books.
Pulay, Gergő. 2011. The Civilized, the Vagabond, the Player and the Fool. Notes on Fieldwork in a Bucharest Neighbourhood. *Studia Universitatis Babes-Bolyai Sociologia* 56 (1): 117–134.
———. 2015. 'I'm Good but Also Mad': The Street Economy in a Poor Neighbourhood of Bucharest. In *Gypsy Economy. Romani Livelihoods and Notions of Worth in the 21st Century*, ed. M. Brazzabeni, M. Ivone Cunha, and M. Fotta. Oxford: Berghan Books.
Quijano, A. 2000. Coloniality of Power and Eurocentrism in Latin America. *International Sociology* 15 (2): 215–232.
Riabchuk, Anastasia. 2009. The Implications of Adaptation Discourse for Post-communist Working Classes. *Debatte* 17 (1): 55–64.
Ruopilla, Sampo, and Anneli Kährik. 2003. Socio-economic Residential Differentiation in Post-socialist Tallinn. *Journal of Housing and the Built Environment* 18: 49–73.
Samara, T.R. 2010. Order and Security in the City: Producing Race and Policing Neoliberal Spaces in South Africa. *Ethnic and Racial Studies* 33 (4): 637–655.

Samson, Melanie. 2010. Producing Privatization: Re-articulating Race, Gender, Class and Space. *Antipode* 42 (2): 404–432.

———. 2015. Accumulation by Dispossession and the Informal Economy – Struggles Over Knowledge, Being and Waste at a Soweto Garbage Dump. *Environment and Planning D: Society and Space* 33 (5): 813–830.

Sandu, Dumitru. 2005. *Comunitățile de romi din România. O hartă a sărăciei comunitare prin sondajul PROROMI. [Roma Communities in Romania. A Community-Poverty Map Based on the PROROMI Survey]*. Bucharest: The World Bank. http://www.anr.gov.ro/docs/statistici/PROROMI__Comunitatile_de_Romi_din_Romania_187.pdf. Accessed 1 Sept 2015.

Sanyal, Kalyan, and Rajesh Bhattacharyya. 2009. Beyond the Factory: Globalisation, Informalisation of Production and the New Locations of Labour. *Economic and Political Weekly* 44 (22): 35–44.

Schwartz, Herman. 2006. Round Up the Usual Suspects! Globalization, Domestic Politics, and Welfare State Change. In *The New Politics of Welfare*, ed. Christopher Pierson, 17–45. Cambridge: Polity Press.

Simionca, Anca. 2012. Neoliberal Managerialism, Anti-communist Dogma and the Critical Employee in Contemporary Romania. *Studia UBB Sociologia* 57 (1): 125–149.

Simionca, Anca, and Sorin Gog. 2016. Sociological and Anthropological Perspectives on Religion and Economy: Emerging Spiritualities and the Future of Work. *Studia Universitatis Babes-Bolyai Sociologia* 61 (2): 5–9.

Slater, Tom. 2004. North American Gentrification? Revanchist and Emancipatory Perspectives Explored. *Environment and Planning* 36 (7): 1191–1214.

———. 2015. Planetary Rent Gaps. *Antipode, Early Online View*. 22 September.

Smith, Neil. 1996. *The New Urban Frontier: Gentrification and the Revanchist City*. New York: Routledge.

———. 1998. Giuliani Time: The Revanchist 1990s. *Social Text* 57 (1): 1–20.

———. 2002. New Globalism, New Urbanism: Gentrification as Global Urban Strategy. *Antipode* 34 (3): 427–450.

Smith, Adrian, Alison Stenning, Alena Rochovská, and Dariusz Światek. 2009. The Emergence of a Working Poor: Labour Markets, Neoliberalisation and Diverse Economies in Post-socialist Cities. *Antipode* 40 (2): 283–311.

Stahl, H. Henry. 1980. *Traditional Romanian Village Communities: The Transition From the Communal to the Capitalist Mode of Production in the Danube Region*. Cambridge: Cambridge University Press Cambridge.

Stănculescu, Manuela S., and Ionica Berevoiescu. 2004. *Sărac lipit, caut altă viață [Poorest of the Poor, Searching for a New Life]*. Bucharest: Nemira.

Standing, Guy. 2007. Labour Recommodification in the Global Transformation. In *Reading Karl Polanyi for the 21st Century*, ed. Ayshe Bugra and Kan Agatan, 67–95. Basingstoke: Palgrave Macmillan.
———. 2011. *The Precariat. The New Dangerous Class*. London: Bloomsbury Academic.
Stanilov, Kiril, ed. 2007. *The Post-socialist City. Urban Form and Space Transformations in Central and Eastern Europe after Socialism*. Heildelberg: Springer.
Stenning, Alison, and Kathrin Hörschelmann. 2008. History, Geography and Difference in the Post-socialist World: Or, Do We Still Need Post-socialism? *Antipode* 40 (2): 312–335.
Stewart, Michael. 1997. *The Time of the Gypsies*. Boulder: Westview Press.
———. 2002. Deprivation, the Roma and the 'Underclass'. In *Postsocialism. Ideals, Ideologies, and Practices in Euroasia*, ed. Chriss M. Hann, 133–157. London: Routledge.
———. 2012. *The Gypsy 'Menace'. Populism and the New Anti-Gypsy Politics*. Oxford: Oxford University Press.
Swanson, Kate. 2007. Revanchist Urbanism Heads South: The Regulation of Indigenous Beggars and Street Vendors in Ecuador. *Antipode* 39 (4): 708–728.
Swinkels, Rob, Manuela S. Stănculescu, Simona Anton, Bryan Koo, Titus Man, and Ciprian Moldovan. 2015. *Atlasul zonelor urbane marginalizate [The Atlas of Marginalized Urban Areas]*. București: The World Bank.
Szalai, Júlia, and Violetta Zentai, eds. 2014. *Faces and Causes of Roma Marginalization in Local Contexts: Hungary, Romania, Serbia*. Budapest: Central European University, CPS Books.
Szelényi, Iván, and Eric Kostello. 1996. The Market Transition Debate: Towards a Synthesis? *American Journal of Sociology* 101 (4): 1082–1096.
Tlostanova, Madina, and Walter Mignolo. 2012. *Learning to Unlearn: Decolonial Reflections from Eurasia and the Americas*. Columbus: Ohio State University Press.
Toma, Stefania. 2009. "Țiganul 'meu' și încrederea – relații economice informale într-o comunitate de romi din România" ['My' Tsigane and Trust – Informal Economic Relations in a Roma Community from Romania]. In *Incluziune și excluziune. Studii de caz asupra comunităților de romi din România*, ed. Tamás Kiss, László Fosztó, and Gábor Fleck, 197–223. Cluj-Napoca: Editura ISPMN.
Tremlett, Annabell. 2009. Claims of 'Knowing' in Ethnography: Realising Anti-essentialism Through a Critical Reflection on Language Acquisition in Fieldwork. *The Graduate Journal of Social Science* 6 (3): 63–85.

Tsenkova, Sasha, and Zorica Nedovic-Budic, eds. 2006. *The Urban Mosaic of Post-socialist Europe. Space, Institutions and Policy*. Heildelberg: Springer.

Uitermark, Justus, and Jan Willem Duyvendak. 2008. Civilising the City: Populism and Revanchist Urbanism in Rotterdam. *Urban Studies* 45 (7): 1485–1503.

Vincze, Enikő. 2014. The Racialization of Roma in the 'New' Europe and the Political Potential of Romani Women. *European Journal of Women's Studies* 21 (4): 443–449.

———. 2015a. Adverse Incorporation of the Roma and the Formation of Capitalism in Romania. *Intersections. East European Journal of Society and Politics* 1 (4): 14–38.

———. 2015b. Precarization of Working Class Roma Through Spatial Deprivation, Labor Destitution and Racialization. *Review of Sociology of the Hungarian Sociological Association* 25 (4): 58–85.

Wacquant, Loic. 2000. Logics of Urban Polarization: The View from Below. In *Renewing Class Analysis*, ed. Rosemary Crompton, Fiona Devine, Mike Savage, and John Scott, 107–119. Oxford: Blackwell.

———. 2008. *Urban Outcasts: A Comparative Sociology of Advanced Marginality*. Cambridge: Polity Press.

———. 2012a. A Janus-Faced Institution of Ethnoracial Closure: A Sociological Specification of the Ghetto. In *The Ghetto. Contemporary Global Issues and Controversies*, ed. Ray Hutchinson and Bruce D. Haynes, 1–32. Boulder: Westview Press.

———. 2012b. Three Steps for a Historical Anthropology of Actually Existing Neoliberalism. *Social Anthropology* 20 (1): 66–79.

Wallerstein, Immanuel. 1974. *The Modern World-System I: Capitalist Agriculture and the Origins of the European World-Economy in the Sixteenth Century*. New York/London: Academic Press.

———. 2004. *World-Systems Analysis: An Introduction*. Durham: Duke University Press.

Willems, Wim. 1997. *In Search of the True Gypsy. From Enlightenment to Final Solution*. London: Frank Cass.

Whitehead, Judy, and N. More. 2007. Revanchism in Mumbai? Political Economy of Rent Gaps and Urban Restructuring in a Global City. *Economic and Political Weekly* 42 (25): 2428–2434.

Wolf, Eric R. 2001. *Pathways of Power: Building an Anthropology of the Modern World*. Berkeley: University of California Press.

2

Working Status in Deprived Urban Areas and Their Greater Economic Role

Norbert Petrovici

The deprived urban areas under scrutiny in this study are *de facto* formed by three categories of people: first, the former socialist working class and their children who could not escape the city in the 1990s during the urban-to-rural internal emigration; second, better-off, qualified Roma workers who, after the 1990s, gradually lost job opportunities in an economically restructuring city; third, qualified Roma workers coming from other cities or towns in search of new job opportunities. The social composition of these areas is highly skewed age-wise. The average age is 26, with 40 per cent of the population being children up to 18 years of age. Few elders can be found in these communities. However, this is hardly a surprise, given that the Roma life expectancy is around 64 years (Romanian Government 2015). Due to living in derelict and polluted places, and places with inadequate housing, these populations are increasingly suffering from morbidity and health issues, and most of the time they are in dire need for health services. Nonetheless, these areas are not strange residues of a system, margins that make visible the unfortunate effects caused

---

N. Petrovici (✉)
Sociology Department, Babeș-Bolyai University, Cluj-Napoca, Romania

by the failure to be integrated. On the contrary, they are integrated in the urban economy and become an important labour pool for three types of jobs: first, unskilled urban workers paid minimum wage for work in new globalized production facilities; second, workers in wage management cycles that provide key components for raw materials production needed by booming industries; third, cheap labour performing reproduction services for the greater working class, either the hyper-skilled labour of professionals or the skilled labour of the service working class.

The aim of this chapter is to link the internal migration of the Roma with greater trends in internal labour migration in Romania in order to show the dynamic of the formation of relatively compact Roma areas, pejoratively labelled by majority populations as *Țigănii*. Moreover, labour migration is linked with key economic transformations of Romania in the European context. I show that the Roma who dwell in spatially segregated areas are employed as unskilled manual workers in the new post-socialist industrial sector in cities that are increasingly becoming hubs for managerial services.

I use here the term "researched areas" in a precise methodological sense. On the basis of the 20 ethnographically identified sites in the 5 cities under scrutiny (see Table 1.1 in Chap. 1), I have identified for each of these sites the corresponding census tracks from the 2011 Census. For the total of 20 sites, there were 58 corresponding census tracks, as their juxtaposition was not perfect. Therefore, in this chapter, the number of dwellers from a certain area, which I call "researched areas", refers to the total population living in the census tracks that contain a given investigated site. I have analysed for the 58 census tracks those dwellers that identified themselves as Roma[1] or spoke a Roma dialect.

Socialist Investment Patterns and Post-socialist Job Losses

The major transformations in employment and housing for the Roma outlined above are strongly connected to the greater transformations in the region and the composition of the labour force in Romania. Eastern Europe experienced a consistent population loss over the past decades

(Gerda Neyer et al. 2013; Kucera et al. 2000), arguably the most persistent population shrinkage in the post-war era worldwide (Romei 2016). This was accompanied by one of the most sustained losses in aggregate employment (Ark et al. 2012; Bell and Mickiewicz 2013). Romania is no exception here, as the total number of wage earners decreased dramatically in the last few decades (Ban 2014; Petrovici 2013). The trend started during the last five years of socialist governance when the share of employees decreased among the total population from 42 per cent in 1985 to 35 per cent in 1990. Another sharp 13 per cent drop happened in the first post-socialist decade and stabilized around 20–22 per cent in the second post-socialist decade. As opposed to aggregate employment, the employment of the occupied population remained relatively stable, around 40 per cent of the total population. Much of this figure can be explained by strong, work-related migration fluxes. In the first post-socialist decade, Romania had significant internal migration from urban to rural areas with a boom in self-employment and familial agricultural work (Rees and Kupiszewski 1999; Rotariu and Mezei 1998, 1999). In the second decade, migration became external, especially towards Western Europe, in various low-paying jobs in informal and formal secondary markets (Andrén and Roman 2016; Sandu 2010).

The decrease in aggregate employment had significant regional variations across Romania. Most employees are found in the cities, where the number of those employed makes up almost 40 per cent of populations. Also, more than half of those employed are concentrated in the top ten most developed counties, out of a total of 41. Some counties suffered major losses in population and jobs, while others, even if hit economic contraction, recovered more swiftly during the second post-socialist decade. For example, in Călărași County, by 2010, the total number of employees was only 43 per cent of the 1990 figure. Cluj County had a milder decrease, where, by 2010, the total number of employees was 73 per cent of the 1990 number. Much of this disparity in job losses can be attributed to socialist investment strategies and their spatial patterning.

The counties with the harshest decrease in employment were those that received the majority of investments in agriculture during the socialist decades (Petrovici 2013). Counties with investments in industry and services retained a greater share of employees across the post-socialist decades. This is somewhat paradoxical given the structure of employment under socialism, in which the greatest share of employees was urban industrial workers. Much of the agricultural labour was done in co-ops with compensation in products and money retribution according to sales and state acquisitions, but not in full-fledged wages (Dobrincu and Iordachi 2009; Kligman and Verdery 2015). Nonetheless, after the demise of socialism, the counties with the biggest job loss were not those with the most employees but those with fewer employees, that is, those which specialized in agriculture.

The paradox dissolves if one takes into account two major policy concepts that regulated investments in Romania in terms of the spatial development of labour pools: commune formation and urban zone formation.[2] First, in 1950, at the dawn of the communist instalment, more that 70 per cent of the Romanian population was rural, dispersed in more than 20,200 villages that made up 4052 communes. By 1990, there were around 13,000 villages that made up 2600 communes. The constant endeavour was to cluster the villages in more compact communities to make investments in amenities and social services more cost-effective and, more importantly, to transform the scattered autarchic villages into grouped localities, suppliers of labour forces for urban factories and rural farms (Stahl 1969). Second, an *urban zone* designated the hinterland of an urban centre that used the rural proximities as supply areas for raw materials and the labour force. Investments were driven by the local natural resources and previous pre-socialist investments (Petrovici 2013) in order to create value chains based on input-output networks connecting urban industries with rural mining, forestry, and agriculture (Constantinescu and Stahl 1970; Stahl and Matei 1966). Therefore, between 1950 and 1990, given the local resources, some counties specialized in industries (especially Transylvania, Banat, and the cluster Ploiești-Argeș-Bucharest), others specialized in agricultural production (counties from the Southern part of Romania), and a small portion specialized in services, being mainly export hubs abroad (Brăila-Galați, Constanța, Bihor).

The consequence of these policies was that the counties benefiting from industrial investments had a more economically integrated settlement system, while counties benefiting from agricultural investments had a less cohesive settlement structure. The contrast between Călărași and Cluj is once again illustrative. Călărași County received one of the greatest shares of agriculture investments across the whole socialist period. Starting at the end of the 1970s, Călărași city received a series of heavy industry investments, hosting, for example, one of the biggest steel factories in Romania (Steel Mill Călărași—Siderca). Nonetheless, this urban industry was uncoupled with the rural hinterlands, which were becoming specialized in grain production and livestock. The suppliers for these urban industries were coordinated directly at the national level. With the collapse of governmental planning, the supply networks became uncertain, hitting hardest the factories that were not locally embedded in their hinterlands. Cluj County, on the other hand, was an important receiver of industrial investments that went into the creation of a strong network of input-output industries located in satellite towns, with its centre in Cluj-Napoca city. Cluj County had a highly integrated rural agricultural production in the urban industrial circuits (Rotariu and Mezei 1998).

Using 2011 Census data based on the available information the census tracks in each city, Călărași, Cluj-Napoca, Miercurea Ciuc, Ploiești, and Târgu Mureș, a clear picture of labour migration emerges. During socialism, those who left these five cities were mostly professionals and skilled workers (see Table 2.1), a pattern that holds across urban Romania (Rotariu and Mezei 1998; Sandu 1984). The skilled labour force during socialism was recruited from large urban centres, while, as mentioned above, rural areas were suppliers of abundant and cheap unskilled labour. This trend was abruptly halted in the 1990s. An important part of the dismantled working force returned to the rural hinterlands in the 1990s as farm workers, cultivating either cash crops on small plots, as was the case with Călărași County, or fresh agricultural products for the local urban markets, as was the case of Cluj County (Petrovici 2013). Other emigrant labourers left the city for smaller towns, most often in the same county, working in 2011 as service workers or industrial workers. But the magnitude of the labour emigration flux was linked to the extent to which the five cities lost their economic supply chains. Călărași was hit the hardest, Cluj-Napoca the least, and Ploiești, Miercurea Ciuc, and Târgu Mureș in between.

Table 2.1 Occupational positions held in 2011 by those who emigrated from the cities of Călărași, Cluj-Napoca, Miercurea Ciuc, Ploiești, Târgu Mureș

Occupational position	1948-1990	1991-2003	2004-2008	2009-2011	Total
Owners and management positions	5%	4%†	6%*	6%*	4,004
Professionals	32%*	25%†	31%*	32%*	22,925
Technicians	10%†	9%†	11%*	13%*	8,041
Administrative functionaries	5%†	4%†	6%*	6%*	3,920
Service workers	12%†	15%*	15%*	15%*	11,229
Farm workers	11%	15%*	9%†	6%†	8,820
Skilled workers	12%*	14%*	10%†	10%†	9,335
Semi-skilled workers	7%	7%*	6%†	6%	5,229
Unskilled workers	6%	7%*	5%†	5%†	4,820
Total	**100% (19,191)**	**100% (28,862)**	**100% (15,646)**	**100% (14,624)**	78,323

*Adjusted standardized residual less than 1.96, indicating a significantly lower percentage than expected under no association hypothesis, at the cell level
†Adjusted standardized residual greater than 1.96, indicating a significantly greater percentage than expected under no association hypothesis, at the cell level. Cell highlighted in grey
Statistical association: contingency coefficient = 0.143, Cramer's V = 0.083; If destination (rural vs. urban) is controlled C = 0.287; V = 0.180
Time cut-points: 1948 is used for the beginning of Romanian socialism and 1990 for the end of socialism; 2004 is used as the beginning of a period of macroeconomic growth; 2008 is used to signal the Great Global Depression, which also affected Romania
Source: National Institute of Statistics, Census 2011. Author's calculations based on data at the level of census tracks

Workers in the New Urban Zones

The first post-socialist decade came with a partial deindustrialization. In the second post-socialist decade, after a steady macro-stabilization driven by an alliance of local capitalists and global capital (Pasti 2006; Petrovici and Simionca 2011; Poenaru 2011), industrial output started to grow steadily once again. After the 2009–2010 economic crisis, the industrial sector registered a boom in production and investments. The growth was driven by the extension of Western European firms' demand for cheap industrial facilities and labour. By 2015, one-third of Romania's GDP was produced by industry and 36 per cent of the workforce was employed in this sector. Also, 40 per cent of the GDP was produced by foreign-owned companies and 90 per cent of the banking system was owned by foreign capital (Ban 2016).

Romania, as many other Central and Eastern European economies, entered the course of a "dependent market economy", as Nölke and Vliegenthart (2009) put it. Romania became an assembly line in the global system of production, as an effect of radical neoliberal policies and privatization, strong property laws on behalf of companies, minimum taxation of profits and dividends, a flat taxation system on income and profit, and heavy taxation of labour in the social insurance system (Ban 2016). While most of the economic decisions were controlled by multinational companies, either directly through the banking system or through intra-company investments, the major competitive advantage of the country became the cheap labour it provided to the transnational supply chains and production.

The former socialist geography of industrial development is still relevant; the areas of Romania that received more investment in industry still received more investments than others after 2008. By 2011, most of the new exporting manufacturing facilities were in Transylvania and Banat and across the corridor in București-Prahova-Argeș (see Fig. 2.1). Either the former factory areas were refurbished and new technological investments were made, or new greenfield investments sprawled into the rural periphery of the major cities. The former socialist industrial platforms were certainly important, but the specificity of the new productive boom was that many factories were in the hinterland of the cities, either in rural areas or in smaller towns. However, the greater logic of concentrating the labour through communes and urban zones was preserved, ironically, by reverting it. The whole purpose of the socialist urban zone was to concentrate industry in urban areas, as well as the workers through urbanization. The communes were methods of concentrating the rural population to make the new rural areas amenable to policies of recruitment and raw material extraction. Much of these policies were reverted, and many industries are now located in the rural hinterland in the proximity of the rural labourer (see Fig. 2.1).

An important portion of managerial and professional positions are concentrated in major cities, while the new manufacturing facilities benefit from the cheap rural force. However, these developments created a new push for the service sector, which resulted in a significant boost. Service-sector-related exports have increased four times in the last ten years. Business-to-business consultancy, especially in Transylvania, and

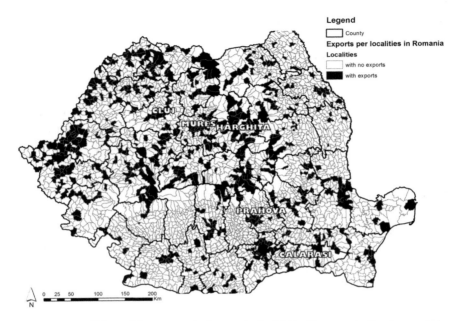

Fig. 2.1 Localities with exports in Romania in 2011. (Source: Author's graph is generated in ArcGIS. Data courtesy to the Romanian National Institute of Statistics and the project Competitive Cities (2013) of the World Bank – Romania Regional Development Program, project coordinator: Marcel Ionescu-Heroiu

engineering-related consultancy are the fastest-growing activities in the service sector (Heroiu 2013). In addition, a new service sector directly linked to the global service sector, particularly the IT sector, flourished in the most important cities. The clear majority of them function as outsourcing outlets for companies located in Frankfurt, Dublin, and Silicon Valley. Most of the labour that came into the five cities after 2004 is highly educated workers and skilled employees in search of higher-paying urban jobs: managers, professionals, technicians, administrative and service workers (see Table 2.2). Therefore, the composition of the cities became even more skewed towards professionals and service workers. In Cluj-Napoca, one in three employees is a professional. In Miercurea Ciuc, Ploiești, and Târgu Mureș, one in four employees are professionals. Cluj-Napoca city, between 2001 and 2011, lost more than 10,000 industrial workers and gained the same number of service workers. Similar changes happened in the rest of the researched cities, yet on a smaller scale. The very composition of workers in these cities has changed significantly.

Table 2.2 Occupational structure of the cities in 2011

Occupational position	Călărași	Cluj-Napoca	Miercuirea Ciuc	Ploiești	Târgu-Mureș	Total
Owners and management positions	3.8%	4.9%	4.5%	3.8%	3.7%	15.336
Professionals	16.5%	32.4%	24.8%	28.4%	26.4%	102.555
Technicians	12.6%	12.4%	13.8%	12.8%	13.3%	45.833
Administrative functionaries	5.3%	6.6%	10.9%	7.5%	6.4%	24.876
Service workers	19.6%	16.9%	17.7%	15.7%	20.0%	62.529
Farm workers	3.2%	0.7%	1.9%	1.5%	1.4%	47.43
Skilled workers	18.1%	13.5%	15.1%	15.8%	15.8%	53.807
Semi-skilled workers	13.3%	7.7%	6.1%	9.5%	8.0%	30.979
Unskilled workers	7.5%	5.0%	5.2%	4.9%	4.9%	18.651
Employees	100% (29.888)	100% (150.119)	100% (18.491)	100% (97.157)	100% (63.654)	359.309
Active population	36.050	163.445	20.313	111.034	69.211	400.053
Active age population (18–65 years)	45.347	243.279	27.304	146.425	96.147	558.502
Population	65.181	324.576	38.774	211.022	137.731	777.284

Definition: Active population, population that is occupied, unemployed, and homemakers
Source: National Institute of Statistics, Census 2011. Author's calculations based on data at the level of census tracks

A related transformation is linked with agriculture. In the last 15 years, the weight of agriculture in the GDP was cut in half and is currently at 6 per cent. Nonetheless, the production of grains and fruits increased constantly. After the 2008 global economic crisis, in parallel with the industrial sector, there was a boom of investments in agriculture, with a new wave of land acquisition and concentration mediated by foreign capital. Romania ranks both in the top five European countries with the biggest agricultural exploitation above 50 ha (the top three biggest farms in Europe are in Romania) and the country with the biggest number of farmers, more than 4 million, working on small plots, less than 5 ha. By 2015, Romania had become one of the most important economic actors exporting grains in Europe, while the city of Constanța became the site of the biggest grain exchange in Europe, opening a debate about whether the government should privatize the whole port (Cimpoi 2016). The most important producer of grains in Romania is Călărași County, yet this area barely appears on any economic map of Romania (see also Fig. 2.1). On the contrary, it is consistently ranked as lagging behind, supposedly competing in the last 25 years for the most undeveloped county. But this is the case for most of the counties specializing in agriculture, since exports are organized by the major cities from the region, where managerial services are located (in the case of Călărași County this city is the Bucharest) as part of the greater service economy. Production is organized locally by local entrepreneurs, and mechanization makes most of the employment redundant, while silo storage and transportation is coordinated by multinational companies (Petrovici 2013)

This labour division has created a specific geography of wage differentials and income strategies. Major cities have become the home of well-paid professionals, as opposed to their hinterlands, which have become places for workers earning minimum wage. Out of the total 4.75 million employees in Romania, 1.6 million are paid minimum wage (Mihai 2016). In this macroeconomic context, businesses in search of a cheap labour force are using three strategies of recruitment. First, major cities in Romania, like Cluj-Napoca and Ploiesti (also Bucharest, Iași, Timișoara, and Oradea) are turning into "metropolitan areas" and use the first and second rings of localities to externalize production in new industrial platforms. The suburbanizing of capital in the hinterlands encounters a population who still have rural households, which makes possible the production of cheap food and some of its energy requirements as part of a strategy of subsistence. The lands and livestock themselves become the object of agribusiness in need for more land area for production of cash crops. Without more investments, there is little chance that most of these producers will be able to rescale themselves outside the subsistence economy and out-compete multinational companies. Therefore, a job in a factory is a welcomed monetary resource for village dwellers.

The strategy of capital to move outside of the cities or in rural areas puts pressure on urban manual workers who are in the difficult position of having to fully cover their daily costs. The pressures to live on wage income on urban or suburban manual workers are very high, since rural workers have at least part of their everyday needs ensured by the rural household. Urban labour, rarely unionized (Guga and Constantin 2015) is losing its bargaining power and the pressure on employers to increase wages is in a general downturn. The most vulnerable workers are the Roma, who, with their low educational qualifications, systematically take the most undesirable jobs. Moreover, it is even harder for the Roma workers to compete with the disposable labour force and members of the reserve army when racial profiling is still a major mechanism of sorting who is deserving of a job and what kind of job.

A second strategy for labour recruitment is to attract commuters from the rural areas around the major cities. Multinational capitalists in the automotive industries, particularly in Cluj-Napoca and Ploiești, rely heavily on employees from the rural hinterlands. In alliance with the local authorities, the multinational (i.e., Fujikura, Ekerle, or Emerson) and major local companies are offering cheap transportation while relying on the subsistence economy to offer workers the minimum wage. A very important fraction of this labour force, who are only paid the minimum wage, combines urban jobs with a rural household and subsistence agriculture. An important portion of these commuters are rural Roma (Gog 2016). The urban labour that cannot combine rural resources with their extended family's income are put in a dire situation—especially if, for example, the household does not own their apartment.

A third strategy for labour recruitment is to disperse production facilities in nearby cities and towns, forming economic clusters that connect certain major localities. Some of these clusters are bigger, as the one formed between București, Ploiești, and Argeș, others are smaller, as is the case of Miercurea Ciuc and the nearby Odorheiu Secuiesc in Harghita County. This clustering strategy offers a wider spectrum of jobs and opportunities, making use both of wage workers and professionals. Ploiești, as a satellite of Bucharest, also has, in addition to manufacturing jobs, a significant number of professionals (from the total number of employees in the private sector 21 per cent are professionals). Similarly, in Ilfov, the Bucharest first hinterland ring, more than a quarter of the employees of the private companies are professionals (Petrovici 2013). The comparative advantage Romania crafted for itself on the European market was a cheap, skilled labour pool (Ban 2014). If all professional jobs are offered in only a few major cities, such as Bucharest and Cluj-Napoca, it would take away Romania's competitive edge. Wages are cheaper in smaller towns, given that the labour force can access non-commodified means of subsistence provided by various local populations. For example, cheaper food produced by the local rural population or the work of various vulnerable strata of the workforce provide informal services such as janitors, handy men, auto mechanics, nannies, and so on. The underpaid Roma play a special role, using their labour to help sustain the urban working class and middle class, with reproduction work needed for higher paid employees to be able to resume their production cycles.

The Evolution of the Researched Areas Between 1992 (Post-socialist Deindustrialization) and 2011 (Uneven Economic Growth Following Increased Capital Investment)

The current situation of urban areas inhabited mostly by Roma should be understood against the above-described context. Between the 1992 Census and 2011 Census, the cities of Călărași, Ploiești, Miercurea Ciuc, and Târgu Mureș lost between 16 per cent and 18 per cent of their total populations. Only the population of Cluj-Napoca remained relatively stable.

Those who left these cities during the 1990s were disproportionately industrial workers, and those who came during the 2000s were professionals and service workers. These population movements constituted themselves in two waves of internal emigration, the first urban to rural, the second an exchange of urban populations. The occupational composition among the Roma was and is highly skewed towards manual jobs. Many of the Roma inhabitants left the cities, including the five cities studied here. Most of them emigrated in the first half of the 1990s, most of them being workers, either skilled or unskilled, who lost their jobs in the systemic downsizing of employment of the 1990s (see Table 2.3).

At the 2011 Census, across Romania, around 19 per cent of the Roma population, as opposed to 14 per cent of the non-Roma population, had their previous stable residence in one of the five cities. These figures vary significantly across the five cities. Both Ploiești and Călărași host sizable and stable Roma populations, yet the Roma left these cities in a much smaller proportion (9 per cent and 7 per cent, respectively) as opposed to the other three cities.[3] Miercurea Ciuc and Târgu Mureș are home to an important Hungarian population, highly mobile across Transylvanian

Table 2.3 Stable city population and emigrants from the five cities between 1991 and 2011

Cities	Non-Roma population			Roma population		
	(A) Stable 2011	(B) Emigrated 1992–2011	(A)/(B) (%)	(C) Stable 2011	(D) Emigrated 1992–2011	(C)/(D) (%)
Călărași	62,221	7466	12	2960	216	7
Cluj	321,153	40,579	13	3423	1083	32
Miercurea Ciuc	38,415	9680	25	359	175	49
Ploiești	205,211	24,815	12	5811	547	9
Târgu-Mureș	133,817	23,920	18	3914	1043	27
Total	760,817	106,460	14	16,467	3064	19

Definition: Emigrants 1992–2011, are persons who are not currently living in one of the five cities, yet she/he had their last stable residence in one of these cities or was born there; Stable 2001, is a person who has the current stable residence in the city

Source: National Institute of Statistics, Census 2011. Author's calculations based on data at the level of census tracks

cities (see Table 2.3); at least a partial explanation for this higher mobility can be linked with the nature of the social ties specific to these two cities. Cluj-Napoca hosts the biggest conglomerate of compact Roma areas from the five cities, with mobile populations that determine the total size of these areas to vary seasonally (Raț 2012).

One-quarter of the Roma who left the five cities, according to the 2011 Census, became rural farm workers (see Table 2.4)—following the greater trend that can be seen among the non-Roma population, yet in a significantly bigger proportion (25 per cent as opposed to 15 per cent). In 2011, another half of the occupied Roma population was employed as skilled and unskilled workers, most of them in small towns. Those who

Table 2.4 The occupations in 2011 of Roma migrants after 1990 and Roma inhabitants in the five cities of Călărași, Cluj-Napoca, Miercurea Ciuc, Ploiești, Târgu Mureș

	Emigrants	Scattered outside of the researched areas		Compact inside the researched areas		
		Immigrants	Stable	Immigrants	Stable	Total
Professionals and management positions	4%	13%*	5%*	3%	1%†	173
Technicians and Administrative functionaries	3%†	7%	10%*	6%	6%†	300
Service workers	14%	18%	20%*	12%	12%†	670
Farm workers	25%*	2%†	2%†	1%†	2%††	262
Qualified and semi-skilled workers	28%†	39%	36%	46%*	37%	915
Unskilled workers	27%†	20%†	28%†	32%	42%*	589
Total	**790**	**326**	**1596**	**145**	**1404**	**4,261**

*Adjusted standardized residual greater than 1.96, indicating a significantly greater percentage than expected under no association hypothesis, at the cell level. Cell highlighted in grey
†Adjusted standardized residual less than 1.96, indicating a significantly lower percentage than expected under no association hypothesis, at the cell level
Statistical association: contingency coefficient = 0.400, Cramer's V = 0.218
Definitions: *Roma*, a person who declared herself/himself or was declared as an ethnic Roma or she/he speaks Roma language; *emigrants*, people who left one of the five cities after 1990; *immigrants*, people who came to one of the cities after 1990; *stable*, a person who came before 1990 to one of the five cities or was born in one of them. *The researched areas* correspond to the 20 sites included in our ethnographic research
Source: National Institute of Statistics, Census 2011. Author's calculations based on data at the level of census tracks

left for other bigger cities were employed, especially, as qualified workers. This last point is seen among those who came and established themselves in one of the researched areas in the five cities—around half of them are qualified workers, and another third are unqualified workers. Nonetheless, the proportion of the Roma immigrants in the cities is significantly smaller when compared with that of the non-Roma immigrants.

In the case of all five cities, the Roma in researched areas have, on average, less education and they are more often unskilled workers, when compared with the Roma who live scattered across the city or those who left the city. The above dynamics supports the argument that the inhabitants of the researched areas were those who were not in a position to move out from that area or to leave the city either for a different locality in Romania or for abroad. Approximately 90 per cent of those living in the researched areas are either born in the city where that area is located, or they came as workers during socialism. In public discourse, most of the time, the Roma from the researched areas are portrayed as mobile travellers coming from outside the cities. Even if this is the case for some of the areas, on average, these places are urban enclaves gradually formed during the post-socialist decades from disenfranchised Roma workers and their children, who were trapped in these very cities, with few alternative opportunities, that is, those who did not have enough resources to move away. More precisely, the two types of resources they lacked were: first, property, social connections, and skills to move to a rural locality in order to benefit from farm work; second, skills, formal qualifications, and social connections to work in new urban factories, logistical facilities, and retail chains. The cities changed, their occupational structure becoming more attuned to their function as managerial hubs dominated by professionals and service workers. Therefore, the areas inhabited mostly by Roma became compact and homogeneous not only in terms of ethnicity but also as concerns their low educational credentials and employment in precarious, labour-intensive jobs.

The percentage of employed (20 per cent) and unemployed (8 per cent) are the same for the Roma dwelling in the researched areas and those scattered across the city. Yet, among the non-Roma population the share of those employed is more than double (42 per cent) and the percentage of the unemployed is less than half (3 per cent). This low aggregate indicator of Roma employment is linked to the very structure of the population. At least four aspects are important in this context. First, approximately 39 per cent of the population in the areas is under 18 years. Among Roma scattered across the city, 31 per cent of the population is under 18 years old. Infant mortality rates for Roma in Romania is four times greater than that of the general population (Bennett 2010). Also, morbidity rates are much higher, more the 50 per cent of children do not receive basic vaccines, which are generally freely distributed and administrated by the state (Bennett 2010). These conditions seem to be exacerbated in the researched areas. Second, only 4 per cent of the Roma population in the five cities is older than 65. Therefore, the percentage of pensioners (8 per cent) is small when compared to the case of non-Roma (23 per cent). In Romania, the life expectancies of Roma men and women are, respectively, 12.1 and 14.4 years lower than for the country's population as a whole (Hajduchová and Urban 2014; Kovats 2004), which is, across the sexes, approximately 64 years (Bennett 2010; Romanian Government 2015). This life expectancy is linked to morbidity and health issues, both of which are for the Roma population all much worse than in the general population (Masseria et al. 2010). Third, 26 per cent of dwellers aged 14 or older in the researched areas have no education, a figure significantly higher than for those living in the cities (14 per cent). In fact, around 98 per cent of the researched areas have at most primary school education. Fourth, the proportion of homemakers (12 per cent), almost entirely women, is much higher compared with the non-Roma population (3 per cent). One-fifth of homemakers have no education, and another fifth has only primary school education.

The new urban relatively compact Roma areas that have appeared in the last two decades accommodate arguably the least protected workers by welfare provisions. The labour of the Roma is used by many businesses in search of manual routine jobs paid with minimum wage. Around 34 per cent of the Roma in the researched areas and 29 per cent from those dwelling scattered across the city are working in manufacturing, as opposed to 19 per cent of non-Roma workers (see Table 2.5). Roma are disproportionately recruited more than non-Roma for the growing, yet still largely unregulated and informal, industry of waste

Table 2.5 Distribution of occupied persons by economic sector in 2002 in the five cities of Călărași, Cluj-Napoca, Miercurea Ciuc, Ploiești, Târgu Mureș

Economic sector	Non-Roma	Roma living scattered in the city	Roma living compact in the researched areas	Total
Agriculture	2%†	4%*	4%*	6,808
Extractive industry	0.8%*	0.4%	0.2%	2,869
Manufacturing	19%†	29%*	34%*	68,900
Production and distribution of amenities	3%†	2%†	1%†	10,355
Sanitation	0.6%†	6%*	17%*	2,525
Construction	7%†	12%*	10%*	26,607
Commerce	24%*	24%	17%†	85,355
Services	43%*	23%†	15%†	154,818
Household's activities	0.2%	1.1%*	0.8%*	917
Total	354.464	2.233	2.457	359,154

*Adjusted standardized residual less than 1.96, indicating a significantly lower percentage than expected under no association hypothesis, at the cell level
†Adjusted standardized residual greater than 1.96, indicating a significantly greater percentage than expected under no association hypothesis, at the cell level. Cell highlighted in grey
Statistical association: contingency coefficient = 0.178, Cramer's V = 0.256
Source: National Institute of Statistics, Census 2011 and 2002. Author's calculations based on data at the level of census tracks

recycling. Around 17 per cent of the Roma in the researched areas are employed in sanitation work, as compared to 6 per cent of those living scattered across the city and only 0.6 per cent of the non-Roma. While some jobs in sanitation and waste cycle management are paid with minimum wage (i.e. waste truck driving or street cleaning), many of them work as day labourers or occasional workers and their revenues depend on their "productivity", meaning that they are often paid depending on how much recyclable waste they manage to collect, with minimum wage barely being reached.

Booming industry needs raw materials, and a very important resource is the waste industry. For many manufactured products, cheap raw materials need cheap extraction methods, placing the workers and the businesses doing this work at the low added-value end of the production chain. Some of the worst paid, toxic, and stigmatizing jobs are precisely in the industry of collecting, disassembling, and sorting waste in order to extract valuable resources that serve to refuel production cycles (Gille 2007; Samson 2010, 2015). Take the case of Tenaris, a multinational company, which has a production facility in Zălau, a town near Cluj-Napoca, specialized in high-end industrial pipes made of various alloys with a major steel component. The ex-pat division is in Cluj-Napoca, coordinating the exchange of highly skilled labour and managerial talents in 140 locations across the globe. In Bucharest, there is a commercial and legal office coordinating sales in the region. In order to streamline raw material procurement, the company bought two steel mills in Romania, one in Călărași (the former Siderca) and one in Câmpina (near Ploiești), with scrap collection points near Bucharest, Călărași, and Ploiești. Most of the raw material inputs come from metal recycling. The metal is bought at the scrap points and purchased according to quantity. This creates the need for autonomous workers capable of finding and sorting waste at very low rates, more specifically, rates that are similar or lower to the iron ore purchased directly from mines across the globe. The vast majority of the researched areas across the five cities are located near such scrap collection points or near landfills. Obviously, metal is not the only type of valuable raw material, various polymers, glass, and paper are very important.

Conclusion

The majority of our researched sites that can be considered compact Roma areas are located in places hardly possible to be made suitable as residential areas due to heavy pollution and the immediate proximity of waste dumps, wastewater plants, out-of-use refinery infrastructure, or similar obstacles, or in derelict urban zones with a major gap between the value of the land and the value of the dwellings. The very gradual formation of these areas is linked with the history of partial deindustrialization during the first post-socialist decade, trapping those Roma workers who could not escape the city.[4] The demographical structure in our researched areas is highly skewed, with a sizable young population and almost no elders, and major health issues among the population. A quarter of the adult population has no education, half of the women are homemakers. If we take as a base the population of active age, only one-third of the Roma adults living in the researched areas are employed, as opposed to almost two-thirds of the non-Roma in the case of our five cities. Purportedly, our results seem to suggest that these areas are cut-off from the city, and that they function as enclaves where the socio-economic processes effective in the rest of the city are suspended. However, this is far from the truth. The clear majority of the Roma dwellers in the researched areas from the five cities have unskilled manual jobs. Arguably, those living in there are the least protected workers, with few benefits and negotiable resources. They are a primary faction of the workers employed in manufacturing, sanitation, recycling, and construction sectors doing the worst-paid jobs in towns and cities that are increasingly oriented towards managerial functions. The larger cites, like Cluj-Napoca and Ploiești, have become important service cities, yet they retain a very important role in coordinating the inner city industrial production and industrial platforms functioning outside of the cities, in suburban or rural areas.

Notes

1. The 2011 Census had an open question on ethnicity which was coded subsequently in categories. There were 19 Roma-related self-identification categories in the Census. Based on the self-identification in 58 census tracks pertaining to the 20 studied locations, I have lumped together as Roma the following categories (ethnic denominators in Romanian original): *rom, țigan, țigan de mătase, spoitor, pletos, gabor, ursar, căldărar, rudar, lăieș*. In the neighbourhood of Obor from Călărași there were 265 self-identified Turks. Based on our ethnographic material and their area of residence in the city, I have indexed them as Roma for this research.

2. These concepts have an important pre-war history. The communes (*comune*) became rural administrative units in the second half of the nineteenth century (Law 394/31 March 1864), as a measure used by Al. I. Cuza to create reasonable spatial divisions for taxing purposes. There was a constant effort to reduce the huge number of villages during the entire twentieth century, and one of the most productive concepts, put forward by the interwar Gusti School, was that of a "communal centre", a cluster of social services provided by the state and amenities (pipelines, sewages, electricity) around which the villagers were incentivized to spatially regroup. This became a major concept during communism when members of the Gusti school, such as Henri H. Stahl and Miron Constantinescu, became responsible for the planning process in the post-1948 Communist government. The urban zone was also an important concept of the interwar Gusti School as part of the developmentalist concepts that prescribed how urban growth could benefit from its specific rural hinterland, with specific localized resources (Constantinescu 1966; Rostás 2000; Stahl 1975).
3. The ethnographical material suggests that Roma from Călărași have migrated abroad on a significant scale after 2002, especially those from the Livada neighbourhood. I could not corroborate this piece of data with the census data. Observations and interviews suggest that in none of the investigated locations this type of migration had a similar scale.
4. There are some notable differences from this pattern. Some of the populations lived in relatively compact Roma areas are those who were evicted from rural areas by the majority. A telling example is the case of some of the families in the "Pork City" informal settlement in Miercurea Ciuc, who were chased away from nearby villages by the Szekler (Hungarian) majority. Or some "corturari" families in the Pata Rât area at the outskirts of Cluj-Napoca, who came from the villages of the present-day metropolitan area, where they had lived for some generations.

References

Andrén, Daniela, and Monica Roman. 2016. Should I Stay or Should I Go? Romania Migrants During Transition and Enlargements. In *Labor Migration, EU Enlargement, and the Great Recession*, ed. S. Esarey and A. Haslberger, 247–271. Berlin/Heidelberg: Springer.

Ban, Cornel. 2014. *Dependență și dezvoltare. Economia politică a capitalismului românesc [Dependency and Development. The Political Economy and Romanian Capitalism]*. Cluj: Tact.

———. 2016. *Ruling Ideas: How Global Neoliberalism Goes Local*. Oxford: Oxford University Press.

Bell, Janice, and Tomasz Mickiewicz. 2013. *Unemployment in Transition: Restructuring and Labour Markets in Central Europe*. New York: Routledge.

Bennett, John. 2010. *Incluziunea Romilor in Servicii de Dezvoltare Timpurie a Copilului*. Bucharest. http://medlive.hotnews.ro/wp-content/uploads/2010/12/Raportul-Național-IRSDTC-pentru-România_rezumat.pdf. Accessed 2 Sept 2016.

Cimpoi, Teodora. 2016. Cioloș Anunță Pregătirea Pentru Privatizare a Portului Constanța. EVZ.ro. http://evz.ro/ciolos-anunta-pregatirea-pentru-privatizare-a-portului-constanta.html

Constantinescu, Miron. 1966. *Cercetări sociologice contemporane [Contempoary Sociological Research]*. București: Editura Științifică.

Constantinescu, Miron, and Henri H. Stahl. 1970. *Procesul de urbanizare în R.S. România: Zona Slatina-Olt. [The Urbanization Process in the Socialist Republic of Romania. The Slatina-Olt Region]*. București: Editura Academiei Republicii Socialiste, România.

Dobrincu, Dorin, and Constantin Iordachi. 2009. *Transforming Peasants, Property and Powers: The Collectivization of Agriculture in Romania, 1949–1962*. Budapest/New York: Central European University Press.

Gille, Zsuzsa. 2007. *From the Cult of Waste to the Trash Heap of History: The Politics of Waste in Socialist and Postsocialist Hungary*. Bloomington: Indiana University Press.

Gog, Sorin. 2016. *The Religious Roma Diaspora in the Context of Neo-Liberal European Governance: Citizenship, Social Inclusion and Political Spiritualities*. Vienna. Working Papers, Vienna: ERSTE Foundation.

Guga, Ștefan, and Camelia Constantin. 2015. Analiza Impactului Noii Legislații a Dialogului Social Adoptate În 2011. Cercetare Sociologică și Juridică. București: Asociatia Conect. http://www.asociatiaconect.ro/upload_res/Cercetare_impactul_legislatiei_muncii.pdf

Hajduchová, Hana, and David Urban. 2014. Social Determinants of Health in the Romani Population. *KONTAKT* 16 (1): 39–43. https://doi.org/10.1016/j.kontakt.2014.01.001. Accessed 1 Sept 2016.

Heroiu, Marcel Ionescu. 2013. *Growth Poles: The Next Phase*. http://documents.worldbank.org/curated/en/857051468332468480/pdf/843270WP0v10RO0t0Box382155B00OUO070.pdf. Accessed 1 Sept 2016.

Kligman, Gail, and Katherine Verdery. 2015. *Țăranii sub asediu: Colectivizarea agriculturii în România (1949–1952) [Peasants under siege. The Collectivization of Agriculture in Romania (1949–1952)]*. Iași: Polirom.
Kovats, Martin. 2004. Accessing Health Care : Responding to Diversity. In *Accessing Health Care: Responding to Diversity*, ed. J. Healy and M. McKee, 237–256. Oxford: Oxford University Press.
Kucera, Tomas, Olga V. Kucerova, Oksana B. Opara, and Eberhard Schaich, eds. 2000. *New Demographic Faces of Europe: The Changing Population Dynamics in Countries of Central and Eastern Europe*. Berlin: Springer-Verlag.
Masseria, Cristina, Philipa Mladovsky, and Cristina Hernandez-Quevedo. 2010. The Socio-Economic Determinants of the Health Status of Roma in Comparison with Non-Roma in Bulgaria, Hungary and Romania. *European Journal of Public Health* 20 (5): 549–554.
Mihai, Adelina. 2016. Distribuția Detaliată a Salariilor Din România. ZF.ro, May 6. http://www.zf.ro/eveniment/prima-oara-zf-prezinta-distributia-detaliata-salariilor-romania-34-000-angajati-castigapeste-10-000-lei-net-lunapolul-opus-70-dintre-salariati-castiga-1-700-lei-lunar-salariul-mediu-economie-15284575
Neyer, Gerda, Gunnar Andersson, Hill Kulu, Laura Bernardi, and Christoph Bühler, eds. 2013. *The Demography of Europe*. Berlin: Springer.
Nölke, Andreas, and Arjan Vliegenthart. 2009. Enlarging the Varieties of Capitalism: The Emergence of Dependent Market Economies in East Central Europe. *World Politics* 61 (4): 670–702.
Pasti, Vladimir. 2006. *Noul capitalism românesc [The New Romanian Capitalism]*. Iași: Polirom.
Petrovici, Norbert. 2013. Neoliberal Proletarization along the Urban-Rural Divide in Postsocialist Romania. *Studia Sociologia* 58 (2): 23–54.
Petrovici, Norbert, and Anca Simionca. 2011. Productive Informality and Economic Ties in Emerging Economies: The Case of Cluj Business Networks. In *Perpetual Motion? Transformation and Transition in Central and Eastern Europe & Russia*, ed. Tul'si Bhambry, Clare Griffin, Titus Hjelm, Christopher Nicholson, and Olga G. Voronina, 134–144. London: University College London Press.
Poenaru, Florin. 2011. Care e problema cu PSD-ul? *Critic Atact*. http://www.criticatac.ro/11683/care-e-problema-cu-. Accessed 27 May 2016.
Rees, Philip, and Marek Kupiszewski. 1999. *Internal Migration and Regional Population Dynamics in Europe: A Synthesis*. Strasbourg: Council of Europe.
Romanian Government. 2015. Strategia Guvernului României de Incluziune a Cetățenilor Români Aparținând Minorității Rome. Monitorul Oficial Al României, 21 jan.

Romei, Valentina. 2016. Eastern Europe Has the Largest Population Loss in Modern History | FT Data. *Financial Times.* http://blogs.ft.com/ftdata/2016/05/27/eastern-europe-has-the-largest-population-loss-in-modern-history/. Accessed 27 May 2016.

Rostás, Zoltán. 2000. *Monografia ca utopie. Interviuri cu Henri H. Stahl (1985–1987) [Monography as a Utopia. Interviews with Henri H. Stahl (1985–1987)].* București: Peidea.

Rotariu, Traian, and Elemer Mezei. 1998. Internal Migration in Romania (1948–1995). In *Romania: Migration, Socio-economic Transformation, and Perspectives of Regional Development,* ed. W. Heller, 121–149. München: Südosteuropa-Gesellschaft.

———. 1999. Asupra unor aspecte ale migrației interne din România. [On Some Aspects of Internal Migration in Romania]. *Sociologie Romaneasca* 1 (3): 5–37.

Samson, Melanie. 2010. Producing Privatization: Re-articulating Race, Gender, Class and Space. *Antipode* 42 (2): 404–432.

Samson, M. 2015. Accumulation by Dispossession and the Informal Economy – Struggles Over Knowledge, Being and Waste at a Soweto Garbage Dump. *Environment and Planning D: Society and Space* 33 (5): 813–830.

Sandu, Dumitru. 1984. *Fluxurile de migratie în România [Migration Flows in Romania].* Bucuresti: Editura Academiei RSR.

———. 2010. Modernising Romanian Society Through Temporary Work Abroad. In *A Continent Moving West? EU Enlargement and Labour Migration from Central and Eastern Europe,* ed. R. Black, M. Engbersen, and Godfried Okólski, 271–287. Amsterdam: Amsterdam University Press.

Stahl, Henri H. 1969. *Organizarea administrativ-teritorială [Administrative and Territorial Organization].* București: Editura Științifică.

———. 1975. *Teoria și practica investigațiilor sociale: Cercetări interdisciplinare zonale [Social Research Theory and Practice. Interdisciplinary Regional Research].* București: Editura științifică și encicolpedică.

Stahl, Henri H., and Ion I. Matei. 1966. O experiență de documentare sociologică în materie de sistematizări teritoriale. [An Experience of Sociological Documentation on Matters of Territorial Sistematizations]. In *Cercetări sociologice contemporane [Contemporary Sociological Research],* ed. M. Constantinescu, 283–296. București: Editura Științifică.

United Nations Development Programme and the Babeș-Bolyai University. 2012. *Participatory Assessment of the Social Situation of the Pata-Rât and Cantonului Area, Cluj-Napoca*. Cluj-Napoca. http://localdevelopmentforinclusion.org/assets/06-undp-ubb_research_report_participatory_assessment_pata_rat_cluj.pdf. Accessed 27 May 2016.

van Ark, Bart, Mary O'Mahony, and Marcel P. Timmer. 2012. Europe's Productivity Performance in Comparative Perspective: Trends, Causes and Recent Developments. In *Industrial Productivity in Europe: Growth and Crisis*, ed. M. Mas and R. Stehrer, 65–91. Cheltenham/Northampton: Edward Elgar Publishing.

3

Ghettoization: The Production of Marginal Spaces of Housing and the Reproduction of Racialized Labour

Enikő Vincze

As a child I lived with my parents in Bufnița colony. This was a Tsigane colony. In the 1960s, the then city leaders decided to demolish it, and to scatter us all over the city. My family made several stops in different homes, but all the locations where we lived were on the city's peripheries. I grew up, made military service and afterwards started working in a factory; therefore I got an apartment in a block of flats in Mănăștur, alongside Romanian workers. Due to a family tragedy, we lost this apartment soon after 1990. Meanwhile I retired and could not afford a private rent in the town. I had no solution but to move with my family to Coastei Street and make a barrack for us near the house of my brother that he rented as a social home from the state. Many of the younger adults from there did not have permanent jobs, but some middle-aged were hired at sanitation and construction companies, some went to work abroad, while many from the older generations lost their jobs as the factories where they worked were closed and they were fired. Altogether, we were doing pretty well, being

---

E. Vincze (✉)
Faculty of European Studies, Babeș-Bolyai University, Cluj-Napoca, Romania
e-mail: eniko.vincze@ubbcluj.ro

close to all the services and schools that one needs in a city, and people could provide acceptable living conditions out of different jobs available in the town. They paid the rent; they paid the utilities. But in December 2010 the police and the City Hall people evicted us early in the morning and moved us into some modular houses newly built especially for us in Pata Rât, nearby the landfill. Since then, on that spot from Coastei Street they built a campus for the Orthodox Theology Faculty of Babeș-Bolyai University and a nice park. But one may still see the marks of the foundation of our houses on the ground. They tried to make the place clean and nice, to please the neighbours, including the mayor, and those who worked in the newly built big office buildings and the new villas. (Interview with a man, former inhabitant of Coastei Street, displaced and relocated to the modular houses of the Pata Rât area, Cluj-Napoca, April 2012)

Stories like this reveal that the formation of marginal urban housing areas is a result of a "long dispossession".[1] This unfolds in several forms under diverse political regimes and is always connected to the histories of the use of the labour force by the dominant modes of production of different times. Departing from such narratives and observations, by addressing ghettoization, I am contributing to the main argument of the book about the interconnectedness of marginal spaces with a racialized labour force and their productive role in the development of capitalism in Romania.

Occurred as a spatial process of enforced disconnection from the rest of the city, ghettoization is entangled with class divisions, respectively with the precarization and pauperization of the working-class Roma (Vincze 2015a, b), who are forced by material conditions and/or by the public administration to retreat into territories where the cost of living is low. Moreover, this is a process sustained by the racialized stigmatization of Roma ethnicity, of poverty, and of penurious spaces, which transforms the inhabitants of such housing areas into an urban assembly of a cheap labour force. Therefore, my study focuses on ghettoization as a political economy of space (Brenner 2000, 2009a, b) that has a role to play in the dynamics of capitalism, because it creates marginalized housing areas where racialized labour power is socially reproduced (Castells 1977). The fabrication of such territories is not only a product of the spatial technologies of displacement and destitution (which I am discussing in the first section of the chapter). But—as I show in the second section—it is a result of the changing political economy of housing under the influence of accumulation by dispossession (Harvey 2003), and of uneven development (Smith 1984, 2002; Harvey 2006). Last but not least, ghettoization creates marginal spaces for the reproduction of the cheap labour force (a process that I describe in section three). The latter is a premise for the accumulation of capital in several domains of economic activity, due to the fact that the impoverished housing areas are the low-cost residential locations where "expropriated labour" (Fraser 2016) is forced to make a living. By making use of the analytical potential of the concept of ghettoization, I conclude that capitalism and racism function through one another in a post-socialist context while creating and justifying a racializing capitalist political economy.

Within the five cities scanned by the means of our research (Călărași, Cluj-Napoca, Miercurea Ciuc, Ploiești, and Târgu Mureș) we mapped the deprived territories from the perspective of several local actors placed in different positions (the inhabitants of these areas, staff of public institutions and non-governmental organizations, journalists). We observed that the formation of deprived marginal spaces for housing in most of the cases overlapped with the enforced ethno-spatial closure of precariatized and impoverished working-class Roma, while the destitute territories (not necessarily inhabited predominantly by persons self-identified as Roma) were culturally stigmatized as *țigănie* (*Tsigane* neighbourhood). Statistical data extracted from the 2011 Census for the five cities covered by our research demonstrate that in all of these cities (and supposedly in several other localities of Romania, too) Roma and non-Roma are distributed unequally across different urban neighbourhoods associated with different degrees of well-being or, on the other side, of pauperization. On the basis of the definition used by the World Bank (Anton et al. 2014) for marginalized urban areas (where disadvantages in terms of human capital, housing conditions, and employment are acting simultaneously) and in the light of 2011 Census data, Fig. 3.1 helps one to conclude that the percentage of the Roma living in such areas out of the total Roma population is higher than that of population dwelling in such areas out of the total population of the localities. This suggests that the political economy creating such housing territories is also informed by structural racism as a mechanism of making distinctions even within the most economically deprived labourers.

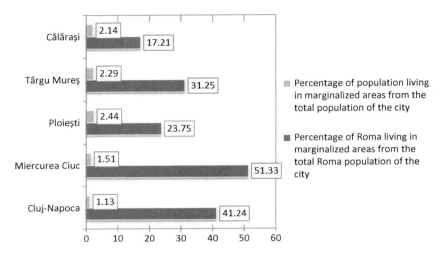

Fig. 3.1 The share of the Roma living in the marginalized areas as compared to the share of the total population in the case of five Romanian cities. (Source: Romanian National Institute of Statistics, 2011 Census. Author's calculations and graph)

However, the ratio between these percentages differs considerably from city to city (Cluj-Napoca: 36.5 per cent; Miercurea Ciuc: 34 per cent; Târgu Mureș: 13.6 per cent; Ploiești: 9.7 per cent; Călărași: 8 per cent), in all of these localities, ethnic Roma persons are affected in larger share by the trend to be pushed towards disadvantaged and marginalized urban areas. Ultimately this shows that class inequalities are not simply the product of political economy but are the consequences of racist social domination (Quijano 2007). All the more, in the localities where this ratio is higher, the ideologies used for justifying such inequalities are appealing to racialization more often and stronger than in the cities where the ratio is lower (see the Chap. 6 from Orsolya Vincze, this volume).

In several cases we also noticed that there was only a thin dividing line between the Roma neighbourhoods formed historically in the localities as a result of their "voluntary" settlement in these areas and their separation from non-Roma dwellers, and between the vicinities inhabited predominantly by ethnic Roma created as a consequence of economic and/or political constraints that kept them segregated from the rest of the locality.[2] However, the territories inhabited in a more or less compact way by different Roma groups (or "nations", *neam*) were not necessarily poorer than other housing areas, and they were definitely not precarious due to the alleged ethnocultural features of their inhabitants. Nevertheless, their stigmatization and deprivation from developmental investments linked to their perception as "*Tsigane* neighbourhoods" played a role in their ghettoization. Once formed, such deprived housing areas are not only the spatial containers but also the territorial manifestations of the condition of a penurious and racialized social class that worsens opportunities for social mobility in all domains of life. The labour force of people belonging to this class is exposed to exploitation insofar as it is restrained in a controlled way on the unsecure peripheries of the localities, and insofar as the social reproduction of both of them (of the labour power itself and of the area that it inhabits) is solely left to their own efforts by the neoliberal urban agenda.

Spatial Technologies of Displacement and Destitution

The series of city maps presented in the Appendix of this chapter (Maps 3.1, 3.2, 3.3, 3.4, and 3.5) reflect that in the five localities of Romania under our scrutiny (see Map 3.6 in Appendix) we discovered four major types of spatial technologies of displacement and destitution that function across city borders and mediate the process of ghettoization of places where dislocated people are settled down due to different constraints. These are the following:

(1) Displacement of individual families and/or of larger groups of families ("communities") without providing alternative homes, from: (a) public-owned blocks of flats due to non-payment of housing-related costs (which contributed to the formation of the *Cantonului* colony from Cluj-Napoca,[3] and of the *Dallas* colony from Ploiești[4]) or under the pretext of public building refurbishment (Târgu Mures: *Marospart* [*Malul Mureșului* in Romanian],[5] Cluj-Napoca: partially *Cantonului* Street); (b)

restituted buildings (Miercurea Ciuc: *Pork city*,[6] Cluj-Napoca: partially *Cantonului* Street); or (c) modest social homes whose value became lower than that of the land on which they were placed (Cluj-Napoca: partially *Colina Verde*,[7] partially *Cantonului* Street).

In each case, these evictions were administered by public authorities without providing adequate and secure alternatives for the displaced Roma, who—during several stages of displacements—retreated into impoverished informal shelters at the periphery of the city with the more or less formal acknowledgement and even technical support from the side of public authorities. People from these ghettoized areas do not consider themselves illegal there, since public authorities know about them; however, the latter, from time to time, through police raids or through the softer means of surveys made by social workers, target them as "illegal residents". Consequently, the non-regulated nature of such spaces (being that they are not registered at the cadastre office and/or are not marked on the localities' maps as housing areas) overlaps with the allegedly illegal status of the dwellers (who do not have a legal domicile, i.e., property documents or rental contracts, and therefore do not have an identity document registered to that address; rather, they have only a temporary identity document without domicile or address or an identity document issued to another address where they actually do not stay, or no identity document at all).

> Well, at first my mother and I were thrown out from the block apartment, then my neighbour was thrown out, after one or two weeks four families were evicted; in total seven families were evicted. We were seven families evicted from Ady neighbourhood, but they let us stay nearby for two years and four months, until the new block was built. And when the new block was finished, City Hall didn't let us stay there in the barracks, so then they moved us to Satul Mureșeni (Mureșeni village) so we would be safe and so we won't bother anyone. But that was not a safe place. People from the village got scared that we would steal from them, and that there would be tussles. So police men with masks were guarding us, the gendarmerie, and they were with us all the time. And then they couldn't do anything, so the commandant came. The mayor, Dorin Florea, was afraid to go there, so he sent the vice-mayor. They kept us there for three weeks, after which they rented this first place for us, near the Mureș River, where

we built our first barracks, for nine families. (Interview with a man, inhabitant in the barracks from *Marospart,* Târgu Mureș, April 2012)

There were approximately fifteen houses here. I remember all the apartments. I moved here in 1995 and lived here until 1996. It was nice here, back then, with a big courtyard; it was very nice. I stayed exactly where you can see that wall. We had two rooms; the rooms were big, 30 square meters. But in the end, they told us that these buildings have an owner, they have to be demolished, because the owner is back and he wants the land back. In November 1996, there was nothing left here, only one small house, where you can see that container. I saw that I had no choice; I started to stay all over town, at the train station, with my children. But in 1997 we moved back there, where you can see that cross there. One of my brothers-in-law was staying here, he had a barrack made out of wood, so I made myself a barrack out of foil; we stayed here until April. In 1998, we started to move to Avram Iancu Street, into an abandoned building, the Executioner House. It was good for a while. But then, one evening, this still remains in my heart, we were threatened, we were told, "On this night you will burn like rats." (Interview with a man, inhabitant of Cantonului Street, Cluj-Napoca, August 2016)

(2) Dislocation of individual families and/or of larger groups of families ("communities") by the authorities with provisions for some alternative homes, from: (a) restituted buildings (Ploiești: *Sub pod* or the container housing zone under the bridge inhabited by ethnically mixed families); (b) refurbished public-owned blocks of flats (Târgu Mureș: the social housing area called in Hungarian by the locals as *Kastély* [*Castel* in Romanian][8] and *Barakoknál* [*La barăci* in Romanian][9]); or (c) deprived social homes positioned on lands whose value increased under the process of gentrification (Călărași: *Obor* district; Cluj-Napoca: partially *Colina Verde* and partially *Cantonului Street;* Miercurea Ciuc: wastewater plant).

In these cases, authorities provided housing alternatives for the dislocated, but precarious and deprived alternatives, located on the city margins, usually on industrial lands or wastelands, that is, in polluted and isolated areas. Occasionally, these legally created poor housing facilities are placed in the proximity of the precarious territories "illegally" inhabited by precariatized working class people, so that all the stigma the former are subjected to is transferred on the latter, too, and the whole larger residential space and all its dwellers are marked as the absolute Other in the city's collective consciousness, as less human, as geographically and culturally remote or inferior, briefly put, as "Tsigane".

> We were outraged and we continue to be outraged vis-à-vis the administrative act, which created the area of modular houses as a residential area. The rest of Pata Rât is declared an industrial area. Reports show that the toxicity of the garbage dump, including also these new temporary storage warehouses, the extent of toxicity is very high. Practically speaking, the authorization to build these modular houses, where people evicted from Coastei Street were moved into, shouldn't have been allowed. (Interview with a woman, former resident of Coastei Street, victim of eviction and relocation to the modular houses nearby the Pata Rât landfill, Cluj-Napoca, July 2016)

> If you know the bank next to the pharmacy, it is in the centre of the city. We stayed there. There were some houses there, nationalized houses, we stayed here until the owner came; after the owner came, he threw us out, and the mayor gave us these places. We were thrown beyond the dead, near the St. Lazarus cemetery. You can see beyond our colony there is only a field. We are at the periphery of the town. The land is in the property of City Hall, only the houses are ours. Everybody built his own house on this land. In Obor there are Turkish Romas and a few *Ursari* Roma and romaniazed Roma. (Woman, inhabitant of Obor district, Călărași, April 2012)

> On the 23rd of November 2000, City Hall and the police came to take us out of there. They were telling us that they will give us thirteen keys for thirteen rooms. They took us to Mănăștur district, on Bucegi Street, but there were not thirteen rooms there; it was a bunker in the basement of a block of flats—very bad conditions, very angry neighbours. Then I started to look for other solutions and discovered the terrain of Cantonului Street. One day, the local police came again and took all of us there. In November 2001, they gave us train wagons to live in. After 2004, some Christian organizations came, and they put here in the Thermo-Pan houses and the

green wooden barracks. By then there weren't so many families here. We were thirteen. After that, City Hall moved 27 more families here, from down there, from the post office. So we were like forty families here. After that, Cantonului Street began to be a colony. City Hall brought every Roma here from the city; they moved everyone here. So now, we are 260 families living here. Nobody has identity documents with this address. (Interview with a man, inhabitant of Cantonului Street, Cluj-Napoca, August 2016)

(3) Spatial destitution of (a) particular peri-urban areas mostly inhabited by precariatized working-class Roma for decades (Cluj-Napoca: *Dallas*[10] and landfill; Miercurea Ciuc: landfill), or (b) abandoned worker dormitories situated in the city centre or on the periphery and occupied by ethnically mixed inhabitants (Călărași: *Doi Moldoveni* and *Cinci Călărași*; Ploiești: *blocul NATO*[11]).

Informally, authorities allow people to live in these areas and sometimes explain this permission as a sign of tolerance or humanitarianism. But they do not provide any resources for the infrastructural development of these spaces and refuse the legalization of these informal homes. Officially, they base this decision on the argument that such territories are not proper for living. In many instances it may turn out that, later in time, the exchange value of such areas increases on the local real estate market. In these cases, their "illegal" dwellers might be easily pushed further through a next cycle of displacement. In the cases of landfill tenants, it is obvious that their working and living on or nearby the landfill is tolerated until there is a need for their cheap and "illegal" labour force, but they are kept in "illegality" (or, differently put, under labour and housing insecurity), and they might be straightforwardly expelled from there when needed (e.g., with the occasion of closing down the non-ecological landfills).

We have been living here since 2000. Everything was devastated here, in the end the factory gave it to us—we bought it from them, in instalments, 2000–3000 lei, however much we could give. Now, nobody takes us into consideration, neither City Hall, nor anyone. We have all the documents for the house, but we don't have any possibility to connect to electricity, which was cut down when the workers left. ... Everything here was devastated, badly, after they left, so there were no doors or windows. These workers initially came here in 1983–84, they were coming from Bolentinu, to work in the factories, and they were accommodated here, in this block, which actually was a worker dormitory. After everything was dissolved, the factory was closed, they left, and everything was devastated here. Poor people entered into this forgotten block; those who needed to make fires, they took the doors, windows. And after that, whoever did not have a place to stay, they came here. And then the factory came and found us here, and the factory forced us to pay. We had a sale-purchase contract. And we have identity cards on this address. (Interview with a woman, inhabitant in the *Doi moldoveni* district in the so-called *Blocul NATO*, Călăraşi, July 2014)

Workers who live in the Dallas colony worked for four decades at the landfill from Pata Rât. The authorities didn't help with anything, leaving people of the third or fourth generation to live on the landfill, to grow up on the garbage dump, to survive on the landfill. This is total indifference. To see that children are born here, generations are born here, for whom no jobs are created, for whom no future is created! To acknowledge that, in 2016, there are still people who live homeless, without electricity. To observe from distance that a Dutch organization is coming and supporting people, while not legally recognizing all this area and keeping people without proper identity documents, only issuing so-called temporary IDs without domicile. (Interview with a man, inhabitant of *Dallas colony*, Cluj-Napoca, October 2016)

(4) Selective development or underdevelopment of peri-urban zones inhabited by groups of Roma families from pre-socialist or socialist times that nowadays are not valuable from the point of view of real estate entrepreneurs or public developers (Călăraşi: *Livada*; Miercurea-Ciuc: *Csíksomlyó* [*Şumuleu* in Romanian]; Ploieşti: *Mimiu, Bereasca, Bariera Bucureşti, Boldeasca*; Târgu Mureş: *Hidegvölgy* [*Valea Rece* in Romanian, meaning "cold valley" in English] and *Hegyutca* [*Dealului* street in Romanian, meaning "hill street" in English; Cluj-Napoca: *Dallas*]).

These areas display a mixture of showcases of allegedly "good practices of Roma inclusion" and of destitute situations. As such, they might be the target zones of projects funded by external funds (offered by private donors and/or via European Funds or via funding schemes provided by other countries' public budgets). On the mental map of the cities, they are also the areas providing the "target groups" where non-governmental organizations, casually in partnership with local authorities, might run multiple series of social assistance or humanitarian aid projects. Even more, these territories with better infrastructural features might be promoted by local authorities as good practices of "poverty alleviation". It happens that the local politicians, via informal or formal "community leaders", try to mobilize these "communities" as sources for their political capital. If the latter numerically makes a difference from this point of view, people might rely on further administrative support; but if does not, they might be always disqualified as a burden due to whom politicians might lose votes from the majority population.

> Before, we stayed in the city centre. In 1981, they demolished our houses; they built there a whole district of blocks of flats. Then we went to Cuza Vodă. In 1982, I came back; I bought another house here on the other side of the river. In 1983, I was demolished again. I was demolished three times. When they demolished us, they gave us permission to take the construction materials from the house. Then I went to Roseți. From Roseți I went to Tonea, from Tonea I came here back to Călărași, in this district, called Livada. Every time everybody was going together in a bunch. We were born and raised in a neighbourhood at the banks of the river. There was no need for us to get separated. But, I asked, why do you take me out of the city, when we were born and raised here, and you take us out to a village? We are not people from the country side, we were born and raised in the city, we know how to stay in line, we respect people, we can lead our lives, we are not outsiders. … Now most of the houses are empty. People go abroad for work. First, people went to Turkey, they stayed there 1–2 years, they worked for 1–2 months, and they didn't give them anything—food or anything. They didn't have money to come home. So they thought that they would go from Turkey to Italy, they saw that people are different there. Then they settled there, they called their relatives from here and they told them to go where they were because it was good. They also went to Germany, Spain, Napoli, Roma. They scat-

tered all over. It has been 17–18 years since this movement started, since they left. Some of them made some good money, but then, for the last 7–8 years it started to decrease. Others died there at a young age and were brought back in coffins. (Interview with a man, inhabitant of Livada district, Călăraşi, July 2014)

For starters, I could tell you that Hegy utca did not exist before. It was a simple pasture, which belonged to City Hall. With time, 13 families came to the brick factory, from Atid, they were employees. But as the population grew, the brick factory couldn't assure them housing there in the courtyard of the brick factory. It was a long barrack; soldiers lived there before when they worked at the brick factory. And then, when the place became overcrowded, there wasn't enough space for the 13 families, back then this place was empty. So those families came here, and they built six or seven houses, for starters. Somewhere between 1956 and 1960. And after that, as the population grew, people got married, so Hegy utca also started to develop, and now there are 100 families, which means about 360–370 people. I was born in Hidegvölgy, which is a historical Roma colony, but my father died, so in 1972 I went into the army, and after I got discharged, my mother already was living here—she sold the house in Hidegvölgy, and she built a house here. So she was already here when I got discharged from the army. Now we are 400 persons here. It took long for City Hall to come and make us a normal street and to connect water and sewerage. They mostly invested in the other area of the town where a lot of Roma live. They arranged that district, demolished quite a lot of old barracks, and built blocks for the people. But one can see, behind the blocks, towards the hill, many of the old barracks without water to the house toe the line. (Interview with a man, inhabitant of Hegy utca, Târgu Mureş, June 2014)

Major Trends of the Political Economy of Housing Creating Marginal Spaces

The spatial technologies of displacement and destitution described above are administered within urban planning, housing, social, and development policies embodied by local decision-makers. But eventually they function as instruments of neoliberal capitalism that create uneven development and whose politics of space (both as a socio-economic and cultural-discursive process) is one of the means of assuring capital accumulation by dispossession. These technologies put into motion the major trends of the political economy of housing, such as:

- the uneven development of the city according to the logic of commodification of urban spaces or to the interests of real estate developers supported by local decision-makers, while the latter are investing less and less from the local budget into the endowment of marginal housing areas;
- the privatization of public lands and buildings, and state support given to the development of a new private housing stock for the use of the better-off middle class, whose contribution to the city's financial and cultural capital is highly valued;
- the gentrification of urban areas as a means by which capital is invested into the built environment with the aim to assure accumulation, and as a result of which the class composition of the population inhabiting the distinguished urban areas is constantly "improved" in parallel with the dislocation of the poor towards the margins of the city;
- dismantling the social housing system as a means of entrepreneurial governance (keeping the public housing fund underdeveloped as a means of cutting the "inefficient" social costs of the city; using social housing distribution criteria that disadvantage the already marginalized and supports the kind of people who are welcomed to the city due to the fact that their labour is recognized as important for its development);
- the restitution of formerly nationalized buildings to their former owners, a means by which property rights are re-enforced and privately owned real estate is connected to the flux of capital with the aim of further accumulation, while the impoverished property-less working class is pushed outside from the visible urban spaces of respectability into penurious margins;
- supporting the industries in need of cheap labour (e.g., sanitation or construction companies) or the services using unskilled labourers, by keeping a reserve army of labour nearby the city, that is, by

pushing them out from the developed housing areas but keeping them at the underdeveloped peripheries where they manage to reproduce their labour power at low cost.

In the localities of our fieldwork we could observe that where the real estate value of urban land increased, or when the exchange value of a piece of land had become higher than the value of the more or less penurious homes placed on it, these areas were "cleaned" of the precariatized inhabitants who became "redundant" (i.e., non-profitable) from the point of view of the capital. In several cases, the authorities justified these actions of dislocations by referring to the need for "slum clearance", or "urban regeneration", or "urban development programs." The displaced were left homeless or were relocated to disadvantaged territories, in turn neglected by public authorities and considered as spaces lacking any investment value by the developers.

In this process, racism operated to conceive those who were not "competitive" on the housing market as non-persons, or as sub-humans who did not fit into the ideal-type personhood, and who allegedly deserved no better than to be placed into dehumanizing spaces whose disgrace was eventually transformed into a dishonour projected onto the bodies of its inhabitants. The impoverished Roma from these cities were often subjected to housing dislocation in groups, while the precarious areas of the city were named "polluting" or "dangerous *țigănie*", even if the majority of their inhabitants were not ethnic Roma. These instances of racializing both the ethnic Roma and the penurious working class served as classification mechanisms, by the means of which both the decision-makers on displacements and those who benefitted from these displacements could justify the distinctions made between those who "deserve" and those who "are not worthy" to belong to the city. In addition, while legitimizing the housing and territorial exclusion of the latter, these processes dispossessed the dwellers of marginalized areas not only from citizenship rights but also from personhood by associating them with trash and/or by relocating them to polluted areas that endangered their health and life.

The quotes below illustrate how ghettoization is justified through racialization by public authorities when, while forcibly evicting poor Roma families, they are constructing "the people" (the "civilized

Romanians") against the "dangerous others" ("the poor Roma"), who are supposedly threatening the former. In December 2010, the Romanian mayor of Cluj-Napoca, who orchestrated the eviction of 76 families (the vast majority Roma) from a centrally placed urban space (Coastei Street) undergoing gentrification, affirmed:

> The eviction from Coastei Street was made due to the fact that the way of life generated a lot of controversies for the inhabitants of the area and for the companies from the area and for everything that the city meant—later they were moved in a zone from Pata Rât. (Press communiqué of Mayor Sorin Apostu, May 2011)

At the same time, the ethnic Hungarian vice-mayor of the city made declarations to the press about

> the need to find a solution for the circa 1500 Roma living illegally on Cantonului Street, Coastei Street and in Dallas-Pata Rât considering the area from the proximity of the landfill from Pata Rât. (Press communiqué of vice-mayor Attila László, March 2010)

At the end of the day, local public administration acquired a piece of land in Pata Rât and defined it as a housing area in the larger sea of industrial lands, where it forcibly relocated the families evicted from Coastei Street. Altogether, the formation of the marginalized residential space called Pata Rât as we know it today is the story of a "long dispossession" (Kasmir and Carbonella 2014). Well before the 1990s, the territory began to be inhabited by the workers informally labouring on the landfill and informally living in Dallas colony. By the 2000s, families displaced from several areas of the city, starting in the middle of the 1990s, were directed by City Hall towards Cantonului Street. As a consequence of marketization, privatization, and financialization of housing, including the dramatic reduction of the public housing fund (from 35.7 per cent in 1992 to 1.3 per cent in 2011), due to the pauperization of a part of the working class, and also due to structural racism, almost 2000 citizens with Roma ethnic background were dislocated from their former homes and settled in the landfill area.

But the Cluj-Napoca case is far from being the only one that illustrates the history of long dispossessions that resulted in the formation of marginal housing spaces. In all of our localities, we could observe that the conditions for the possibility of the formation of ghettoized urban areas included the following processes as part of the current political economy of housing:

- the former worker dormitories abandoned as a consequence of dismantling socialist industries, are disconnected from utilities, allowed to deteriorate from lack of maintenance or from the hidden politics of destitution in order to be sold later at a higher price, and are occupied by homeless persons and families who do not have resources to revitalize them;
- some initially formal settlements are extended with informal housing improvisations, or informal settlements are expanded due to the fact that new generations cannot afford moving out of these areas or buying/renting homes on the housing market under conditions in which the development of public social housing stock is dramatically reduced and their position in the labour market is precarious;
- in cases in which there is an interplay of interest between real estate companies, multinational or national firms, and banks in occupying the urban areas whose value as land is higher than the value of the houses settled on them, local authorities clear the inner city's so-called "poverty pockets" through eviction and relocate the displaced dwellers to underdeveloped urban areas that are not targeted by developmental capital at the time being.

Pauperized and Racialized Labour Reproduced in Marginal Spaces of Housing

As soon as the deprived residential areas are formed and fixed on the physical and mental maps of the localities, they grow as spaces of adverse incorporation, as well as zones of aggregated informal housing. Their inhabitants are integrated into the local society through these marginal positions/locations, while being discursively produced as "redundant", "unworthy", or "non-persons" who allegedly do not qualify as "civilized" and "productive" humans or full humans due to their presumed individual or cultural traits.

The identified deprived residential spaces in and across the five localities display variations of ghettoization. These are characterized by different degrees to which they cumulate material deprivation, racialized stigmatization, and spatial seclusion. Most of the time they are legally unrecognized homes, while all of them host people situated on the continuum between the exploitable and the expropriable subject positions: some of them are performing contractual labour, but for wages much less than the cost of their own and their family's reproduction; others are working on the informal market where they are fully dependent, unprotected, and regarded as "illegal"; and still others are performing labour for social benefits on behalf of the municipality being simultaneously expropriable and exploitable.

Nowadays, approximately a quarter of the 1500 inhabitants of the Pata Rât area in Cluj-Napoca are landfill workers.

> These people are very important for the city; it was and it will be like this, because for 40 years now, since this landfill has existed, people were sorting the waste, working with their hands, and they survived doing this kind of work. And so did those people who transport the selected waste from the landfills, given the fact that a very large amount of waste was sorted—papers, plastic bottles, iron. It is a good thing, given the fact that people could make a living out of their hard work on the garbage dump. If these people would not exist, to sort the garbage, Cluj would perhaps be three times more crammed with garbage than it is now. Now, with the new landfills, they have hired thirty people, and the conditions that should be put into place for the people from Pata Rât should be: a stable workplace, bonuses for the toxicity, higher wages, bonuses for the shameful work they do, mothers who work and are hired should have a place where they can leave their children, these people should have medical assistance, a family doctor, and they should be consulted, because the landfill is very toxic. And of course the Romanian state, or RADP (Autonomous Company of the Public Domain), who owns the landfill, should be close to the people who sort the waste, and who work for the benefit of the RADP and the city of

Cluj. These people who worked here they were like working machines! Working machines, working with their own hands… without the authorities coming here to ask them about their health! Without giving them something! Without knowing! There have been accidents, dead bodies; people were run over by cars, without a family doctor! Without secure wages! Giving them nothing! And I cannot say that even now we are working in better conditions. (Interview with a man, inhabitant of Dallas colony, Cluj-Napoca, October 2016)

Other Pata Rât inhabitants, mostly from Cantonului Street and modular houses are underpaid employees at the local sanitation companies or at companies administering the green urban spaces. Many of them are informally labouring at different smaller or bigger waste recycling firms or in construction or cleaning jobs at firms or private homes. According to Romanian law, the adults of families benefiting from the so-called guaranteed minimum income are performing labour "in the benefit of the local community". The latter shared with us stories about the hardest and dirtiest work that one can imagine, among such work is assisting local police in evicting other impoverished people from buildings or from the forests in the close vicinity of the city. People from the Pata Rât area acknowledge bitterly that they are tolerated here without legal forms until somebody important becomes interested in the land. They are also aware of the fact that their low wages or income from unwaged labour will never be enough to provide an adequate home on the private market, and the system of allocation of the altogether reduced number of apartments from the public housing fund is excluding them from this resource of belonging to the city.

People whom we met during our fieldwork in the residential spaces formed as a result of the processes of dislocation and destitution often emphasized that invisibility and informality were the essence of their being, both in matters of housing and labour. What for them was making a living from one day to another out of scrap metal, plastic, or paper collection, a labour that does not provide for the labourer any sort of social security, for the small waste recycling firms where they sold this commodity, was a source of profit predominantly kept under invisibility (or produced outside the realm of taxation).

> We make our living out of a small amount of scrap iron. I go where that factory is, that mine pit. Eight, ten, fifteen kilos I collect so I can buy bread, potatoes, so I can manage. I carry it on my back, as I can. So I can live from one day to another, so I can buy a loaf of bread or two, a kilogram or two of potatoes, so I won't starve. I live on the streets. I have no income; I am 59 years old, after working for 28 years and 88 days, but I cannot retire yet, because I am not old enough. What can I do? One day I eat, then I don't eat for the next two or three days. I have to keep my mouth shut, what can I do? I have to wander around for a slice of bread. I collect boxes, I collect paper, plastic, I take them all in, I get 5-6 lei, as God helps me. I can buy two breads, that's it, this is all my income for today. (Interview with a woman, inhabitant of the barracks from Marospart, Târgu Mureș, June 2014)

Some of the adults performing these tasks still remembered the times when the cities where they lived provided jobs for them in different industries, and at the time such a job also meant an apartment granted by the state-owned factories. They told us about how their housing histories were related to their labour histories and how they lost their secure homes in parallel with the vanishing away of the units where they worked. They became long-term unemployed while the infrastructure of the factories was demolished and sold out as scrap iron by the actors who were privatizing the former state-owned companies.

> I worked at the brick factory for 34 years, out of which I worked 10 years under difficult conditions, so this was considered as 42 years, but only at the brick factory. This was our richness, our wealth, the brick factory. It functioned and it was good. We had to struggle a lot, it was a hard work, but we were safe, we had a home, we had running water, we had electricity, we could get along. What is even more painful today for me is that I do not know what will happen with the youth, with my children? When they opened the "Prefabricate" factory in Ungheni, they could build a room easily, from two or four pieces. We lost a lot because of this, from a sales point of view. But the brick factory still went on, until it was closed for good in 2011–2012. But since 2002 it worked very poorly, a new owner bought it in that year. This new owner, he is Romanian, but he lived in Germany for a long time. He came, he made some changes, and everything

became automatic. So because everything became automatic, half of those employees were sent away. Those families don't work at all now, they don't have jobs; those families go to the garbage dump, to Cristeşti, they dig for iron, plastic, paper, everything that can be sold. There are certain places where they collect these things. This is their job, they earn money from this. This is still good, because if one earns his money from work, that's honest money. But if one steals from someone, that's no longer honest. (Interview with a man, inhabitant in a family house in Hegy utca, Târgu Mureş, June 2014)

Ceauşescu,[12] he gathered here, at the Siderurgic factory, he gathered thousands of people. He made them apartments, for single men, for those with families, with free electricity, everything, and they had jobs. When Ceauşescu was no more, the Siderurgic also disappeared. Somebody bought the factory and moved everything to Năvodari. Where did he start the business? In another country … He broke everything. This is what Iliescu[13] did. If he were smart, he would have said that CAP stays here, all the farms, everyone who was working here, they keep working here. Everything would have stayed the same … would not have been broken. But what the hell did he do? In one year, he started to give passports to everyone, so everyone can leave to other countries. … They could have been obliged to do something. They could have done the uprising of the peasants; they did this once more, between Domniţa Maria and Perinu commune. They said, you either let me work on your land, or you give me two hectares, if you have 20, give me two. But now, how is it? There are owners everywhere. Owner, owner, owner, and the owner does whatever he wants, he cuts, he kills. Before, when I was working for the landlord, with my parents, I was 12–13 years old, there were only two landlords in this county. If there were two, maybe there was only one, and everybody was working there. Everyone worked there, at the landlord. But now, there are thousands of landlords. The patrons, they are also landlords, no? (Interview with a man, inhabitant of Livada colony, Călăraşi, July 2014)

Besides, interviewed people acknowledged that the search for income-generating activities shaped by the economic opportunities provided by the different political regimes they went through was always driving their options regarding the acceptance of available housing arrangements.

Therefore, the lack of alternatives behind the cities where they lived today (and which, maybe except Călărași due to its proximity to the country capital, were the economically most promising localities of the micro-regions to which they belonged) was a force that kept people in the urban deprived areas even if the infrastructural conditions of the latter were hard to endure.

> I worked in places where I learned how to do it. I know how to do everything in construction. I made everything here in this house with my own hands. The only thing is that I didn't finish school, so I can get a degree. I know how to do anything, but if you don't have a degree, you are not allowed to work without a certificate. Maybe they hire you as a utility worker. It doesn't matter if I say that I have a profession if I don't have a degree. I finished school, but not professional school, not for a profession. So I can manage things. And I am from this city, so I will continue looking for making a living here, even if we are going to continue living here where we are, in the barracks near the river. We just want to let us being here peacefully. (Interview with a man, inhabitant in the barracks from Marospart, Târgu Mureș, April 2012)

Authorities justified keeping the marginal urban housing areas infrastructurally underdeveloped by appealing to racist explanations according to which these "undeserving Tsiganes" who live in such areas "like living in poverty" (without water, electricity, etc.) or do not mind living nearby "dangerous sites" (such as landfills, polluted environments, water treatment plants). The dwellers of ghettoized spaces were not considered by decision-makers (or by the mainstream population) as being part of the urban space that needed to be regenerated and developed, but they were, at the most, tolerated on the margins or on the territories that were tried to be made invisible or non-existent and, as such, did not require or deserve administrative attention or socio-economic development. However, as we observed, people living in the marginal urban spaces are providing the cheapest labour force for the entrepreneurs seeking capital accumulation. Therefore, we might assume that the so-called tolerance of public administration towards them will not last, only until the land where their homes are placed will have less or no value from the perspective of urban development, but also until such a cheap labour force will be needed in the city.

Conclusions: Ghettoization as Constitutive of Racializing Capitalist Political Economy

We could see that the inhabitants of the territorially isolated and materially deprived urban areas belong to the property-less working class that underwent precarization and pauperization during the post-socialist transformations and whose histories of long dispossession knew several stages even before. Nowadays, they are engaged in poorly paid formal but unsecure employment; or in informal labour, either domestically or abroad, while lacking any form of social protection; or in "community work" performed for the so-called guaranteed minimum income; or in unpaid domestic labour performed under the conditions of housing deprivation (e.g., the lack of running water and electricity in the homes). Forced into such positions, the pauperized and precariatized labour power is pushed to find cheap housing solutions at the margins of the cities under conditions when gentrification, the privatization of the public housing fund, and the commodification of housing by developers are shaping the scene of urban development. Eventually, this process of spatial marginalization further deepens the precarization of their labour power and housing conditions, and as well as their racialization.

The Roma pushed into the conditions of a precariatized working class and racialized as inferior beings are classified like redundant social categories, but actually they are marginalized on the edge of society from where their labour is easily exploited and expropriated without a consistent investment into its reproduction. This happens in a larger context where the formation of neoliberal capitalism is upheld by a state that withdraws from its role of sustaining collective consumption (Castells 1972): instead of financing adequate public housing for its citizens (by which it would have assumed a role in the reproduction of their labour power), the state supports a type of urban development that serves the interests of real estate investors and developers, and implicitly transfers the whole responsibility of social reproduction on individuals and families. The uneven development of the localities, within which the precarious Roma are forced to live in the most disadvantaged and/or isolated housing areas (whose underdevelopment is also a result of local investment and development policies), is used discursively not only to deny the accountability of the state towards its citizens but also to associate the negative connotations of underdeveloped areas with the (allegedly biological or cultural) features of the people inhabiting them.

The practice of coupling "the Roma" perceived as the racial Other with "the poor" is even stronger in cases when a distinction is made among the people themselves, between the poor who "deserve" and the poor who "do not deserve" social protection (respectively, the ethnic majority on the one hand and Roma minority on the other). Or, put differently, between the poor who deserve to live in poverty (like the Roma who "do not like to work") and the poor who became poor through no fault of their own (the non-Roma who "are victims of economic restructuring or of the financial crisis"). In addition, the racialization of "the Roma" means the displacement of poor Roma from the inner cities and of entrapping them into segregated and dehumanizing marginal/deprived spaces. As we saw, the latter usually lack proper infrastructure, are polluted and isolated, and of course stigmatized, so that the disgrace attached to the space becomes the dishonour projected onto people and internalized by them (Vincze 2013), and eventually this leads to further dehumanization. In this process, the racialization of Roma ethnicity, the racialization of the poor, and the racialization of precarious spaces culminates in the creation of an inferiorized, dehumanized subject.

Last, but not least, it must be mentioned that the territories inhabited predominantly by ethnic Roma (or the so-called compact Roma communities) are not necessarily ghettoized spaces in the sense used in this chapter. Even if they are characterized by ethnocultural seclusion, they do not always interfere with severe material deprivation; that is, they are not precarious, and likewise their inhabitants are not precariatized either. But where it occurs as a result of uneven development and accumulation by dispossession, ghettoization racializes its inhabitants' labour and ethnicity, and at the end of the day the territories that it carves out from the rest of urban space are stigmatized as *țigănie*. Racialized labour reproduced in and by the ghettoized areas is created as an inferior labour or a labour performed by people considered less than persons or less human than their fellow citizens. Racialized labour is precarious, that is unsecure, underpaid, and dehumanizing, and most importantly is conceived as expropriable. Racialized labour includes different types of labour that are considered less valuable labour, or not labour at all, such as: informal labour, labour performed for the "guaranteed minimum income" of the "socially assisted", exploited day or seasonal labour, and underpaid labour on stigmatized domains. By ghettoization, people are not only pushed into and enclosed in underdeveloped territories as an undesirable population, but they are also controlled (or kept within a controllable frame) and abused if needed as a cheap informal labour force, as a mass of political voters, as "wild people" naturally associated with a distressed area of induced structural violence and insecurity, or as racialized subjects blamed for becoming "black labour force" or "socially assisted" or "criminal" due to alleged individual, natural, or cultural deficiencies.

The process of ghettoization in Romania mirrors a larger phenomenon happening across borders under the impact of globalized financial capitalism and is part of the broader politics of dispossession of working classes (Kasmir and Carbonella 2014). This phenomenon is endemic to capitalism, because it serves the interests of the capital, which transforms the post-socialist urban landscape while pushing towards the underdeveloped areas the city dwellers who cannot pay for the commodified adequate housing in other urban spaces. But marginal housing areas are not only products of the capitalist political economy of space; they are premises of capital accumulation in other domains, too. They are the home where the precariatized and penurious labour power is socially reproduced as subject who might easily be exploited in the formal economy or expropriated outside of regularized wage contracts. As part of these processes, racialization plays the role of making distinctions between social classes, and even more so within the working class, as well as of justifying the violence of dislocations and, generally speaking, the disciplination of the dispossessed.

Appendix

Map 3.1 Municipality of Călărași, Călărași County, South Development Region

- Obor
- Doi Moldoveni, Cinci Călărași
- Livada

Total population of the city: 65,181
82.91% Romanians, 3.15% Roma, 0.04% Hungarians (Census 2011)

88   E. Vincze

Map 3.2 Municipality of Cluj-Napoca, Cluj County, North-West Development Region

- 🔴 Partially Cantonului street, partially Colina Verde
- 🔵 Partially Colina Verde, partially Cantonului
- 🟢 Dallas, Landfill
- 🟡 Dallas

Total population in the city: 324,576
75.71% Romanians, 1.008% Roma, 15.27% Hungarians (Census 2011)

Ghettoization: The Production of Marginal Spaces of Housing... 89

Map 3.3 Municipality of Miercurea-Ciuc, Harghita County, Central Development Region

- 🔴 Pork city
- 🔵 Wastewater plant
- 🟢 Landfill
- 🟡 Csíksomlyó (Şumuleu)

Total population in the city: 38,966
16.77% Romanians, 0.86% Roma, 78.54%, Hungarians (Census 2011)

E. Vincze

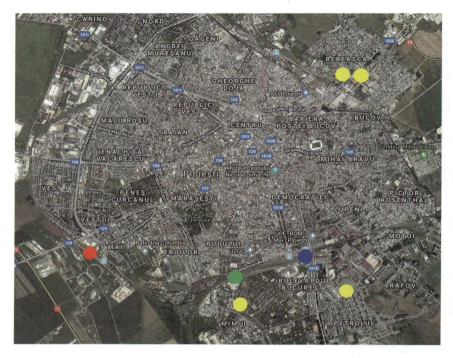

Map 3.4 Municipality of Ploiești, Prahova County, South-East Development Region

🔴 Dallas
🔵 Container housing zone under the bridge
🟢 Blocul NATO
🟡 Mimiu, Bereasca, Bariera București, Boldeasca

Total population in the city: 209,945
90.64% Romanians, 2.40% Roma, 0.08% Hungarians (Census 2011)

Ghettoization: The Production of Marginal Spaces of Housing... 91

Map 3.5 Municipality of Târgu-Mureș, Mureș County, Central Development Region

- 🔴 Marospart (Malul Mureșului)
- 🔵 Social housing area Kastély (Castel), Barakoknál (La barăci)
- 🟡 Hidegvölgy (Valea Rece), Hegy utca (Dealului street)

Total population in the city: 134,290
49.17% Romanians, 2.32% Roma, 42.84% Hungarians (Census 2011)

Map 3.6 Romania, counties and county centres

Marked with red bullets on the map	Percentage of ethnic Roma (2011 Census) (%)
Călărași county	8.05
Cluj county	3.46
Harghita county	1.71
Prahova county	2.33
Mureș county	8.78
Romania	3.3

Notes

1. The term is used by Kasmir and Carbonella (2014) in order to highlight the long process of the fragmentation of the working class from the United States. In my article, I am adopting it to reflect the *longue durée* nature of ghettoization and to suggest that the spatial dislocation of the penurious working-class Roma consists of multiple series of displace-

ments, and that—as Carbonella and Kasmir say in the context of their analysis—these are not cases where we are dealing with a one-time enclosure or related event.
2. This is an observation that recalls the conclusions of another research project, conducted in 25 localities from Romania, entitled *Faces and Causes of Marginalization of the Roma in Local Settings: Hungary—Romania—Serbia. Contextual inquiry to the UNDP/World Bank/EC Regional Roma Survey 2011*. A joint initiative of the United Nations Development Programme (UNDP), the Open Society Foundation's Roma Initiatives Office (RIO) and the Making the Most of EU Funds for Roma Inclusion program, and the Central European University/Center for Policy Studies (CEU CPS). October 2012–June 2014. See more about it in Szalai and Zentai (2014).
3. The inhabitants of the informal homes from Cantonului Street call the area Cantonului colony. Since this was formed starting at the end of 1990s as a result of a series of relocations of evicted people from the city, it illustrates the case of an area constituted as an outcome of different kinds of spatial technologies of displacement.
4. Details of the formation of disadvantaged housing areas inhabited predominantly by Roma in Ploiești, including the area informally named *Dallas* are given in the chapter of Berescu, this volume.
5. Since the Roma from Târgu Mureș are Hungarian speakers, they use Hungarian names for the territories where they live. *Marospart* is a geographical denomination expressing the fact that the shelter area where they live is on the shore of Mureș River.
6. The locals are naming this area using the English term "Pork city." The name refers to the fact that, before 1990, dwellers of blocks of flats used this territory as a location for small animal farms.
7. *Colina Verde* means "Green Hill" in English, and this was the name given to this area by the local public administration that actually created it in 2010 as a "residential area" placed less than one kilometre from the non-ecological landfill of the city. This denomination was a way to avoid making explicit the fact that the modular houses provided for Roma evicted from a centrally placed area of the city were actually located in the landfill area called *Pata Rât*. Moreover, in fact not all the evicted families were provided with alternative homes there. The latter were allowed by public officials to build "illegally some improvisations" on the land nearby the modular houses.

8. The Hungarian-speaking local Roma call this area *Kastély* in Hungarian, which means *Castel* in Romanian and Castle in English; it was actually the building of a former slaughter house.
9. The Hungarian name for the area means *La Bărăci* in Romanian, both referring to the fact that the houses from here are actually improvised barracks, in fact being metallic container-like housing spaces.
10. Also encountered in other localities, the denomination *Dallas*, according to the inhabitants of these areas, has its roots in the American television series titled *Dallas*, which played in Romania in the 1980s. By this, people expressed in an ironical way the huge discrepancy between their actual living conditions and the luxurious life of the very rich oil company owner family depicted in the show.
11. The term *bloc NATO* in Romanian or NATO block of flats is used in several towns of Romania for denominating buildings formerly owned by the state that after 1990 were abandoned by their former tenants and were disconnected from utilities and allowed to deteriorate. The name recalls the horrendous situation of blocks of flats from areas hit by the war where NATO interfered.
12. Nicolae Ceaușescu, General Secretary of the Romanian Communist Party from 1965 to 1989 and Romania's head of state from 1967 to 1989, embodies in the memories of the locals the period of real socialism in this country, marked by industrialization and urbanization.
13. Ion Iliescu served as President of Romania from 1989 to 1996 and also from 2000 to 2004, representing first the National Salvation Front and afterwards the Democratic National Salvation Front that split from the former, which later evolved into the Party of Social Democracy in Romania, and then into the Social Democratic Party. Altogether, these periods (likewise all of the post-1989 era) are marked by the privatization of the state-owned units of production as well as the public housing stock, and by the integration of Romania as an emergent market into the scene of global (neoliberal) capitalism.

References

Anton, Simona, Bryan Koo, Titus-Cristian Man, Sandu Ciprian Moldovan, Manuela Sofia Stănculescu, and Robertus A. Swinkels. 2014. *Elaboration of Integration Strategies for Urban Marginalized Communities: The Atlas of Urban*

Marginalized Communities in Romania. Washington, DC: World Bank Group. 27 August, 2016. Retrieved from http://documents.worldbank.org/curated/en/668531468104952916/Elaboration-of-integration-strategies-for-urban-marginalized-communities-the-atlas-of-urban-marginalized-communities-in-Romania

Brenner, Neil. 2000. Urban Question as Scale Question. *International Journal of Urban and Regional Research* 24 (2): 361–378.

———. 2009a. What Is Critical Urban Theory? *City* 13 (2–3): 198–209.

———. 2009b. Restructuring, Rescaling and the Urban Question. *Critical Planning* 16: 60–79.

Castells, Manuel. 1977 [1972]. *The Urban Question. A Marxist Approach* (translated from French by Alan Sheridan). London: Edward Arnold.

Fraser, Nancy. 2016. Expropriation and Exploitation in Racialized Capitalism: A Reply to Michael Dawson. *Critical Historical Studies* 3 (1): 163–178.

Harvey, David. 2003. *New Imperialism*. Oxford: Oxford University Press.

———. 2006. *Spaces of Global Capitalism: Towards a Theory of Uneven Geographical Development*. New York: Verso.

Kasmir, Sharryn, and August Carbonella, eds. 2014. *Blood and Fire. Toward a Global Anthropology of Labor*. Oxford: Berghahn.

Quijano, Aníbal. 2007. Questioning 'Race'. *Socialism and Democracy* 21 (1): 45–53.

Smith, Neil. 1984. *Uneven Development: Nature, Capital, and the Production of Space*. 1st ed. New York: Basil Blackwell.

———. 2002. New Globalism, New Urbanism: Gentrification as Global Urban Strategy. *Antipode* 34 (3): 427–450.

Szalai, Julia, and Viola Zentai, eds. 2014. *Faces and Causes of Roma Marginalization in Local Contexts*. E-book. Budapest: CEU Center for Policy Studies, Central European University.

Vincze, Enikő. 2013. Urban Landfill, Economic Restructuring and Environmental Racism. *Philobiblon – Transylvanian Journal of Multidisciplinary Research in Humanities* 18 (2): 389–406.

———. 2015a. Adverse Incorporation of the Roma and the Formation of Capitalism in Romania. *Intersections. East European Journal of Society and Politics* 1 (4): 14–38.

———. 2015b. Precarization of Working Class Roma Through Spatial Deprivation, Labor Destitution and Racialization. *Review of Sociology of the Hungarian Sociological Association* 25 (4): 58–85.

4

Social Citizenship at the Margins

Cristina Raț

Introduction

The political embracement of the social citizenship project has been historically tied to the expanded reproduction of labour (Harvey 2003) beyond the means of individual workers and their families. The "fictitious decommodification" (Standing 2007) provided by welfare states has turned into overt forms of workfare, where the new icons of "activation" and "social investment" (Morel et al. 2011; Hemerijck 2015) guide the making of social policies. Throughout this book, we look at the impoverished residents of *Țigănii* (Tsigane neighbourhoods) as a racialized category of workers whose productivity is actively denied and whose work is portrayed as lacking commodity value, and we try to demonstrate how, in various forms, their labour is part and parcel of contemporary Romanian capitalism.

Within this larger endeavour, the present chapter takes up the task of unfolding how the workings of social policies put forth pathways of

C. Raț (✉)
Sociology Department, Babeș-Bolyai University, Cluj-Napoca, Romania

(re)commodification (Bugra and Agartan 2007) and "adverse inclusion" (Sen 2000) that reinforce participation in productive work without relieving it from precariousness and insecurity. While neoliberal policies across the globe typically feature this dynamic, and precarious workers appear, as a rule, racialized and constrained to reside in deprived areas at the peripheries (Wacquant 2000, 2011), our case is more specific and illustrative for Eastern Europe, given the historical persistence of societal divisions even under self-declared communist rule and their rapid deepening after the change of political regime in 1989. Moreover, the relation between the evolution of social policies and social inequalities might become particularly twisted when the disadvantaged disproportionately belong to a heavily prejudiced ethnic minority, such as the Roma.

The first section of this chapter briefly presents the evolution of national legislation on social assistance benefits targeting the deprived segments of the population in relation to policy developments at the European level. It investigates the disciplinary elements contained in the Romanian legislation, with a focus on those regarding formal employment, community work, and various forms of precarious labour. The second section reveals bureaucratic contradictions leading to adverse effects upon dwellers from impoverished and marginalized areas. The third section discusses the interaction between national legislation and local practices with emphasis on social workers' understandings of work and welfare rights that bring in forms of local-level discretion that is, at times, incongruent with the "activation agenda" of the so-called social inclusion policies.

The Push Towards Greater Commodification Within European and National Social Policies

When applying for EU membership in 1997, Romania received the clear-cut conditionality of "solving" the situation of the Roma minority, whose members are disproportionately more subjected to multiple forms of deprivation, and reforming child protection, in particular services for children in state care.[1] The EU's pressure to address poverty, and more specifically poverty among the Roma, intensified with the Lisbon agenda (2000) that explicitly requested national reports and action plans to tackle what was defined as "the risk of poverty and social exclusion".[2] In the case of Romania, the first national action plan to combat poverty and promote social inclusion for the general population,[3] issued in 2001, had to be accompanied by a specific strategy for improving the living conditions of the Roma,[4] which also contained affirmative action on ethnic grounds in various domains, most notably education and health care. As elsewhere discussed (Raț 2013), the structure of the latter document turned out to resemble the strategy developed by state-socialist Romania in the late 1970s in order to address the socio-economic situation of the "Tsigane population" (National Demographic Commission 1977) with the very important exception of the overtly assimilationist objectives of the Communist Party. Both the *anti-poverty social inclusion strategies*, requested by the EU from member states and candidate countries as a form of the "soft pressure" in accordance with the Lisbon 2000 agenda (under DG Employment, Social Affairs and Inclusion), and the *Roma inclusion strategies* first expected only from Eastern European candidate countries, and much later in 2011 from all member states as part of the European Platform for Roma Inclusion[5] set up in 2008 (under DG Justice), created new arenas for policy design and, implicitly, for identity politics regarding very heterogeneous categories such as those "at risk of social exclusion" and "the Roma". Simultaneously, the transnationalization of "the Roma issue" induced alternative forms of subjection and racialization, insightfully analysed by Vincze (2015). For our present purpose, it is important to note the interplay between precariousness and Roma ethnicity and the ways in which the concept of "social inclusion" obscures some of the most relevant processes leading to the racialization of precarious work and the concentration of underprivileged workers in marginalized and severely deprived areas, as discussed in the previous two chapters of this book.

Historically, the rationale for social inclusion marked a compromise between the principles of social justice and the goals of economic growth. The early ideas of "productive social policy" (see Morel et al. 2011: 4–5), embedded in this compromise, were set forth in the 1930s by the very same Gunnar Myrdal who introduced the troubled concept of the "underclass", originally defined as those who lost their employability and fall outside of the class system, and used mainly in the context of the

United States (Wilson 1987; Gans 1990; Katz 1992). The concept would later gain temporary traction among Eastern European scholars working on the issue of Roma poverty and marginalization (see Emigh and Szelényi 2001; Ladányi and Szelényi 2006), but lost ground as its meaning became trivialized in populist discourses to blame "the ghetto-poor" for their own disadvantage. As European documents adopted the perspective of "social exclusion" in explaining poverty across member states, this approach served as an alternative for analysing deprivation and marginalization in the case of the Roma too (Stewart 2002).

Despite the change in the discourse on poverty and the acknowledgement of its structural causes, in the case of social benefits and services the emphasis shifted from defining them as compensations for structural disadvantages (or societal "disservices") towards "investments" in the future, both terms eventually coined by Titmuss in a memorial lecture from 1967 (Titmuss 2000[1967]). At that time, Keynesian views prevailed in economic thinking, and redistributive social policies consistently followed the logic of demand-side economics. By the mid-1980s, the left-leaning goals of social cohesion and solidarity became largely rebranded as "social investment" (Morel et al. 2011; Hemerijck 2015) and "activation" (Bonoli and Natali 2011) in an effort to defend the welfare state against intensified attacks from the neoliberal right. In the policy documents of the European Union, "social inclusion" meant, from the very beginning, fostering participation in the formal labour market (Begg and Berghman 2002; Ferrera et al. 2002) primarily through subsidized vocational training and child care services to "activate" women's labour power (Bonoli and Natali 2011). The tendency to abandon vertical redistribution and embrace the new aims of "activation" accelerated after disappointments with the Lisbon process, as the "social investment package" issued by Lászlo Andor, EU Commissioner for Employment, Social Affairs and Inclusion, illustrates well. While some authors (most notably Morel et al. 2011) argue that "social investment" should be seen as a novel "paradigmatic shift" (as defined by Hall 1993), I would rather join voices with those claiming that it only marks a turn towards increased neoliberalization of social policies.

Confronting the contradiction between the consistently high welfare spending throughout the EU and the intensifying political rhetoric of work disincentives allegedly created by social benefits, Pierson (2001) argues that welfare states have not undergone processes of retrenchment as such, but they have changed via cost containment, recalibration, and recommodification. This becomes obvious after analysing increased conditionality, narrowed-down eligibility, and the replacement of old ideals of work and needs decommodification (Esping-Andersen 1990) by a more straightforward push for recommodification (Standing 2007). The patterns of these changes do not point at a paradigmatic shift in social policies. Even in the "golden ages" of modern welfare states in the 1960s and early 1970s, decommodification remained "fictitious" (Standing 2007), as benefits and sometimes even social services had been for a long time tied to participation in paid employment or formal training and job-searching in Western Europe as well as in the Eastern state-socialist bloc (Ferge 1997; Popescu 2004). Thus, redistributive social transfers and subsidized services (social, educational, medical, etc.) mainly served as means of "expanded reproduction" (Harvey 2003) closely tied to the interests of capital. This remained so not only in the case of workers in the formal labour market but also in the case of precarious workers with irregular, unsteady, and labour-intensive jobs, sometimes without a contract or without any form of social insurance. Ironically, in the case of the latter, social assistance is often framed in terms of "social inclusion", although "beneficiaries" are actually well integrated in various forms of unsecure labour relations, and consequently, they still need state support precisely because of the precariousness of their labour.

Romanian social assistance policies serve as good illustrations of policies developed in accordance with European "soft" recommendations on social inclusion, which subsidize the reproduction of precarious labour and simultaneously push for greater commodification. Built on the former law on social aid[6] issued in 1995, but also inspired from French Law on the Minimum Revenue for Insertion, the Law on the Guaranteed Minimum Income (GMI)[7] was presented as a key programme of the first national action plan for social inclusion (2002), and it has remained in place with some modifications since then.[8] GMI set from the very beginning a low eligibility threshold and imposed several conditions linked to the "activation" agenda: registration at the county-level Labour Force Office, undertaking vocational training or completing education within the "Second Chance" programme, and performing community service work (after a schedule established by the municipality). Allegedly to demise corruption accusations, but actually with a strong stigmatizing effect on beneficiaries, the list of GMI recipients was obligatorily posted at a visible location in the municipality building, along with the schedule of community work.[9] Exemption from community work and a bonus of 15 per cent was established for GMI beneficiaries who were gainfully employed. However, given that the minimum net wage is five times higher than the GMI for a single person (as of 2016), having an employee in the family hardly allows for eligibility. While the type of the community work performed has been as a rule labour-intensive and dirty, interviews with GMI beneficiaries revealed that the very majority of them perceived it as *labour* performed in order to *earn* the benefit: "it is normal to work for the money you get" (see World Bank Report on GMI in Romania 2009).

Most importantly, local councils used to have the prerogative to establish the approximate value that could be potentially earned by undocumented seasonal day-labourers in agriculture, forestry, or construction, for example, or from independent gainful activities such as picking and selling wild berries or mushrooms. This potential income had been imputed, according to the GMI rules, to all families who had able-to-work members, leading to considerable diminishment or even suspension of paying any social assistance benefit at all, which was reflected in the seasonal fluctuation of GMI beneficiaries (Statistical Bulletin of the Ministry of Labour 2002–2016). Thus, potential, estimative, and irregular income from undocumented labour was actually imputed similarly to the earnings from contractual labour, although the former lacked any social insurance protection. Even if they did not receive any financial provision at all, those entitled to GMI scheme continued to submit all documents needed to maintain their formal entitlement, as it granted them health insurance paid from public funds.

The 2010 austerity package of the democratic-liberal government hit hard the pillars of social protection and even attempted to delete the very notion of the "welfare state" from the Romanian constitution (Popescu et al. 2016). It tightened eligibility for means-tested social assistance benefits, leading to a 65 per cent drop in the number of families receiving support allowance for dependent children[10] and a 33 per cent reduction

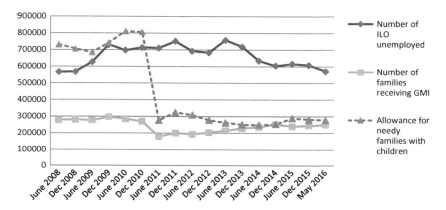

Fig. 4.1 The evolution of ILO unemployment and the number of families receiving means-tested welfare benefits 2008–2016. (Source: The Statistical Bulletin of the Ministry of Labour and INS 2016. Author's graphs)

of GMI beneficiaries (see Fig. 4.1). The decrease was also influenced by the conditioning of all social benefits upon the full payment of local taxes, a regulation introduced in December 2010. In the same period, the new law on social assistance[11] redefined the scope of welfare as providing *minimum* subsistence (and not *decent* resources, as stated in the initial legislative proposal). Importantly, our fieldwork took place exactly in the years following this wave of welfare retrenchment, in the context of heated political rhetoric on welfare dependency, corruption, and criminalization of poverty.

The highly restrictive regulations on social assistance benefits eventually started to soften in October 2012, following the coming into power of a social-liberal coalition cabinet,[12] as the means-tested family allowance for needy children was no longer imputed as income for establishing the GMI and it could be cumulated with the social aid. Furthermore, as of 2015, earnings from contractual day-labour were exempted as well, giving the possibility to legally compensate deregulated labour with GMI benefits.[13] Indirectly, this law reinforced an already existing dual system of social protection for workers. On the one hand, there is the working class of employees (including the low-paid proletariat) who benefits from the institutionalized system of social insurance funded from earmarked taxes and some limited tax reliefs for their children. On the other hand, the category of precarious workers who may opt to self-finance their social insurance, or, if their low earnings do not allow that, they may prove the scarcity of their economic resources and apply for a minimum protection in the form of social assistance benefit (GMI), public health insurance, and means-tested family allowance. In other words, whereas the commodification of employees' labour force is somewhat tempered by historically entrenched social rights (a prevalent object of trade unionism and political unrest), in the case of day labourers and other irregular workers there is a clear commodification of both work and needs.

Put differently, the role of the state in the "expanded reproduction" (Harvey 2003) of labour power changed significantly. It no longer imposes on private capital the same sort of commitment to long-term state welfare via contributions to the social insurance system. Instead, it demands the payment of income taxes necessary to subsidize labour via social assistance benefits, health insurance, support for children born into deprived families, and in particular their school education. In its functionality, the GMI programme seems closer to the old Speenhamland system of subsidizing labour (Polanyi 1944; Bugra and Agartan 2007; Block and Somers 2014) than to the idea of citizen's allowance promoted by the basic income network.[14]

Similarly, means-tested allowance for low-income families with children "invests" in future workers, while its poverty reduction for the most deprived and remote settlements is left at the discretion of charity organizations, at times with some public subsidies (Raț 2013). Despite critiques that point out the adverse effects of conditioning the benefit on regular school participation of *all* school-aged children (UNICEF and Save the Children Romania 2012), this restriction has not only been maintained, but turned stricter in 2011. School absenteeism was one of the main reasons for losing the right to this allowance in the case of severely deprived families from the segregated areas we have visited, as parents could not afford proper clothing for their children and feared discrimination in school (see also Vincze and Harbula 2011) or simply lacked warmer outfits for the cold season. At the time of our fieldwork in 2012, nationwide 60 per cent of persons from households of two adults and three or more dependent children (the most widespread family composition to be found in our marginalized settlements) had been living in financial poverty, as measured by Eurostat.[15] By 2014, this figure grew to 73 per cent. The poverty-reduction effects of social transfers remained lower than the EU average: in 2012, only 12.5 per cent of persons living in low-income households with two or more dependent children avoided poverty as a result of receiving social benefits, whereas in 2014 this measure of relative poverty reduction dropped below 5 per cent (Eurostat 2016, author's calculations). After 2014, we have witnessed an increase in the values of almost all family benefits, but not enough to effectively combat poverty. The percentage of children below 16 years old who avoided poverty as their families received social protection benefits decreased from 19.7 per cent in 2012 to as low as 10 per cent in 2014, and somewhat improved to 16.4 per cent in 2016. Similarly, for the total population, this indicator of relative poverty reduction decreased from 19.8 per cent in 2012 to 12.2 per cent in 2014, and then increased to 15.9 per cent in 2016 (Eurostat 2018, author's calculations). In-work poverty remained the highest within EU countries, at 18.8 per cent in 2015 (Eurostat 2018). The introduction of the voucher for regular kindergarten attendance in 2016, following a pilot-project of a non-governmental organization,[16] further illustrates the turn towards "activation" and "investment in children".

"Adverse Inclusion" and Bureaucratic Contradictions

The fact that social inclusion policies may hide pathways towards "adverse" (Sen 2000) or "disempowering" (Anthias 2001) inclusion, stigmatization, and ultimately a reinforcement of exclusion have become, by now, common currency in social policy analysis (Dean and Taylor-Gooby 1992; Fraser 1997; Lister 2004). However, less attention was given to the various forms under which these processes occur. In the case of the Roma ethnic minority, the structural disadvantage of a history of discrimination and negative stereotyping translates into the adverse effects of turning "Tsigane" into a rhetorical device performed in order to discredit welfare claims as abusive reliance on state support. These discursive strategies developed on the fertile ground of nationalistic demographic fears over the increase of the Roma population, at times resembling legacies of the interwar Eugenic thought (Bucur 2002; Turda 2009). Their new shape reveals a fusion with the neoliberal quest for productivity, self-discipline, and individualization, which the "Tsiganes" allegedly lack (van Baar 2012). Furthermore, the fact that persons living in marginalized informal settlements cannot prove that they have a formal residence prevents them from obtaining valid identity cards; instead, they must identify themselves by using temporary identity papers. As elsewhere argued (Raț 2013), this form of *dividing identification* allows a stricter surveillance of the deprived and limits their possibilities of setting up autonomous businesses or travelling abroad. Consequently, they factually cannot live up to the neoliberal ideal of being entrepreneurial and mobile, and they remain constrained into precarious employment at the discretion of private capital.

In the previous section, we discussed how Romanian social policies echo the scaling back of social citizenship into the new policies of "activation" and "social investment", when state support takes mainly the form of subsidies for precarious work and maintains the constraint of commodifying work and needs. However, not all precarious workers are covered by these schemes. Bureaucratic contradictions embedded in welfare regulations limit or deny their access to social provisions that they, in principle, would be entitled to receive. Welfare bureaucracies typically contain such inconsistencies, mainly stemming from the contradiction between substantive and formal rationality (Weber 1978[1922]). Understanding the manifestations of these incongruencies is crucial for establishing whether such adverse effects only randomly appear or if they systematically disfavour certain groups in contemporary Romania.

A widespread form of bureaucratic contradiction resides in the setting of a seemingly minimalistic eligibility condition that actually turns out to be a major barrier to access for a sizeable part of those who need it most. For example, in order to submit a request for heating allowance during the cold season,[17] claimants must present the proof of their residence (a rental lease or an ownership document). However, many of the families from these marginalized areas reside in shacks or improvised extensions of older buildings, and, consequently, they cannot prove a legal residence and thus fail to qualify for the heating allowance. Interviews held in Pata Rât, but also in the other informal settlements such as those from Somlyó (Șumuleu) Street in Miercurea Ciuc or on the shore of the Mureș River in Târgu

Mureș, where families cannot prove they have a formal residence, revealed their worried preoccupations to ensure the supply of wood or some other fuel for the winter. A similarly frequent example of hidden exclusion regards the case of obtaining medical certificates of disability that could qualify the family for specific benefits and services. The social-medical commission entitled to issue such certificates requires a medical letter from the family doctor based on a previous examination by a medical specialist. However, the latter two documents can be obtained for free only by persons with valid health insurance, while those uninsured need to pay a considerable fee. With the exception of GMI beneficiaries, whose health insurance is coved within the GMI programme, precarious workers from marginalized areas hardly hold health insurance. If they lose the capacity to work (following work accidents or other problems related to their vulnerable position), they neither will have access to subsidized public health care services, nor could afford paying for them.

Another form of bureaucratic contradiction manifests in disciplinary conditionings for maintaining the welfare entitlement, which beneficiaries cannot fulfil precisely because of their precariousness and impoverishment. As Culpitt inspiringly phrased it: "the double bind of welfare is struck: welfare recipients ought not need that which demonstrably they do need" (Culpitt 2001: 194). Blaming assumptions about beneficiaries' alleged inadequate behaviour penetrate these conditionings, envisaging that they should unlearn that in order to "enable" them to shift out of poverty. Control over their behaviour materializes in the obligation to submit once a month the proof of being a registered jobseeker or, as mentioned before, in making public on the walls of the town hall the list of families receiving social aid and the schedule of public work. The support allowance for needy families with children contains similar disciplinary regulations: in the case of repeated absences from school, the allowance is diminished or cut altogether. At first sight, this may be interpreted only as state paternalism oriented towards children's rights and control over parenting, but actually it produces counter-effects, leading to a vicious circle where the poorest families cannot afford sending their children to school and, instead of receiving state support, they are penalized.

The above-described bureaucratic contradictions have been persistent in time and remained systematic, thus holding lasting effects on the adverse inclusion of families from marginalized areas. Their endurance needs to be understood in a societal context that racializes poverty and associates the use of social assistance benefits with being "Tsigane". Moreover, there is a *demographic phobia of uncontrolled high fertility* among the most impoverished Roma and the latent expectation that social policies should limit that. A national survey carried out in 2006 by the Department for Interethnic Relations reported that almost half of the respondents agreed that "the state should take measures to stop the increase of the number of Roma" (DRI 2006), referring to birth rates, as Roma immigration towards Romania is totally atypical. Some leading demographers also expressed concerns of differential fertility, though not in ethnic terms, but with reference to the significantly higher fertility among the less-educated women, a situation common to other European countries as well, but not to the remarkable extent registered in Romania (Ghețău, interviewed in 2007 by *Adevărul*). Despite the historical pronatalism (Kligman 1998) and child-orientation of the Romanian welfare state, which was consolidated during the process of EU accession (Inglot et al. 2012), family policies have long reflected concerns for differential fertility, incorporating clear disincentives for families to raise more than four children. The value of the means-tested support allowance for needy families with children has flattened after the fourth child (no additional provision granted for the fifth, sixth, etc.) since its first legislation in 2003.[18] The birth grant[19] introduced in 2002 had been given only for the first four children, but this provision was eventually phased out in 2010 as part of the government's austerity package. Tax relief for low-income employees with dependent children has been available only up to four dependents.[20] Paid child care leave[21] was granted until 2014 only for the first three births, and only after that it was extended for all children, regardless of rank. However, given the strict eligibility condition of 12 months' continuous employment, the precarious workers from marginalized settlements hardly qualify for paid child care leave.

In the next section we move closer to the institutional settings through which social policies operate and analyse the everyday interactions between persons living in severely impoverished *Țigănii* and welfare workers, seen not only as agents who embody state bureaucracy, but also as actors who shape the local workings of the welfare state.

The Shadows of the Welfare State: Insights from Our Local Ethnographies

In our interviews with social workers and other local-level policy actors, we have tried to explore their own judgements of social justice, as well as their visions for national legislation and local-level initiatives. We paid particular attention to the "conflict zones" between social workers' mindsets and official regulations. Such conflicts play out in discretionary decisions concerning families from marginalized settlements, motivated at times by charitable feelings, and at other times by the desire to shape beneficiaries' behaviour in accordance with normative beliefs about "deservingness". As we will later see, local standards of "deservingness" do not necessarily coincide with the attributes of neoliberal subjects portrayed in political discourse or embedded in welfare regulations.

In all our cases, social workers shared the perception that the overwhelming majority of welfare beneficiaries were of Roma ethnicity, and that they had been receiving these provisions since the very beginning of the programme in 1996. Despite the fact that welfare records do not contain data on ethnicity, our questions on the ethnic distribution of beneficiaries resulted in prompt answers:

> Not only the Roma receive it [the GMI], but they are the majority and they have been receiving it continuously, since the benefit was introduced.
> *They represent the majority?*
> Yes.
> (Interview with a former social worker of the Miercurea Ciuc Welfare Office, at the time working in the non-governmental sector. May 2012)

> *What is, approximately, the percentage of the Roma among the social aid beneficiaries?*
> 90 per cent.
> *And are these families receiving the benefits since 1996?*
> Some of them yes, others don't ... but the majority of them yes.
> (Interview with social workers of the Ploiești Welfare Office, August 2012)

Social workers were aware of the fact that beneficiaries earn some money from informal labour, and that without this undeclared income they would literally starve, as the amount of benefits at the time of the interviews, in the summer of 2012, were very low:

> Well, they don't have another choice [but to apply for the GMI]. They go and search for [recyclable] stuff in the garbage bins, and sell further what they found… […] And some settled near the waste dump, but only two families, and actually they are slightly further away from the dump. But more families go for scavenging there. And the city is divided among them. Let's now say the truth … They placed containers [for selective waste collection], but those have been broken …
> *So they divide the city among themselves?*
> Yes, yes. Everybody has a job, everybody has a territory …
> (Interview with a former social worker of the Miercurea Ciuc Welfare Office, at the time working in the non-governmental sector. May 2012)

Moreover, in 2012, income from contractual day-labour still had been imputed from the amount of social assistance benefits granted under the GMI scheme. Given the necessity to combine earnings from irregular work with social assistance benefits, and also the fact that contractual day-labour does not confer health insurance, beneficiaries preferred to work undocumented, so they could safely maintain health insurance granted for GMI beneficiaries. However, social workers hastily qualified them as being work-shy, rather than acknowledging that they took an apparently reasonable, strategic decision from their position. As previously mentioned, three years later it became legally possible to cumulate income from contractual day-labour with social aid, but back in 2012 it was not the case.

> I know someone, he has a brick factory and employs Roma. But actually they do not want to sign the employment papers … He tried to hire them using the law on daily labourers, so that he would be covered, the employment would be official. But they [i.e., the Roma] told him: "Look, if you want us to sign something, be careful, because we do not want to lose the social assistance benefit. We won't come to work for you…" So they simply don't want to work. (Interview with a social worker of the Miercurea Ciuc Welfare Office. May 2012)

At the same time, social workers internalized the expectation that work should be "properly" commodified as documented labour, and they defended the "advantages of a contractual job" despite evidence that, in particular circumstances, the strategic choice might be in favour of unregulated labour.

> They were very reticent to enter this project [of vocational qualification]. Approximately 100–150 persons from Pata Rât took part in the project, and 10 were trained as commercial workers, for room service and cooking. Others, around 25 persons, were employed by cleaning companies and the employers are satisfied with them. We expect them to approach us, and we are here to help them. Those who were willing to get a job were hired, and today we still have jobs, but there are also persons who refuse getting employed on minimum wage because they obtain higher revenues from working on the waste dump. We have to work on their motivation in order to let them understand the advantages of a contractual job. (Interview with a social worker of the Cluj-Napoca Welfare Office. June 2015)

Social workers' discourse often reproduces the division between the established working class and the precariat, the latter being seen as "the poor" (economic bystanders) and "the Tsiganes" (racialized cultural outsiders), whose allegedly unproductive work is merely proof of their simultaneous willingness to work but inability to do so in a disciplined and productive manner. Thus, in this discourse, it is their effort and need that should receive (or that "deserves") some societal response. And this response is not framed as a right,[22] but as an act of charity (Wilenski 1964). Kasmir and Carbonella (2014: 6) see the division between "the stable working class" and "the poor" as a result of old "class maps or memories" that lost relevance for contemporary global capitalism, when labour remains a contingency revolving around the movements of capital and when dispossession should be understood as a "holistic notion" depicting "varied acts of disorganization, defeat, and enclosure that are at once economic, martial, social, and cultural and that create the conditions of a new set of social relations" (Kasmir and Carbonella 2014: 9). Dispossession from welfare as a *right*, undoubtedly much easier to be done in the case of a racialized group that for centuries has been rendered as "undeserving", creates the conditions for an instrumental use of social services and benefits as "social investment" aimed at better "activation" and more profitable use of the present and future labour force.

Furthermore, the logic of neoliberal "expanded reproduction" (Harvey 2003) does not necessarily overlap with the normative judgements of welfare workers, who see their role rather as distributers of charity than as administrators of state subsidies for the labour force that would ultimately serve the interest of capital. Consequently, they framed as "help" from "us" (the taxpayers of the municipality) any kind of public service provided for "them" (the residents of marginalized settlements). This further contributed to making invisible their status as precarious workers and projected upon them, instead, the derogatory portrait of "idle" recipients of welfare, as Enikő Vincze rightly observed during our joint research.

Baseline facilities, such as minimal housing, water supply, electricity or heating, were often defined as generous provisions granted for free by local authorities, and not as basic means of survival as a human right.

And does it matter [for the access to social housing] whether someone is a GMI beneficiary or not?

Of course it matters. If someone already benefits from GMI, he gets a lower score, as we consider that he has already received…

A form of social benefit…

A form of help.

(Interview with the social workers of the Ploiești Welfare Office. August 2012)

In almost all of the marginalized areas that we visited, public water pumps located on the street provided free drinkable water. However, the water supply eventually turned into a means of disciplining the inhabitants, as local authorities blamed them for excessive use of water and inability to safeguard the pumps from damages. Consequently, they occasionally stopped the flow of water in order to remind inhabitants that access depended on their disciplined behaviour and on the local public officials' benevolence. Similarly, the housing of evicted families in atrociously small and badly equipped container houses, often much worse than the improvised barracks built in other settlements, was seen as an act of generosity for families who were considered "outsiders" to the local society:

But many of these persons [who were evicted from the city and relocated near the wastewater plant] do not have identity cards issued in our city, and they are not going to get one either. Because they cannot prove, according to the law, that they have a residence in the city [...]. We have rental contracts with them for the barracks [small metal container houses without sewage, improper for dwelling] and based on the law on social marginalization we provide them social protection. We pay for their use of electric power, we pay for the water, we ... I mean the municipality pays ... for waste collection at the barracks. The children receive free food, but conditioned upon school attendance, otherwise they don't get anything. (Interview with the social worker of the Miercurea Ciuc Welfare Office, May 2012)

Counter-intuitively, social workers often position themselves as gatekeepers to "unmerited" social assistance benefits, rather than taking the side of claimants. This is reinforced by the complicated bureaucracy of the claiming process, which often remains incomprehensible for applicants, but it seemingly absolves social workers from potential feelings of guilt because of not being able to respect their own normative beliefs about "deservingness". For example, GMI regulations do not differentiate in terms of benefit amounts between home-owner applicants and those living in rented spaces or informal accommodation. The strict means-testing of household resources, which narrows down eligibility to those lacking any kind of valuable asset, except one's home, discloses a recommodification of needs that nonetheless may fail to pass through the maze of conditionings and bureaucratic requirements. Nonetheless, the process of proving one's total deprivation brings about a loss of self-esteem and a form of social disqualification (Fraser 1997).

(About the decrease in the number of families receiving support allowance for needy families with children): [the number of beneficiary families] decreased not because we have fewer cases [of needy families], but because they don't bring the documents that could help them, that we need in order to be able to help them ...
What kind of documents are you referring to? The certificate of school attendance?
Yes. And in the case of social aid, they don't go the Labour Office. So they are not registered at [vocational training] programs ... I tell you honestly: they prefer to stay at home, to take the social aid instead of going to

work. I know one case, he resigned from a cleaning company in order to receive the social aid. As simple as that.
(Interview with social workers of the Ploiești Welfare Office, August 2012)
Well, most of the time they respect the requirements [for maintaining entitlement to social assistance benefits]. Only those who go to work abroad fail to comply, but this occurs mostly during the summer. And they no longer get the benefits.
(…)
Probably some of them [i.e., social assistance beneficiaries] gain some earnings from occasional labour, but we cannot check this. And the truth is that, if so, it is not that bad, actually.
Yes, I see …
It is not that bad if they do …
(Interview with a social worker of the Târgu Mureș Welfare Office, May 2012)

Frequent checks of the county-level social inspection,[23] notoriously uninterested in field visits in deprived areas but carefully checking every paper involved, put particular stress on social workers, who conversely see their roles reduced to that of welfare accountancy within a heavily understaffed national system. As we saw in the previous section on bureaucratic contradictions, regulations that might seem reasonable from the desk often prove, on the ground, to contain adverse effects for the most deprived. Overall, precarious workers ought to find ways to commodify both their work and their needs in order to make ends meet, and they do this at the expense of being portrayed as "beneficiaries" of "social inclusion" measures, instead of their efforts as precarious workers, productive for capital and well integrated into an increasingly deregulated labour market, being acknowledged.

Conclusion

The logic of the Romanian welfare state at the margins is neither a logic of class compromise via social insurance, nor a logic of targeting benefits to the most needy as a last-resort safety net embroiled by the moral unacceptability of poverty. Even less so is it a universalistic logic of societal cohesion and equality through extensive redistribution and public services. Instead, we see increasingly conditional access to a limited number of provisions and subsidized services that ultimately facilitate the commodification of work through maintaining employability (via financial benefits, vocational training, counselling, etc.) and subsidizing the costs of living and raising children (via social assistance benefits, family allowances and provisions tied to schooling). In other words, we assist at the neoliberalization of the welfare state that is most visible at the margins. Roma and non-Roma families living in segregated, impoverished settlements, labelled as *Țigănii*, provide productive workforce for labour-intensive, weakly regulated sectors of basic services (sanitation, reparations, gardening, etc.), manual work in construction sites, or selective waste collection in polluted and often dangerous settings. The possibility of contracting day labourers in these sectors, and by that exempting them from the payment of social contributions, opened up a parallel system of relations between workers, capital and the state, the latter basically subsidizing deregulated labour for private capital via social aid and health insurance. New forms of local-level discretion emerged in the administration of welfare, revealing bureaucratic contradictions and diverging views over "deservingness".

"Social inclusion" policies obscure the adverse forms in which precarious workers from segregated and severely deprived urban peripheries participate in productive labour and relate to a strictly conditional and disciplinary social assistance framework, which is nonetheless obstructed by local-level discretion, at times in favour of those rendered impoverished for generations, at times blaming them as undeserving, but most often racializing them as *Tsiganes*. As their work and needs enter processes of commodification outside of the historically institutionalized labour rights and social insurance, their effort and plight remain discarded.

Notes

1. The Opinion of the European Commission on the Membership Request of Romania, Accessed June 5, 2011. http://ec.europa.eu/enlargement/archives/pdf/dwn/opinions/romania/ro-op_en.pdf
2. "We consider to be poor those individuals, families, and groups whose resources (material, cultural and social) are so limited as to exclude them

from a minimum acceptable way of life in the member state in which they live" (85/8/EEC: Council Decision of 19 December 1984 on specific Community action to combat poverty).
3. The first *National Action Plan to Combat Poverty and Promote Social Inclusion* was adopted by governmental decision No. 829/31.07.2002, and it explicitly mentions compliance with the EU recommendations following Lisbon 2000. The strategy lists the Roma minority among the vulnerable categories at risk of poverty and social exclusion, along with persons with disabilities and children in remote rural areas.
4. *The Strategy of the Romanian Government for Improving the Situation of the Roma.* 2001. Bucharest: Ministry of Public Information.
5. The European Platform for Roma Inclusion. Accessed May 25, 2016. http://ec.europa.eu/justice/discrimination/roma/roma-platform/index_en.htm
6. Law 65/1995 on means-tested social assistance benefits.
7. Law 416/2001 on the Guaranteed Minimum Income.
8. At the time of writing (May 2017), the government issued new legislation that combines the three main forms of social assistance benefits (GMI, family allowance, and heating subsidy) into one benefit. Conditionings on "activation" remained in place.
9. All families receiving GMI should assign a family member to undertake community work depending on the amount of the benefit, but not more than 72 hours per week. Persons caring for children below the age of seven or ill and frail family members had been exempted from this rule (Law 416/2001).
10. Law 277/2010 on the means-tested allowance for needy families with children reformed earlier legistation on this provision introduced by governmental executive order O.U.G. 105/2003.
11. Law 92/2011 on Social Assistance.
12. The new social-liberal coalition government hijacked the parliamentary debate on the emergency ordinance OUG 124/2012 designed by the former democratic-liberal government in order to considerably alter its text to transform it into the new Law 166/2012, which stated explicitly that the amount of the means-tested family allowance (Law 277/2010) should be imputed from GMI. This allowed the acceleration of an otherwise lengthy process of issuing a novel emergency ordinance and waiting for it to be endorsed as a law by Parliament. These changes occurred in the last quarter of 2012, shortly after we completed our fieldwork.

13. OUG 25/2015 allowed cumulating earnings from day-labour (Law 52/2011) with social assistance benefits granted under the GMI scheme.
14. See the platform of the Basic Income European Network, founded in 1986, Accessed October 1, 2016. http://basicincome.org/research/basic-income-studies/
15. The threshold of being at risk of poverty and social exclusion, set at 60% of the median household income per equivalent adult, OECD-2 equivalence scale (Eurostat 2016).
16. The pilot project was carried out by the *Ovidiu Ro* foundation, mainly in rural areas, with the co-financing from the 2014 European Economic Area grant from Norway, Iceland, and Liechtenstein. The text of the law refers to the success of this programme (Law 248/2015). See the Ovidiu Ro Foundation, Accessed September 1, 2016. http://www.ovid.ro/en/our-work/programul-fcg/
17. Heating allowance is regulated by the government's executive order O.U.G. 70/2011.
18. The first regulation on means-tested allowance for needy families with children consisted of the governmental executive order O.U.G. 105/2003. From the very beginning, it granted higher amounts for de facto single-parent families.
19. The birth grant was introduced by the very same law (416/2001) as the GMI programme.
20. The initial version of the new fiscal code was introduced by Law 571/2003. Subsequent modifications maintained the limit of four dependent persons for computing tax reliefs for low-income employees.
21. Paid child care leave was introduced by Law 120/1997, and it limited the benefit for the first three children.
22. "The essence of the welfare state is government-protected minimum standards of income, nutrition, health and safety, education, and housing assured to every citizen as a social right, and not as charity" (Wilenski 1964: XII).
23. Local welfare offices ought to report and comply to regular audits of the county-level Agency for Welfare Payments and Social Inspection, established in 2008 under the Ministry of Labour.

References

Anthias, Floya. 2001. The Concept of 'Social Divisions' and Theorizing Social Stratification: Looking at Ethnicity and Class. *Sociology* 35 (4): 835–854.

Begg, Iain, and Jos Berghman. 2002. Introduction: EU Social (Exclusion) Policy Revisited? *Journal of European Social Policy* 12 (3): 179–194.

Block, Fred, and Margaret Somers. 2014. *The Power of Market Fundamentalism. Karl Polanyi's Critique*. London: Harvard University Press.

Bonoli, Giuliano, and David Natali. 2011. *The Politics of the New Welfare States in Western Europe*. EUI Working Papers, RSCAS No. 17. Florence: European University Institute.

Bucur, Maria. 2002. *Eugenics and Modernization in Interwar Romania*. Pittsburgh: University of Pittsburgh Press.

Bugra, Ayse, and Kaan Agartan, eds. 2007. *Reading Karl Polanyi for the 21st Century*. Basingstoke: Palgrave Macmillan.

Culpitt, Ian. 2001. *Michel Foucault, Social Policy and 'Limit Experience'*. PhD dissertation, Victoria University of Wellington.

Dean, Hartley, and Peter Taylor-Gooby. 1992. *Welfare Dependency: The Explosion of a Myth*. Hemel Hempstead: Harvester Wheatsheaf.

Department for Interethnic Relations (DRI). 2006. *Climat interethnic în România, în pragul integrării europene*. [*Interethnic Climate in Romania on the Verge of European Integration*]. Bucharest: The Department for Interethnic Relations of the Romanian Government.

Emigh, Rebecca, and Iván Szelényi, eds. 2001. *Poverty, Ethnicity and Gender in Eastern Europe During Market Transition*. London: Praeger.

Esping-Andersen, Gosta. 1990. *The Three World of Welfare Capitalism*. Cambridge: Polity Press.

Eurostat. 2016. *Population and Social Conditions Database*. Brussels: The European Commission. http://ec.europa.eu/eurostat/data/database. Accessed 1 Nov 2016.

Eurostat. 2018. *Population and Social Conditions Database*. Brussels: The European Commission. http://ec.europa.eu/eurostat/data/database. Accessed 27 Mar 2018.

Ferge, Zsuzsa. 1997. The Changed Welfare Paradigm. The Individualization of the Social. *Social Policy and Administration* 31 (1): 20–44.

Ferrera, Mario, Manos Matsagaris, and Stefano Sacchi. 2002. Open Coordination Against Poverty. The New EU Social Inclusion Process. *Journal of European Social Policy* 12 (3): 227–239.

Fraser, Nancy. 1997. *Justice Interruptus: Critical Reflections on the "Postsocialist" Condition.* New York: Routledge.
Gans, Herbert J. 1990. Deconstructing the Underclass. The Term's Dangers as a Planning Concept. *APA Journal* 1990: 271–277.
Ghețău, Vasile. 2007. Interview by S. Iordache and N. Zaharia. "De ce nu mai fac copii româncele?" [Why Romanian Women have Babies No Longer?] *Adevărul*, August 24.
Hall, Peter. 1993. Policy Paradigms, Social Learning, and the State: The Case of Economic Policymaking in Britain. *Comparative Politics* 25 (3): 275–296.
Harvey, David. 2003. *The New Imperialism.* Oxford: Oxford University Press.
Hemerijck, Anton. 2015. The Quiet Paradigm Revolution of Social Investment. *Social Politics* 22 (2): 242–256.
Inglot, Tomasz, Dorottya Szikra, and Cristina Raț. 2012. Reforming Post-Communist Welfare States. Family Policies in Poland, Hungary and Romania since 2000. *Problems of Post-Communism* 59 (6): 27–49.
Kasmir, Sharryn, and August Carbonella. 2014. *Blood and Fire: Toward a Global Anthropology of Labor.* London/New York: Berghahn Books.
Katz, Michael B. 1992. *The "Underclass" Debate. Views from History.* Princeton: Princeton University Press.
Kligman, Gail. 1998. *The Politics of Duplicity.* Berkeley: University of California Press.
Ladányi, János, and Iván Szelényi. 2006. *Patterns of Exclusion: Constructing Gypsy Ethnicity and the Making of an Underclass in Transitional Societies of Europe.* New York: Columbia University Press.
Lister, Ruth. 2004. *Poverty.* Cambridge: Polity Press.
Morel, Natali, Bruno Parlier, and Joachim Palme, eds. 2011. *Towards a Social Investment Welfare State.* Oxford: Oxford University Press.
Comisia Națională de Demografie [National Commission of Demography]. 1977. *Studiu privind situația social-economică a populației de țigani din țara noastră* [*Study on the Socio-economic Situation of the Gypsy Population in Romania*]. București, 29.11.1977. http://www.militiaspirituala.ro/detalii.html?tx_ttnews%5Btt_news%5D=189&cHash=17bcd59f589de31d0c4c3576da0 72f02. Accessed 5 May 2016.
Pierson, Paul. 2001. *The New Politics of the Welfare State.* Oxford: Oxford University Press.
Polanyi, Karl. 1944. *The Great Transformation.* New York: Farrar & Rinehart.
Popescu, Livia. 2004. *Politici sociale Est-Europene între paternalism de stat și responsabilitate individuală* [*East-European Social Policies Between State Paternalism and Individual Responsibility*]. Cluj-Napoca: Presa Universitară Clujeană.

Popescu, Livia, Valentina Ivan, and Cristina Raț. 2016. The Romanian Welfare State at Times of Crisis. In *Challenges to European Welfare Systems*, ed. Klaus Schubert, Paloma Villota, and Johanna Kuhlmann, 615–645. Berlin: Springer.

Raț, Cristina. 2013. Bare Peripheries: State Retrenchment and Population Profiling in Segregated Roma Settlements from Romania. *Studia UBB Sociologia* 58 (2): 155–174.

Romanian Ministry of Labour, Family, Social Protection and Elderly Persons. 2016. *Statistical Bulletin of the Ministry of Labour, 2002–2015*. http://www.mmuncii.ro/j33/index.php/ro/transparenta/statistici/buletin-statistic. Accessed 1 Nov 2016.

Sen, Amartya. 2000. Social Exclusion: Concept, Application and Scrutiny. *Social Development Papers* 1: 1–60.

Standing, Guy. 2007. Labour Recommodification in the Global Transformation. In *Reading Karl Polanyi for the 21st Century*, ed. Ayshe Bugra and Kan Agartan, 67–95. Basingstoke: Palgrave Macmillan.

Stewart, Michael. 2002. Deprivation, the Roma and 'the Underclass'. In *Post-Socialism: Ideals, Ideologies and Practices in Eurasia*, ed. Chris M. Hann, 133–155. London: Routledge.

The World Bank. 2009. *Report on the Guaranteed Minimum Income Program in Romania*. Bucharest: The World Bank.

Wacquant, Loic. 2000. Logics of Urban Polarization: The View from Below. In *Renewing Class Analysis*, ed. Rosemary Crompton, Fiona Devine, Mike Savage, and John Scott, 107–119. Oxford: Blackwell.

Wacquant, Loic. 2011. A Janus-Faced Institution of Ethnoracial Closure: A Sociological Specification of the Ghetto. In *The Ghetto: Contemporary Global Issues and Controversies*, ed. Ray Hutchison and Bruce Haynes, 1–31. Boulder: Westview Press.

Wilenski, Harold L. 1964. *The Welfare State and Equality*. Berkeley: University of California Press.

Titmuss, Richard. 2000[1967]. Lecture at the National Conference on Social Welfare, London, April 1967. In *The Welfare State Reader*, ed. Christopher Pierson and Francis G. Castles, 42–49. Cambridge: Polity Press.

Turda, Marius. 2009. 'To End the Degeneration of a Nation': Debates on Eugenic Sterilization in Interwar Romania. *Medical History* 53 (1): 77–104.

UNICEF and Save the Children Romania. 2012. *Manifestul pentru copii [Manifesto for Children]*. http://www.stepbystep.ro/images/unicef/manifest_copii_unicef_salvati_copiii.pdf. Accessed 1 May 2013.

van Baar, Huub. 2012. Socio-Economic Mobility and Neo-Liberal Governmentality in Post-Socialist Europe: Activation and the Dehumanisation of the Roma. *Journal of Ethnic and Migration Studies* 38 (8): 1289–1304.

Vincze, Enikő. 2015. Processes of Subjectification and Racialization of 'the Roma'. In *Modes of Appropriation and Social Resistance*, ed. Gabriel Troc and Bogdan Iancu, 30–60. București: Tritonic.

Vincze, Enikő, and Hajnalka Harbula. 2011. *Strategii identitare și educație școlară [Identity Strategies and School Education]*. Cluj-Napoca: EFES.

Weber, Max. 1978 [1922]. *Economy and Society*. Berkeley: University of California Press.

Wilson, William J. 1987. *The Truly Disadvantaged*. Chicago: University of Chicago Press.

5

Framing the "Unproductive": A Case Study of High-Level Visions of Economic Progress and Racialized Exclusion

Anca Simionca

Introduction

This chapter[1] looks into the formation and maintenance of spatially and socially marginalized categories of people through the lens of imageries of city development. Spatial segregation of the poor in urban areas that lack most basic facilities is an outcome of various structural forces operating at levels ranging from global capital flows and fixes to the aggregated individual racist views and practices. Convincing arguments have been made showing the fact that urban slums concentrating the poor (who many times share a certain ethnic or racial background) had been formed under interwoven system-level causes such as deficient redistribution, housing policies, commodification of commons, neoliberal market policies.

The contention of this book is that such multilevelled marginalization is not simply an unintended consequence of uneven or carelessly implemented development. Far from being a redundant category of the system, or a consequence of structural violence that is a by-product of larger

---

A. Simionca (✉)
Sociology Department, Babeș-Bolyai University, Cluj-Napoca, Romania

© The Author(s) 2019
E. Vincze et al. (eds.), *Racialized Labour in Romania*, Neighborhoods, Communities, and Urban Marginality, https://doi.org/10.1007/978-3-319-76273-9_5

structural dynamics, these segregated areas and the racialization of their populations are an integral and productive part of the current dynamic of capital. The angle from which this chapter will address the importance of marginality for the productive system is that of the imaginaries guiding the development of the city and the labour market as they become visible in the discourses of several institutions producing city-level policy. The positive visions of city growth, development and integration that these institutions operate with only occasionally and marginally discuss poverty itself and are not explicitly acknowledging the damaging effects of ethnic prejudices and latent racism. Yet they have an immense impact on the range of possibilities opened and closed for the disadvantaged through the fact that they are the very setting of the limits between desirability and non-desirability, normality and abnormality, worthiness and unworthiness. The operation of drawing these boundaries constitutes itself into the basis of an epistemic injustice (Fricker 2007; Samson 2015), as the inhabitants of these marginalized areas are being denied their quality as knowing subjects. They become by definition unemployable and redundant in the dominant categories, while their epistemic and material contributions to the larger functioning of the economic system are being from the start made impossible to recognize. In the overall neoliberal logic of justification of individual wealth and well-being as being based on individual merit, will and ability to make oneself useful and productive, this a priori denying of people's quality of knowing and working subjects clears the path of permanent symbolic exclusion and material exploitation.

This chapter seeks to describe the ways in which the current hegemonic discourses of economic development (centred on attracting foreign investment to cities) and those of the neoliberal subject (the worthy entrepreneurial autonomous and creative individual) constitute the material and symbolic context in which the pre-existing marginalized situation of many of the ethnically Roma is further legitimized and constitutes the starting point of a new wave of exclusion from the positive visions of society. Thus, it provides a tentative explanation of the ways in which the particular nodal points on which the dominant vision of development operates create the basis for the definition of certain actors and possible alternatives that excludes from the onset certain categories of people when attempting to manage and to better the life of the cities. It creates a dichotomy between a world of "the developed" and one of "the undeveloped," based on meritocratic ideology. All individuals within this societal project need to prove their worthiness. However, the setting in which this worthiness can be proved is structured a priori by including a category of the external to development.

I will first describe the research questions that have guided this analysis and the type of material the conclusions are built on. Then, I highlight the commonalities in the visions of positive governing and prosperity of the five cities researched and the centrality that a subject endowed with certain features has for the possibility of achieving the goals of such government. In the third section, I show how the failure to meet the standards of development (both by cities and by individuals) is constructed as a category belonging to a different order of reality, to which different rules apply, and that lacks even the potential of becoming part of the positive "developed world." It is to this category that the inhabitants of marginalized areas are relegated to. Finally, I show how this separation and relegation to the sphere of underdevelopment is operated on a discursive level by the city officials interviewed.

The Research and Research Questions

Within our joint research, briefly presented in the Introduction, interviews were conducted with inhabitants of marginalized impoverished settlements, NGOs, politicians, representatives of local authorities and social workers, as well as with a set of representatives of decentralized institutions that are not particularly focused on the urban poor but have an important role in shaping the economic future of the cities, namely, the County Agencies for Labour Force Employment (AJOFM) and the County Commerce and Industry Chambers (CCI).[2] The idea behind including the latter category of interviewees in the sample was, on the one hand, to have the opportunity to access more detailed factual information about the main parameters of the local economy and employment. On the other hand, the interviewees were rightfully expected to be able to provide an important insight into the imaginary of development and of the desirable future for the city as a whole, therefore allowing us to gain a different perspective over the situation of the urban poor by placing it in the wider context of the cities in which they live and the type of problems, struggles and solutions that are sought.

The main "speaking actors" in this analysis will therefore be the representatives of AJOFM and CCI from the five cities of Călărași, Cluj-Napoca, Miercurea Ciuc, Ploiești and Târgu Mureș, whose interviews are used primarily for discourse analysis. The factual information that they provide and that is included here as such has been cross-checked with statistical data (see also Table 1.1 in Chap. 1 and Chap. 2). While limited in their comparability across cities, public documents produced by these institutions (missions and vision, reports) have also been analysed in order to arrive at the most recurring themes and to be able to place the narratives of the interviewees in a more general discursive context. Also, the interviewees' assessment of various situations concerning the people living in the communities was confronted with the multiple accounts gathered through the discussions with the people themselves. The point was not, however, to assess the accuracy of the information provided by the representatives of the two institutions, but exactly to gain some knowledge about the main gaps between the representations that the officials operate with (when putting together reports and strategies for development) and the experiences of the people themselves.

The five cities provide the necessary diversity for analysing the recurrence of nodal points of the dominating vision of development, growth and employment. They are county-level capital cities, both from Transylvania and from the southern part of Romania, of different sizes and ethnic composition (Vincze 2013; Petrovici 2013).

There are two main dimensions on which cities differ, and that could have a significant impact upon the visions and discourses of the authorities regarding the desirable outcomes for the future. The first one is *the diversity of the industrial profile of the city before 1989*. This dimension has the potential of introducing important differences in the type of situation the city is confronted with: in case of monoindustrial background, the crumbling of one industry can easily lead to the overall paralysis of the entire production, while a more varied profile can result in different paths for parts of the economy. Călărași and Ploiești were the two cities in the research that could be best described as having a single-industry profile before 1989, while Târgu Mureș, Cluj-Napoca and Miercurea-Ciuc had a more diverse economic background. Categorizing a city as monoindustrial does not imply that only one industry was operating in these cities, but that the core of the productive activities was represented by one plant or platform and that most of the remaining production was at least in part linked to it. This had a significant impact on both the level and the structure of unemployment after 1989 (Petrovici 2013; Simionca 2013).

The second one is *the current level of foreign investment*. We could have expected that it is those cities that have a strong share of foreign investment that place such a great importance on them, while those more unsuccessful are coming up with alternatives. Or, on the contrary, that those cities which have a high share of foreign investment might be more sceptical with the actual positive impact they may have on the city economy. On this dimension, Ploiești, Cluj-Napoca and Târgu Mures are all examples of cities currently having relatively high levels of foreign investment. On the side of the cities with less foreign investment is Călărași, which is the clearest example of a city whose crumbled industry has not been replaced by any alternative massive investment in high-scale production. While similarly missing an impressive share of foreign capital, Miercurea-Ciuc is a more peculiar example on both dimensions. While it had a rather varied industrial profile during socialism, it also had a rather lower rate of proletarization than the other cities. Currently, it does not have a high rate of foreign investment, but it has a rather varied sector of production, in contrast to Călărași (Petrovici 2013).

Development as Moving Away from Socialism and the Productive Worker

The general parameters in which the interviewees describe the past and future of their localities are remarkably similar, despite the fact that we have purposefully selected the localities so that to maximize the chance of obtaining variety.[3] The overall narrative is that of a grandiose unsustainable industrial past, whose crumbling leaves cities with lower productivity rates, unemployment and the need to seek alternative productive arrangements.

Another commonality refers to the fact that the centralized and large-scale industrial project that constituted the backbone of the socialist economy is unsustainable in the longer run and that it is only the market (as the aggregation of private interests) that can overcome its shortcomings. Further, in the three cities that have been successful in attracting foreign investment, the transition between the two models is a clearly positive one, highlighting the imperative and the advantages of, on the one hand, large-scale investments and, on the other hand, entering global circuits of production and consumption. On the side of cities with a less successful project of insertion in these circuits, it is rather the degree of optimism that differs than the desirable vision itself.

In the wider context of city rescaling following the US fiscal crisis of the 1970s, and Romania's intricate subsequent relationship with IMF (Ban 2014), it is hardly a surprise that the dominant strategy of the cities included in this sample is that of attempting to make themselves into the localization of global fluxes of capital in order to be able to maintain and enhance the well-being of their inhabitants. Becoming progressively entangled in the global fluxes of capital through the attraction of foreign investors—the backbone of all the visions of desirable development of the cities—is synonymous with departing from a communist past. This equivalence further adds legitimacy to the process and delegitimizes any alternatives. The market becomes central: an impersonal mechanism that is objective and is able to organize productive activities and make the subsistence and prosperity of society possible. Much more than this, however, it is viewed as the very mechanism that coordinates human energies in such a way as to also produce the effects of just and meritocratic distribution of resources and rewards. The economy and its tool— the market—become the starting point for any solution sought for either material or non-material problems identified in the society. This understanding of the market is in sharp contrast with the state, seen as corrupt and a remnant of the past.

This vision of development comes with a certain definition of the actors capable of successfully operating in this "dynamic" world, which is the entrepreneurial flexible and autonomous employee. While certain important mutations of this dominant visions can be documented (Simionca 2013), the commonality lies in the way in which responsibility is shifted to the individual level. Therefore, the agenda for progress is not fully articulated in structural terms (attracting capital and investment) but also in subject-making terms (making sure that individuals are fit to participate in the new arrangement).

One of the most frequently recurring criterion along which the inhabitants of a city are evaluated by their planners is the degree of their flexibility, their capacity and willingness to adapt to the ever-changing conditions of the dynamic economy and labour market. One of the institutional responses that both the CCIs and the AJOFMs have in this respect is the increasing numbers of training and retraining courses that they offer, partly with the support of European funds for "human capital development." The underlying assumption of the need to have flexible careers and individuals in order to maintain a flexible economy (Binkley 2009) is clearly echoed by the interviewees. All the CCI representatives I have interviewed offered me very similar versions of the same narrative: it is no longer reasonable to expect to be working in the same domain for one's entire life, because the economy is dynamic, production is volatile and restructuring is permanent. Therefore, individuals need to be able to reinvent themselves and their skills accordingly in order to be employable (Binkley 2009; Ten Bos and Rhodes 2003; Sennett 1999).

Through their discussion about the spirit of capitalism, Boltanski and Chiapello (2005) draw our attention to the fact that the normative visions about a desired social order operate with two central figures: that of the *Great* person, the person as one should be, and that of the *Little* person, the one that does not manage to acquire the desirable features. The *Great* people are the ones who manage to understand the premises of the new structural requirements and to adapt. The *Little* ones are those who "expect everything from the state, just like during communism, without exiting their comfort zone a bit, without doing their share" (AJOFM representative, M, 40 years old, interviewed in 2012). These institutions, therefore, imagine their role to be double: create the structure of opportunities and create the right type of subject. This type of binary was present also in the situation of the otherwise innovative project put forth by the Cluj county AJOFM regarding the cooperative for the former employees from Câmpia Turzii (Simionca 2013). The right type of subject is, in the institution's vision, capable of adapting, with internalized control, responsibility and mastering a high variety of skills. The people who would be part of the group of beneficiaries needed to prove not only their potential of learning new technical skills, but also their leadership qualities. In order to eliminate the potential of corruption and to maximize the probability of success for the project, the people from the target group (the former employees of the factory) were administered several computer-led tests. The major concerns about the selection were whether the people would be able to adapt themselves and learn a brand new occupation and also to adapt themselves to their new status of co-owners of an enterprise. The non-interference of human "subjectivity" was insured through the computer tests, the accuracy and validity of computer results was beyond any doubt. Apart from the selection, there were several other major concerns about the proper functioning of the factory once it would be set up, all of them related to the labour control and responsibility. For example, the hypothetical situation of a worker coming to work drunk was mentioned, and the solution was thought to come from the common ownership and individual interests of all those involved.

The "Tsiganes": Are They Productive or Not?

The extent to which the entire population of Roma ethnicity was seen by the interviewees as being outside of the world endowed with potential for normality depended greatly on the degree of open racism that they had. I will briefly refer below to the most recurring types of descriptions I was offered in regard to those seen as "Tsiganes" in relation to work.

In one of the interviews with a representative of AJOFM, I was explicitly told that while their institution does have some programmes like the "Job fair for Roma", in his opinion all these attempts are doomed to fail and are a waste of precious resources of time and money.

> What to say about the Roma's employment? They are unemployable, that's what they are, let's stop being polite about it. (AJOFM director, male, 45 years old, interviewed in 2012)

When I confronted him with the counterfactual of the socialist period, in which it is a well-known fact that many of the ethnically Roma were successfully employed, for example, in various positions in factories all over the country, his city included, he replied that:

They were forcing them back then, that's why it was happening. It's not because they wanted to! There, with a broom in their hands or stealing, that's all they're good at! (AJOFM director, male, 45 years old, interviewed in 2012)

Apart from this straightforwardly racist account, which this official had no problem openly giving to me (an outsider coming from the academia), most of the replies I got were more nuanced. When asked about the range of jobs open to, or currently taken by people belonging to the Roma ethnicity, the first workplace to be mentioned was the city cleaning company. Clearly confirmed by the various discussions we as researchers had with the people in the community, working in the city cleaning industry was the major option for formal employment. Another commonality in the discourses of officials and that of the people themselves was the fact that this opportunity for employment was really an opportunity to be cherished and be enthusiastic about being able to have. The difference most of the times, however, comes from the degree to which the officials on the one side and the members of the vulnerable community on the other side think it is a widely available one. On the officials' side, the very scarcity of these positions is not a salient feature: as these jobs are available and they do not exclude ethnically Roma from them, it follows that if all people living in marginalized impoverished areas actually wanted to have jobs, they would be able to get them. On the side of those facing deprivation and marginalization, it appears clear that this is hardly the case, and that having a job in these companies is actually a hassle, going way beyond their willingness or ability to take up a job with a structured schedule that requires discipline. Reportedly, access to these jobs is also conditioned by offering bribes (around 200 euro in Ploiești, for example) to the middle management in charge of personnel selection.

It was only in one of the cities where the city cleaning company was described by the authorities as an employer in the same way in which the other, more "productive" employers were described. In this case, I was explained that since 2007, when the company was taken over by a new owner, it also delivers high-quality employment opportunities: adequate work protection gear and machinery. This came out as a duty of the employer. In the other accounts, the companies providing services of cleaning for the city were depicted by the authority almost as a branch of the social work benefits available to the poor: the fact that they offered jobs for those seen as "unemployable" by others is a service that the company provides intrinsically to the city. The fact that these companies operate within the same logic of profit and that they are far from being in the position of distributing benefits to the poor was completely ignored.

Another recurrent story that the people in the various communities that were visited during our fieldwork brought to surface was the fact that getting such jobs was in many cases made very difficult by the existence of a type of entrepreneur: people either working in the companies or just having close ties to them, who operated a market in which the goods were the jobs themselves. This means that in many cases people had to pay the equivalent of one, two or even three months' salaries in order to become employed legally. Far from being the regular capitalist "selling one's labour power for the salary," these jobs were seen and exploited as the bunch of other benefits that they bring along: the fact that in order to get unemployment benefits, medical insurance, state pensions and other retirement benefits, one needs to have been employed for a number of months or years. The salary becomes secondary. Also, many of these jobs require some educational credentials (e.g., eight years of basic education are mandatory in order to gain a driving license but also for the majority of training courses organized by the AJOFM) and therefore they are not open for everyone. In the thus established hierarchy, people from marginalized settlements only have access to the lowest layer of job hierarchy. None of these complications were on the radar of the authorities, who viewed the labour market niche of the cleaning sector as an open, transparent and equitable one.

This image of openness, fairness and transparency of a business that is actually rarely so in practice is very instrumental in solidifying a certain image of the Roma worker. If the business is available and fair, and there are still people who are unemployed, it follows that it is their direct individual responsibility and failure. The explanation that is quickly mobilized is that of the stereotypically lazy, undisciplined and unwilling to work "Tsigane", who tries to get as much benefits from the state as possible, avoiding the socially acceptable and desirable ways to earn a living by putting in effort through work. None of the interviewees qualified collecting iron or plastic bottles as work, or as an activity that requires self-control, sustained effort and will. These qualities are considered essential for a person being able to hold a job, and they are completely separated from the image of the "petty activities" undertaken by the people living in marginalized areas. The same categories are internalized and used by the people themselves, who also mention only the formal employment that they hold as being "work", while the rest of the working activities that they are involved in are indexed as "doing what we can to have something to eat."

Another occupational niche that was presented by the authorities as being frequently occupied by ethnically Roma women was the informal sector of domestic cleaning, especially the staircases from block of flats. This is, however, a much worse scenario, because their status as employees is not legally recognized and, consequently, it does not qualify the workers for health insurance or other type of benefits. The conditions of pay are also left to the individual negotiations and therefore (in the majority of cases) the women doing this kind of work have a very vulnerable status and very little job security. Even the representative of CCI that most eloquently described the vulnerability of such position to me, proving a real awareness of the shortcomings of the situation, finished this account by presenting it in a positive light: "they can do it, however, it's an opportunity that is out there for them, people seek their services" (CCI director, female, 50 years old).

Most of the discourses of the officials interviewed are rather ambiguous in placing the blame for the situation of exclusion in which the impoverished Roma from the segregated areas we were interested in were living. The main rhetorical tool that organizes this ambiguity in such a way that the stereotypical image of the lazy and unwilling to work "Tsigane" can be still mobilized is the well-known distinction between the "good" and the "bad" Roma.

The "good" Roma are those who managed to become "integrated" into mainstream society, by which most of the time is meant that they exhibit individual traits that make them worthy: willingness to put in effort and discipline into a job, to "make a living." The people living in the areas of our ethnographic fieldwork rarely qualified in this category. The examples I was given were those of people who, despite the fact that they might have a Roma ethnic origin and live in marginalized areas, manage to have "normal" jobs: hairdresser, selling in a shop or working in the factory. These examples are mobilized to prove an individualistic argument, in which a "token" success case from a category is being brought forth in order to weaken any systemic pattern: there is hardly anything different in the type of challenges in getting a job that people have regardless of their ethnicity, the difference lies in the type of attitude that individuals have towards success; and the examples of those who made it are there to prove this point. In addition to this, I was told several times that it is not the Romanians who are racist, but it is the Roma themselves who use the card of discrimination in order to make excuses for themselves.

Underdevelopment Because of the Non-Productive Worker, Not Systemic Functioning

Starting from the conclusion of that analysis, I argue that it is important to understand that the representation offered about the livelihoods and the role in the productive economy of the people living in the impoverished segregated areas is skewed in a way that makes their contribution to the system invisible. While showing that their daily activities are actually quite productive for the overall capitalist system, the official representation of these activities does not allow them to make claims of being worthy citizens that are recipients of the benefits of taking part of the system.

The representatives of AJOFM and CCI were asked during the interviews to help us put together the economic and labour market history of their locality, as well as to give us a detailed description of the current situation, as much as possible. They were invoked as experts on the global situation of the city. However, they were also introduced to the overall aims of the research and to the fact that our interest focuses on the situation of the segregated impoverished Roma communities that live within their cities. We expressed our interest in understanding how their institution views their situation and their own role in dealing with the shortcomings of these communities' livelihoods. The reaction of one of the CCI directors to this framing of my request was, while singular, rather telling:

Madam, our business here is development, not ... underdevelopment! What could I tell you about poverty?! Go to ... Social Work, it's them who deal with such things. (CCI director, female, 45 years old, interviewed in 2012)

In this straightforward account, "underdeveloped" and "developed" are not two states of the same variable, but two completely distinct realities, with a different set of institutions responsible for their management.

How does it happen that an institution whose aim is to foster the growth and the consolidation of a prosperous productive environment is thought to have nothing to do with the very failure of its aim? It is not that examples of various types of failure of their attempts to better the situation in their cities were absent in the discourses of the officials interviewed. On the contrary, I was offered several analyses of situations in which foreign investors cannot be attracted due to various (objective or not) reasons, of small firms that do not manage to keep afloat due to the competition or to the weak markets they operate in, or of individuals that do not manage to become integrated on the labour market even after having completed training for different jobs than before. However, all these are happening in that part of society that has, for the dominant view, at least the potential of development, the potential of success. The impoverished segregated Roma communities are not part of the limits drawn around the world with the potential of normality. Their situations of poverty, unemployment, and precarious living conditions are not recognized as failure of the activity of these institutions because they are from the onset and by definition seen as belonging to a different reality and are, therefore, not even considered.

These institutions are primarily operating with those people that can at least in theory be transformed to "Great people" of the new order, who have the potential of being the flexible desirable subjects. Within this category, there is failure and success: there are people who manage to put their potential into practice and those who do not manage. People participating in a course on how to become an entrepreneur may open successful businesses, may be able to keep them for long, or they might fail to do either. There are, however, other people that are from the beginning outside of this category of potentially "Great people."

And Who Decides That?

A discussion I had with one of the representatives of AJOFM is very telling in regard to the way in which the distinction between "the good" and "the bad" Roma operates. After I was told that the main reason why workers of Roma origins are not sought by employers is the bad experience they had in the past with allegedly Roma people who were not disciplined enough to carry on work, I asked whether the implication of this is the standard meritocratic one: regardless of their ethnic background, it is people with the best qualifications and work discipline that succeed in finding and keeping good jobs. The answer was an affirmative one: "of course, many of them have gone through schooling, or they have a particular skill and they could work at any given point, of course. I didn't mean that if they're Roma they're incapable of working" (CCI director, female, 50 years old, interviewed in 2012). And, in order to make the argument about the lack (or shallowness) of racism clearer, I was given the example of a very successful workshop organized especially for the professional qualification or requalification of Roma. Unlike what I would have expected, the success of this event came not from the fact that people managed to find a job afterwards (indeed, none of them had, to the knowledge of my interlocutor), but from the fact that the participants were disciplined enough to go through the classes and they showed the willingness to better themselves and put efforts into increasing their chances of finding formal employment.

Although this story was actually about ethnically Roma people who do not manage to secure a formal working position even after going through the trainings, the person from AJOFM presented it to me as a case of success. What would have been otherwise reported as a failure of such a programme was in the case of the impoverished ethnically Roma considered a success because they had managed to enter the category of those who have the potential of being successful. The fact that they did not achieve the actual purpose of the programme—that of increasing the employment rate among the participants by means of professional training—becomes less significant than the fact that a process of disciplining was carried out.

This discussion shows one of the mechanisms that contribute to the invisibility and normalization of racism, achieved through double standards of success: while unemployment is a failure generally speaking, it can still be a success in the case of ethnically Roma in case they have managed to prove that they are "employable" unemployed, owning the attributes that could make them worthy of a labour contract. This image of elevating people from their state of complete lack of employability, presumably due to individual traits making them unfit for formal employment, would not be possible unless the actual work that people from these communities do on a regular basis for their survival is not dismissed as unworthy.

There were the interviews conducted with the spokespersons of the county-level police departments that made even clearer the ways in which the impoverished Roma living in the segregated areas belong to the jurisdictions of different institutions, being made into altogether different types of entities. While CCI and AJOFM are only in special conditions preoccupied with the situation of the Roma, the police take them as particularly important for their activities and mission. "Ethnicity" cannot be used as an official category in the police departments' reporting of crimes; therefore no statistics are available for the past years indicating the proportion of different types of criminal activities that have been undertaken by ethnic Roma. However, the lack of statistical data is compensated by the informal knowledge of the employees and, in most of the cases, the dwellers of impoverished segregated areas visited during our fieldwork had a special place.

The police spokesperson from Călărași and Miercurea-Ciuc were very surprised to find out that I was interested in their institution's experience and problems with the people living in the impoverished segregated areas in their cities. While they politely answered all my questions, I was also repeatedly reminded that the type of petty offences they were routinely involved in did not constitute "the real Roma problems." The "real" problems were in the rural areas and I was encouraged to redirect my interest to those situations. In the Harghita county, for example, some violent incidents involving ethnic Roma villagers had been widely known and documented by the media, and it was to them that I should have referred to. After reaffirming my interest in the Roma people living in our particular locations, I was first told that "no, the police has no problem with them" (female, 45 years old). However, my more targeted questions (regarding the situations we had learned about from different sources, like begging, stealing iron, prostitution, illegal usage of carriages) were answered affirmatively.

Discrimination and racism become less visible in this apparently benevolent discourse that defends the urban Roma from the accusations of being "truly" delinquent. By this discourse, however, a certain degree of crime is normalized for any person of the ethnically Roma. In the definitions of the police, the "good" Roma are those that are involved only in petty offences (that are, consequently, a "normal" feature for this population), while the "bad" Roma are only those that are violent or involved in large-scale trafficking of people or drugs, as well as the violent interactions between "neamuri" (clans based on kinship). Several such incidents (in Valea Rece, Târgu Mureș and Harghita county) resulting in the intervention of police officers from the special troops are mobilized as examples of what "bad" Roma deliquency means.

The situation of the impoverished segregated areas and their populations falls completely out of the self-definition of institutions such as CCI and AJOFM. These institutions are conceptualized as the agents of development, of implementing positive and constructive projects. Only those situations in which the unemployed have passed a test of meritocracy and have earned their right as an insider are taken up as belonging to their area of jurisdiction and are made into their own failures. Their "work," that is the "productive" activities they are involved in, are rather under the jurisdiction of the police. Gathering plastic bottles or iron (and sometimes transporting it with carriages that are illegal in the city) being considered "non-work," it becomes assimilated to the category of petty crime, which falls under the interest of the police as an institution. The fact that the recycling is done mainly through the hard work of hundreds of people who barely manage to live out of the money earned is not visible in most of the discourses. Neither the public utility nor the individual effort, discomfort, discipline and skill inherent in these activities are recognized. The alleged lack of these features is, however, used exactly to exclude these people from the world of those having the potential of being productive, those who are the target of the programmes and policy envisaging the well-being of the city.

One could view this situation as a paradox: from the point of view of imageries of development, it is people's ability to constantly transform themselves and make themselves useful that gives their relevance to the system and their right to make demands. However, what constitutes productive work is outside the power of definition of the people themselves. There are at least two types of productive work that the people we look at are systematically involved in: reproductive work in the domestic sector (e.g. cleaning of blocks of flats) and highly productive involvement in one of the most lucrative industries, that of waste management.

The dimension that most rudely seems to escape the discourses analysed is the fact that "recyclable materials that may initially be sold informally to intermediaries [...] are transformed into inputs for formal production as they are sold upwards into highly globalized value chains" (Samson 2015: 816). The case of the South African garbage dump is a very telling one for the complex intermingling of individual informal survival strategies that articulate into semi-formal sectors of activity (recycling) that are then open to the neoliberal state to attempt to privatize (Samson 2015). The waste dump in this case study started off by being very similar to the ways in which the waste and the waste dumps in our fieldwork were viewed: as a redundant place in relation to the productive system, in which informal activities were tolerated. However, as the centrality of the waste management industry increased, the privatization of the waste dump was sought, excluding in this way the people who had before earned their livelihoods doing the work of transforming waste into new resources. Transforming the waste dump into a "resource mine" was done by individuals who had and cultivated the skills of knowing not only what to pick up, in which way, but also where to sell it further to higher value chains or how to integrate the goods into their circuits of reproduction (Samson 2015; de Angelis 2007). The entire legal action that was taken in order to prevent the dump to become privatized was centred on the claims of the "scavengers" to their autonomy and skill, of their quality as knowing and skilled subjects. In the case of the collection of plastic bottles and iron, the same type of skills is involved.

The case of Pata Rât in Cluj-Napoca speaks of a similar trajectory, albeit with a different ending. There were several stages in the evolution of the garbage dump. In the first one, between 1989 and 2000, it was a rather small-sized and less industrious area. However, the changes in the city production and consumption practices around year 2000 seriously impacted both the volume and the content of the garbage taken to Pata Rât and the type of resources and raw materials it could be further transformed into by selective picking. Slowly plastic and copper, aluminium and iron became the main materials sought. In this second period, the legal status of the dump was many times unclear, as it had been recurrently closed due to lack of conformity with the legal norms and later on reopened after the private firm that administered it had paid the fines. The workers themselves were legally tolerated, as they were free to pick as much materials as they could and further sell them to intermediaries.

In 2015, the dump was officially closed and two new ones, a private and a public one, were opened nearby. Also, a special place was put together through European Structural Funds financing for handling the first stage of the recycling process, employing around ten people. The legal status of the workers has changed; as they are now legally employed, they pay profit taxes but not social contributions and their capacity to further sell the product of their labour is limited, as at the end of the day they need to declare everything they have gathered. Many of the families who had worked there before 2015 moved away, but the majority of them remained and continued to work there, together with their families, living in the informal settlements from the highly polluted Pata Rât area, without any urban infrastructure.

In none of the stages that the garbage dump went through did the experience or the existence of the people making it a productive site mattered.

This type of epistemic injustice (Fricker 2007) is not only clear in the discourses of the representatives of the institutions concerned with "productivity" and "development", but internalized and further reproduced by the people themselves. A crucial operation leading towards this outcome is the misrecognition of the productive activities that the inhabitants of these segregated communities are involved in. Similar to what Samson (2015) shows for the case of a South African garbage dump, the activities that make possible the sustaining of livelihoods of the impoverished Roma are based not only on effort and discipline but also on a wide variety of skills and abilities. Not recognizing their activities as work is a crucial aspect that further makes possible the appropriation of the added value produced in the process by the globalized and highly profitable value chains of waste management. I argue that the importance of the fact that the underprivileged, mostly ethnic Roma persons, living in the segregated and marginalized areas fall outside of the "normal world" should not be underestimated or regarded as a mere symbolic aspect.

What makes individuals worthy of entering the area of concern of these institutions is their having the potential of being a productive worker. I have attempted to show how, through an act of epistemic injustice (Fricker 2007) none of the activities and ways of making a livelihood, available for the poor living in the segregated areas, are understood as belonging to the latter category. In most of the cases, working for the cleaning companies is conceptualized closer to being welfare beneficiaries than full-fledged workers. Collecting plastic or scrap metal is thought of as petty illegalities at hand rather than hard, skilled, precarious and exhausting work. Further, making a living by these means is naturalized as a cultural or ethnic preference of the Roma. The contradictions that arise from the examples of people of Roma ethnicity who earn their living in ways that are closer to the mainstream (formal employment in other areas than city cleaning) are alleviated through the distinction between "the good" and "the bad" Roma. They are further used as arguments to show that it is indeed a matter of personal discipline and will rather than institutionalized racism that traps certain people and communities in situations of deprivation, exclusion and poverty.

Concluding Remarks

I have described the ways in which policy actors' imaginaries are centred on the neoliberal ideals of a flexible economy and subsequent outsourcing of risks and responsibility at the individual level. Foreign investors, who are seen as the rational actors seeking to increase their profits through the fair and objective mechanisms of the market, are viewed as the solution for development and for ensuring large-scale yet flexible productive activities that would allow the worthy subjects to be employed and therefore make a living. This imagery draws much of its force from the fact that it is juxtaposed to the former communist orders and economy, which is most times viewed as being inefficient and unsustainable in the long run, bringing along much more sources of dissatisfaction than advantages. At the individual level, the fact that employment was available to everyone presumably encouraged a lack of personal involvement, and lack of responsibility on the employees' part, which ended up expecting everything from the state.

The starting point of my argument was the vision guiding the development of the city and the labour market as they become visible in the discourses of CCI and AJOFM, two of the important institutions producing city-level policy. The positive visions of city growth, development and integration that these institutions operate with only occasionally and marginally discuss poverty itself and are not explicitly formulated in ethnic or racial terms. Yet they have an immense impact on the spaces of possibilities opened and closed for the disadvantaged through the fact that they are the very setting of the limits between desirability and non-desirability, normality and abnormality, worthiness and unworthiness.

Notes

1. An earlier version of this chapter was previously published as Simionca (2013).
2. For example, CCI in Cluj offers the following description of its mission as a legal entity that is an organization of public interest and utility, non-governmental, autonomous: "CCI represents a force that: proposes (CCI CLUJ is a laboratory of ideas for local development, taking part, for example, in the formulation of the annual and long-term development programmes), represents (because it defends and supports the interests of the business community, making available practical and informational tools for enterprises), formation (through the courses it organizes, where it attracts specialists from the academia as collaborators) and implementation (through its examples of clear, successful initiatives, through its presence at the local, regional, national and international level, through its economic missions abroad, the participation of the CCI Cluj representatives in Local Administration structures, representatives of the business environment in the administrative boards of hospitals)." Source: http://www.ccicj.ro/ (accessed: November 2013). Author's translation.

3. I have offered elsewhere (Simionca 2013) a more detailed analysis of the discourses provided by these state officials, highlighting how the past of the city and the desirable direction for the future are represented, which are the more concrete ways in which achieving this direction is sought for and who are the actors and which are the features of the actors that appear as important in making this vision feasible.

References

Ban, Cornel. 2014. *Dependență Și Dezvoltare. Economia Politică a Capitalismului Românesc*. Cluj-Napoca: Editura Tact.

Binkley, Sam. 2009. The Work of Neoliberal Governmentality: Temporality and Ethical Substance in the Tale of Two Dads. *Foucault Studies* 60. https://doi.org/10.22439/fs.v0i0.2472.

Boltanski, Luc, and Eve Chiapello. 2005. *The New Spirit of Capitalism*. London/New York: Verso.

de Angelis, Massimo. 2007. *The Beginning of History. Global Capital and Value Struggles*. London: Pluto Press.

Fricker, Miranda. 2007. *Epistemic Injustice: Power and the Ethics of Knowing*. Oxford: Oxford University Press.

Petrovici, Norbert. 2013. Neoliberal Proletarization along the Urban-Rural Divide in Postsocialist Romania. *Studia Universitatis Babes-Bolyai Sociologia* 58 (2): 23–54.

Samson, M. 2015. Accumulation by Dispossession and the Informal Economy – Struggles Over Knowledge, Being and Waste at a Soweto Garbage Dump. *Environment and Planning D: Society and Space* 33 (5): 813–830. London: Sage.

Sennett, Richard. 1999. *The Corrosion of Character: The Personal Consequences of Work in the New Capitalism*. New York/London: W.W. Norton.

Simionca, A. 2013. Development, Underdevelopment and Impoverished Roma Communities. A Case Study of High-Level Visions and Agendas of Economic Progress in Urban Romania. *Studia Universitatis Babes-Bolyai Sociologia* 58 (2): 55–75.

Ten Bos, René, and Carl Rhodes. 2003. The Game of Exemplarity: Subjectivity, Work and the Impossible Politics of Purity. *Scandinavian Journal of Management* 19 (4): 403–423.

Vincze, Eniko. 2013. Socio-Spatial Marginality and the Roma as a Form of Intersectional Injustice. *Studia Universitatis Babes-Bolyai Sociologia* 58: 217–242.

6

Segregated Housing Areas and the Discursive Construction of Segregation in the News

Hanna Orsolya Vincze

Introduction

The attention of the news media is rarely captivated by issues of poverty or segregation. In a rare reflection on the nature of the gaze turned towards, or rather turned away from, marginalized people, a Romanian journalist explains:

> We turn our attention away from them if they come our way on the street. We try not to breathe around them, as if their mere presence might contaminate us. We try hard not to become aware of the fact that they exist, too, in this world, in this city, and in our way.[1]

Dedicated to the work of a Dutch charity helping the homeless of Târgu-Mureș, and published during Christmas, the piece sets an emotional tone otherwise uncharacteristic of news reports. The article is also a

---

H. O. Vincze (✉)
Department of Communication, Public Relations and Advertising,
Babeș-Bolyai University, Cluj-Napoca, Romania

© The Author(s) 2019
E. Vincze et al. (eds.), *Racialized Labour in Romania*, Neighborhoods, Communities, and Urban Marginality, https://doi.org/10.1007/978-3-319-76273-9_6

clear example of what literature calls charitable framing, a device typically used during holidays and after disasters. Such articles focus on helping those in need, but also assign such actions to special occasions rather than presenting them as a continued, sustained effort (Kendall 2011, 18). Thus, the very fact that such pieces are published at special times makes the coverage of poverty out of the ordinary and distances the problem from everyday experience and preoccupations.

The rare pieces that report on the life of people living on the physical and symbolic fringes of society also tend to highlight the physical and symbolic distance between the world of the journalist and that of those covered. Thus, Pata Rât, a segregated housing area of Cluj, becomes part of a different world:

> To reach them, you cross over the city's boundaries, into a sort of parallel universe, inappropriately called "district". It is a miserable area, with a terrible stink, with children and people here and there whose features one cannot distinguish because of the dirt.[2]

This chapter analyses the discursive construction of segregation in the news in segregated housing areas of five Romanian cities: Călărași, Cluj-Napoca, Miercurea-Ciuc, Ploiești, and Târgu-Mureș. Previous analyses of public discourse undertaken within our research project focused on media and policy discourse on the Roma. Enikő Vincze addressed in several papers the processes of subjectification that construct a Roma ethnicity resulting in a disempowered Roma political subject (Vincze 2014). In what follows, we shall be looking at the media coverage of these segregated areas, in order to describe how the news media articulates the issue of segregation, how it covers those inhabiting these spaces, and in doing so what its role is in their construction as distant and unproductive, segregated from the city not only spatially, but also ontologically.

The analysis is guided by two central questions. First, it aims to identify the main themes raised when covering these locations and their inhabitants, the contexts in which they appear in the news, and the way their newsworthiness is constructed. Second, it aims to describe the effort referred to in the introductory quotation as trying hard "not to become aware of the fact that they exist," to identify the discursive features of news coverage that contribute to the further symbolic marginalization of these areas, to creating a sense of them being out of the ordinary, distant, and detached from everyday experience and endeavours. In particular, we shall investigate how the everyday endeavours of these people, the ways they make ends meet by undertaking various forms of informal labour, are made either invisible or out of the ordinary.

News coverage can only be generated by issues that are perceived as newsworthy in the newsroom, that is, which are connected to the interests, fears, or aspirations of a readership that in our case is not coextensive, indeed in most cases does not even intersect with the social groups covered. This also means that analysing the thematic structure and discursive features of the coverage of segregated housing areas also offers an insight into wider public debates, the role of marginalized spaces and people in these, and the more general nature of public discourse in contemporary Romania.

Covering the Marginalized: The Possibilities and Constraints of News Discourse

Analyses of media content, verbal and visual, cannot in themselves fully explain how media discourse affects policies, campaigns, or even commissioned research. However, they can help us understand the main concerns involving the groups represented; the logic of their representation itself; the social, cultural, and historical complexities involved; and the agendas promoted. These representations are forms of public knowledge that also determine the issues that are kept on or off the public's and policymaker's agendas, and thus are forms of hegemony.

Literature on news media portrayals of deprivation, poverty, or marginalization generally agrees that such studies are scarce, especially in Europe (Larsen and Dejgaard 2013). A more prominent research tradition exists in the United States, focusing predominantly on the negative portrayal of African American welfare recipients, as well as classist stereotypes (Kendall 2011; Bullock et al. 2001; Iyengar 1990). A recurrent finding of such studies is that

> the poor are either rendered invisible or portrayed in terms of characterological deficiencies and moral failings (e.g. substance abuse, crime, sexual availability, violence). Either way, the poor are defined as "outsiders" who deviate from middle-class values and norms. (Bullock et al. 2001, 231)

Less obviously stigmatizing practices also act towards distancing the already marginalized. News reports of segregated areas have been shown, for example, to imagine and represent the journalist and the audience as situated outside of the world depicted, with "the media providing a window into this place from which the audience themselves are socially distant" (Devereux et al. 2011, 510). The articles we have quoted in our opening paragraphs have also set the scene of their reports as distant, by describing, for example, the long and even perilous trip one needed to take to reach the deprived areas.

One of the trajectories through which deprivation may become visible in the news is through coverage generated by actions of various authorities, accompanied by their specific news management techniques. The language used in the news coverage of various social inclusion measures or programmes in such cases intersects with policy discourse on poverty, which, in turn, has also been shown to focus on deviance rather than the processes and relations that lead to deprivation. The poverty analysis offered especially by economic development reports, with their newsworthy scales and quantitative indices, portray poverty abstracted from the people living in poverty, and push to the background the processes these people are subjected to. At the same time, such reports, and the media relying on them, rarely focus on wealth:

> This is not because wealth and poverty are unconnected, far from it, but because such approaches are essentially concerned with a normalising vision of society that is premised on the elimination of what is socially accorded the status of deviant or pathological. (Green 2006, 1112–1113)

In terms of news reporting, this results in the naturalization of such relations, with journalism rarely discussing social relations or capitalism, for example (Richardson 2007, 116).

Thus, critically oriented social sciences have long found the news wanting in terms of covering social processes. Apart from the above reasons related to the position of journalists and the types of sources journalists tend to cover, a more structural reason has to do with the very definition of news. In his frequently cited study on the assignment of responsibility for poverty, Shanto Iyengar pointed out that television news, for example, was "an inherently 'episodic' or event-oriented medium" (Iyengar 1990, 21). This means that news as a format favours individual actors and distinct actions rather than the coverage of underlying social, economic, or historical processes. The textbook definition of news grammar as "who, what, when, where, why, and how" clearly requires journalists to feature individual actors. As Herbert J. Gans summarized this position, "journalists often say that the news ought to be about individuals rather than groups or social processes; and by and large, they achieve their aim" (Gans 1979, 8). Moreover, Gans pointed out, journalism prefers the "Knowns" to the "Unknowns," and in general those who are in official roles. This implies that actors with various official roles, from local officials to NGO actors or experts, will figure more prominently, for example in titles, leads, photographs, and captions than the people they might be trying to help, for example, in anti-poverty or social inclusion campaigns. This discursive feature of the news can be expected to have implications on the assignment of agency in the coverage of deprivation, in the sense of assigning agency to the actors possessing names and voices rather than the "Unknowns."

The prominence of individual actors in the news also explains the prominence of a particular type of news story in covering deprivation, the story of the individual struggling against hardship and adversity (Gans 1979, 50). When appealing to the audience's sympathy and empathy, that is, appealing to strong emotions, these pieces also belong to the larger category of human interest stories (Semetko and Valkenburg 2000, 96). When covering deprivation, it is in these stories that individuals belonging to the deprived categories are more likely to appear possessing names, faces, and voices, and children are also likely to figure prominently. However, the human interest story has also been shown to possess an inherent capacity of "symbolic marginalization," if the vivid depictions and individual stories are coupled with a denial of agency, presenting stories of individuals who are helpless, or rely on the help—and even the voice—of benefactors to act and speak for them (Kleut and Milinkov 2013, 82). Of similar importance is the general lack of the voice of the poor, with their experience being framed by official or expert voices, a tendency especially true of female subjects. Although human interest stories do cite such voices, these tend to serve to strengthen the emotional appeal of the story, but they do not shape the general perspective of the report (Bullock et al. 2001, 242).

One of the central issues in the study of representation of poverty in the news is the assignment of responsibility, both in terms of causes, and in terms of control or solutions. The way the question of causal responsibility emerges in the news is important, because it is connected to the envisioned solutions. In their analysis of public discourse on the global economic crisis, for example, Norman and Isabela Fairclough have identified two ways of defining economic problems. In the first case, the problem is systemic and requires, in its turn, systemic solutions. In the second case, the problem is particular; for example, it is blamed on intellectual or moral failures of particular individuals. In such cases, the solutions asked for are also local or particular: correcting the specific failure, like ensuring people do their jobs properly, would allow the system to function as it was meant to or "to get back to normal" (Fairclough and Fairclough 2012, 9). The way responsibility is assigned is also crucial in debates on social problems, as such debates tend to involve competing interests, and the way responsibility is framed determines the directions efforts towards change will take or the interests that will prevail (Kim et al. 2010, 563–565).

The assignment of responsibility has also been connected to the episodic or thematic framing of the news. In his above-cited study, Shanto Iyengar found that when poverty was covered thematically, that is, in pieces that discussed it as a general phenomenon, using abstract and impersonal information that provided the issues with wider, government, or society-level context, people tended to assign responsibility to the government. By contrast, when coverage was episodic, focusing on concrete events and individuals, people tended to hold the individuals responsible (Iyengar 1990). However, in a later study analysing Dutch news media, Semetko and Valkenburg found that episodic news could also cast the government as responsible for social issues, suggesting that Iyengar's results might be culture-bound (Semetko and Valkenburg 2000, 106). Thus, the issue of the assignment of responsibility will need to be addressed anew when analysing local news media representations in an Eastern European context.

A central element of the way the problem is defined is the way in which those marginalized are represented. There is a well-documented tendency both in mass-media and in social research to represent people living in poverty as "Others," distanced from the majority (Krumer-Nevo and Benjamin 2010). Elements of such "othering" might include cultural or behavioural references like talking about "a culture of poverty" or moral references to the "deserving" and "undeserving" poor, highlighting deviant behaviour like crime, promiscuity, or violence (Bullock et al. 2001, 231–232). In the case of Romanian discourse, Enikő Vincze has pointed to the way the public discourse on poverty intersects with those on Roma, thus racializing and even dehumanizing those affected by forced relocations as excluded from "the civilized people" (Vincze 2014, 233).

A prominent discursive mechanism of segregation pertains to articulation. Referential or nomination strategies employed by the media, that is, the names attached to groups of people and labels attached to their actions, can serve as forms of othering via discrimination, as in using derogatory terms for people (Reisigl and Wodak 2001, 45). Apart from othering, however, such use of language can also contribute to dispossession, and such dispossession is both material and epistemological. In several analyses of South African reclaimers, for example, Melanie Samson has shown how the referring to people working on garbage dumps as "scavengers" made their role in the recycling business invisible, and indeed made it impossible to articulate their experience as "work," hence denying them a role in policy discussions on the way the landfills should be exploited (Samson 2009, 2015).

Apart from the above features of the news media in general, pertaining to the languages available and the structural features of news discourse, in recent decades, several developments in the media industry also have shaped the reporting on social processes. In the context of the advent of online news sources and the global economic crisis, which both undermined the business model of the news industry, the decreasing possibilities of journalism to perform its watchdog function have been noted both in the United States (Gans 2010) and by the BBC's own inquiry into the future of news. In this news context, the latter notes, "vast swathes of modern life are increasingly unreported or under-reported," especially combined with the contraction of local media (*Future of News* 2015, 6).

The commercial pressures that brought about the tabloidization of the news, in the West as in Romania, also favour an emotional framework, which will have consequences on our topic as well. In media studies, the role of emotion is the subject of an ongoing debate on the nature of the public sphere. On the one hand, the appeal to strong emotions, and the related focus on the individual, has been described as journalism renouncing its social responsibility (Allan 2010, 256). In this sense, charity-framing and "neediest-case" pieces fail to draw attention to the larger processes behind the specific stories (Kendall 2011, 111). On the other hand, defenders of the role emotions play in public life argue that the appeal to emotions offers new ways of engagement, and that the description of such stories as "soft" or "tabloid" is a demarcation functioning to deny these possibilities (Richards 2012, 303–304).

In Romania, several peculiarities of the country's media industry increase the difficulties inherent in the current nature of the media when covering poverty. Covering social processes beyond the episodic news, looking for relationships between the social, economic, and political domains would call for investigative journalism. However, in Central and Eastern Europe in general, investigative journalism has been weak even prior to the disruption caused by the Internet and the economic crisis. This holds both in terms of the resources available and in terms of the impact of investigative journalist's work (Stetka and Örnebring 2013). Beyond issues of audiences and revenue, the problem also has to do with the fact that the post-communist media industry emerged hand in hand, and variously interlocked, with the new political and economic system and its actors (Preoteasa and Schwartz 2015). With political and business elites instrumentalizing the media, journalistic autonomy tends to be limited, and issues deemed risky or problematic can be kept off the agenda. This appears to be especially the case with local media (Örnebring 2013, 8).

The News Corpus: Sources and Thematic Structure

In what follows, we shall look at the thematic and discursive features of the Romanian media coverage of segregated housing areas, looking at how contemporary Romanian news media contributes to casting the poor as marginalized and unproductive and to creating the symbolic distance reflected upon by the local journalistic voices cited in the introduction.

In order to compile a corpus of news covering deprived housing areas, we searched online news archives for the names of locations that constituted the sites of our fieldwork, which covered five cities: Călărași, Cluj-Napoca, Miercurea-Ciuc, Ploiești, and Târgu-Mureș.[3] The timeframe of the inquiry was 2011–2013, resulting in a material covering three years. A three-year period, with a starting date coinciding with the start of the project, is long enough to avoid the possibility that a single news wave should dominate a specific location, that is, the possibility that coverage of a location be dominated in a shorter period of time by news of a single event or a series of similar events (Vasterman 2005).

For all locations, online archives of both national and local news sources were searched. The national sources were *Adevărul,* one of the largest Romanian generalist papers, which also provides local news from all regions of the country, and the Hotnews.ro news portal. For retrieving news from local media, we used ziare.com, a news aggregator that covers local news outlets from all our locations. In a first step, all articles using the location designators searched for were retrieved, resulting in 552 articles. In a second step, articles that did not make reference to the inhabitants of these locations were deleted from the sample, to allow the analysis to focus on how deprivation affects people. This resulted in a smaller sample size of 325 articles. This methodological constraint means that we shall not be addressing articles that covered, for example, development efforts or investments into infrastructure if these were discussed without reference to the people of the deprived areas.

Investments into infrastructure, like waste management systems, however, do have an impact on people making a living by reclaiming recyclable materials. The large number of articles on such topics that were disregarded for not making reference to the residents (41 per cent of the total articles mentioning the locations) points to a first characteristic of the media coverage of segregated residential areas: the tendency to discuss problems of infrastructure or development without making reference to the people living in the areas that are undergoing the interventions. This tendency is a more general feature of local development discourse, shared by policymakers as well. For example, when analysing interviews with representatives of the County Commerce and Industry Chambers active in our cities, Anca Simionca has shown how the segregated communities and their living conditions were absent from their preoccupations. One interviewee cited defined poverty as the preoccupation of social services, excluding this sphere of life from the "business" of development. Thus, the segregated communities of people living in these areas "are from the onset and by definition belonging to a different reality and are, therefore, not even considered" (Simionca 2013, 67). Similarly, in our inductively developed coding scheme for the themes of the articles that were included in the analysis, that is, the ones that made reference to the people of these areas, the economy did not emerge as a value (see the coding scheme below). Thus, a first feature of media coverage is that it reinforces public policies that disregard a category of the poor, making them invisible by not featuring them at all.

Our sampling pattern resulted in a total number of 30 news outlets, some of which were searched directly, and some of which were found by using a news aggregator, as described above. Although these results are influenced by the aggregation algorithm of the site used, as well as the uneven number of specific locations searched for in each city, the resulting outlet and article numbers are quite close to each other for the three mid-range cities of Călărași (55 articles from 8 outlets), Ploiești (47 articles from 9 outlets), and Târgu Mureș (65 articles from 7 outlets), while the articles from Cluj-Napoca are more numerous (135 articles from 13 outlets), and those from Miercurea Ciuc are much less so (23 articles from 3 outlets). These differences in numbers correspond to differences in the size of the cities, with Cluj-Napoca being the largest and Miercurea Ciuc the smallest of them in terms of population (for further data on the size and other relevant characteristics of the cities, see Vincze and Rat 2013). From all our locations, the Pata Rât area from Cluj-Napoca proved the most visible: as the single Cluj-Napoca location searched for, it alone generated a higher number of articles than the several locations searched for in the other cities. The Pata Rât area also received international coverage, with the local media reflecting on articles on the BBC, in *The Sun*, and in *The Independent* reporting on living conditions in the area.

In order to structure this data, we started from a content analytical approach and combined it in a second step with a closer textual reading of characteristic passages. The content analytical level of analysis also provides an operationalization for our first general research question concerning the predominant themes of news of deprivation. Codes for the themes of articles were developed inductively, based on the preliminary reading of a subsample. The major themes of articles on deprived areas thus identified were: eviction, life, crime, social, and other. Our analysis will proceed along three of these thematic dimensions:

- THEME: *eviction* refers to all stories of evictions, various protests against these, actions meant to sensitize public opinion concerning the living conditions of those evicted, etc.
- THEME: *life* designates articles focusing on living conditions in the deprived areas, including problems of pollution or infrastructure and services, human interest stories, stories of accidents, and in general of the dangerous nature of the environment.
- THEME: *social* designates news of social interventions, including news of charitable giving, aid received, social housing, and other benefits and various social inclusion programmes.

Our second research question refers to the discursive construction of segregation in the news, to the way news discourse articulates the issue, and the specific window it provides on reality. In news media analysis, this "specific window" is referred to as a "frame." A news frame can be defined as "a cognitive 'window' through which a news story is 'seen'" (Pan and Kosicki 1993, 59). One of the most frequently cited definitions of news frames is that of Entman:

> To frame is to select some aspects of a perceived reality and make them more salient in a communicating context, in such a way as to promote a particular problem definition, causal interpretation, moral evaluation and/or treatment recommendation for the item described. (Entman 1993, 52)

For the purposes of operationalizing the window the Romanian news media provides on these segregated areas, we have coded elements of the problem, defined them as themes, actors, voices, and the presence of ethnical indexing, and coded the presence and type of responsibility—whether it emerges primarily in terms of causes or solutions—and the presence and nature of evaluative language, whether neutral or balanced, negative, or positive. However, such elements of an interpretive frame could only be coded for longer pieces that engaged in contextualizing events or providing explanations for them. Thus, we divided the articles into a thematic and an episodic corpus. Pieces that focused on events of a specific day, without offering contextual explanations were coded as episodic, whereas issue-oriented pieces that provided context, referred to multiple points in time, and offered interpretations were coded as thematic (Semetko and Valkenburg 2000, 100–101). Pieces that occurred in our sample because of the presence of a location designator we searched for, but where the reference was only marginal, were also coded as episodic.

The above variables and their values used are summarized in Table 6.1:

The stories were relatively evenly distributed between the domains of eviction (26 per cent), life (25 per cent), crime (24 per cent), social (20 per cent), other (5 per cent). Concerning their syntax, news of segregated housing areas tended to be episodic (71 per cent) rather than thematic (29 per cent). These ratios are in fact very close to what Iyengar found in the US poverty stories: in 1986, studying television news, he found that 72 per cent were episodic and 28 per cent were thematic. However, the nature of the coverage varied by cities: thematic pieces weighed much less in the news from Călărași (16 per cent) and Ploiești (11 per cent) than in news from Miercurea Ciuc (52 per cent), Tg. Mures (35 per cent), and Cluj (33 per cent). One of the reasons is the relatively high ratio of news of crime in the former cities, as news of crime tended to be more episodic in general (75 per cent). Stories of evictions received the largest thematic coverage: 40 per cent of the eviction stories were thematic, as compared to the "life" (29 per cent thematic coverage) or "social" (32 per cent thematic coverage) domains.

Actors, voices, evaluations, responsibilities, and ethnical indexing were coded for the thematic corpus. In what follows, we shall look in detail at the structural and discursive features of the thematic news of deprived areas.

Table 6.1 Coding scheme

LOCATION: Călărași	ACTOR: resident
LOCATION: Cluj-Napoca	
LOCATION: Miercurea Ciuc	VOICE: company representative
LOCATION: Ploiești	VOICE: ecclesiastic
LOCATION: Târgu Mureș	VOICE: expert
	VOICE: foreign observers
SYNTAX: episodic	VOICE: health/social worker
SYNTAX: thematic	VOICE: local official
	VOICE: NGO
THEME: crime	VOICE: other locals
THEME: life	VOICE: police/law enforcement
THEME: social intervention	VOICE: politician
THEME: eviction	VOICE: resident
THEME: other	
	EVALUATION: negative
ACTOR: central government	EVALUATION: neutral/balanced
ACTOR: private actor	EVALUATION: positive
ACTOR: public company	
ACTOR: ecclesiastic	RESPONSIBILITY: none
ACTOR: health/social worker	RESPONSIBILITY: causal
ACTOR: international	RESPONSIBILITY: treatment
ACTOR: local government	
ACTOR: NGO	ETHNICAL INDEXING: Roma
ACTOR: police/law enforcement	ETHNICAL INDEXING: none
ACTOR: politician	

News of Evictions

Under THEME: *eviction*, we grouped all stories of evictions, various protests against these, actions meant to sensitize public opinion concerning the living conditions of those evacuated, and so on. In the timeframe of our research, the media reported in one case on an eviction notice served in Călărași (1 article), several evacuations or threats of evacuations in Târgu Mureș (20 articles), and made references to the evacuation to Pata Rât of the residents of the Coastei Street (55 articles). The most salient case is clearly the latter: although the actual evictions in Cluj-Napoca took place before our timeframe, in 2010, 65 per cent of the 83 eviction stories came from Cluj-Napoca. Evictions were also the leading story type for Cluj-Napoca, and the relocations to Pata Rât in general were the largest thematic group of our corpus, making the issue the most salient.

Evictions were clearly framed as an administrative issue. Responsibility, both in terms of causes and treatments, was primarily assigned to the local authorities. Neither politicians nor representatives of the central government made an appearance. The only national agency that appeared as an actor in the news was the National Council for Combating Discriminations, which applied fines for discriminating against the Roma community. The issue was also far from the preoccupations of the national media. The national news agency Agerpres figured only once among the sources, with a story featuring Amnesty International. The news value of the story was constructed in the lead by making reference to the global nature of the organization and its activists. Thus, the rare case when the issue of evictions came to the interest of a national news organization was due to the presence of an international actor.[4]

Among the actors, local officials were the most frequent (21), followed by NGOs (12), residents (9), police/law enforcement, including the judiciary (7), private individuals (4), the anti-discrimination agency (3), and one publicly held company (1). The frequency of voices cited was similar: NGO voices (24) surpassed local officials (15) and were supplemented by voices of residents (9), experts (5), other locals (4), police/law enforcement (2), ecclesiastic (2), and one social worker (1).

Descriptions of the Cluj-Napoca evictions were disputed: official voices preferred to designate their actions as "moving" or "relocating" rather than "evacuating," as the latter term implies coercive action. In their turn, activists tended to highlight the enforced and inhumane nature of the action that involved the deployment of police forces and took place in full winter.

Apart from the referential strategies involved in the choice of words, news discourse also contributes to backgrounding the coercive nature of evictions by the practice of agent deletion. Agent deletion contributes to casting social practices as acceptable by suppressing some of their less desirable components (van Leeuwen 1996), in our case the use of force against those evacuated. A typical description of the events is the following: "Three years ago, the Roma from Coastei Street were evacuated and moved into housing modules in the Pata Rât area."[5] The passive voice makes it possible to exclude the agents and means of the evacuation, and hence the relatively low number of police or law enforcement actors in the texts proper. The tendency of deleting or pushing to the background law enforcement agents is also characteristic of accompanying images, which hardly ever feature them.

Evictions were also emphatically framed as a Roma issue. With three exceptions, all news of evictions indexed the ethnicity of those affected as Roma. The exceptions included the only eviction news from Călărași, which made reference to "residents," coverage of a Cluj-Napoca petition that framed the issue in terms of human rights, referring to those evacuated as "families," and coverage of a Cluj-Napoca public debate on the issue, which also discussed possibilities of legal action against the measure, referring to those affected as "tenants."

The ethnic indexing characteristic of the news of eviction partly originates from definitions of the situation by the actors themselves. Several NGOs that appear as actors in the news define themselves as representatives of the Roma community (e.g., the Community Association of Roma from Coastei) or as Roma rights organizations (e.g., the European Roma Rights Centre). The fine applied by the anti-discrimination agency to the Cluj-Napoca authorities was also applied for the ethnic discrimination of the Roma from Coastei Street, a decision triggered by a petition started by local NGOs. In Cluj-Napoca, official voices avoid ethnical indexing and prefer to legitimate their actions by reference to the legal status of the residents, or to the precarious or outright dangerous state of their housing. For example, when the National Railway Company filed for freeing up the lots in Cantonului Street, Cluj-Napoca, occupied by the residents and their constructions illegally according to their claim, the news coverage of the petitions started by NGOs to provide appropriate housing to those affected defined them as "the Roma community living in Cantonului Street."[6] One consequence of mixing the two types of descriptions, one referring to the eviction of "the Roma" or "the Roma community" and one referring to illegal or otherwise improper occupants of public spaces is thus the association of the two.

Such indexing serves to activate two characteristic frames that serve as explanations of the events. One is discrimination against an ethnic community, which can lead to calls for integration and fighting racism, the main theme of several Cluj-Napoca protests staged by local NGOs and widely covered by the media. Fighting discrimination is also the topic of a rare editorial on the Pata Rât community not occasioned by the protests. In a section with the subheading "Roma pushed to the margins," the author explicitly argues against racism and discrimination:

> I don't know how we could make citizens understand that there is no alternative to accommodation and understanding between ethnic groups. That you cannot be integrated into a majority that refuses to know you. That you cannot work in a community that refuses to shake your hand.[7]

However, even such well-meaning pieces, again characteristically published a few days before Christmas, point to the unavoidable logic of ethnic indexing. When arguing for the acceptance of the Roma, the author refers to the community of those that need to know and understand "the others" as "the citizens." Clearly this is just a slip on the part of the author who goes on to designate the Roma as parts of a "common Romania" and to the Pata Rât community as part of Cluj-Napoca. Nevertheless, when calling upon "the citizens" to accept the Roma, the logic of exclusion that the author argues against resurfaces and reinscribes itself into the text, as if the Roma were not part of the citizenry.

A second, very different type of explanation, characteristically employed in legitimating evictions, makes reference to the behaviour of the Roma. This frame legitimates evictions by references to various types of conduct deemed socially unacceptable, ranging from accusations of dumping garbage on the streets to "scandalous" behaviour involving shouting at and threatening journalists, as well as children of other residents. These instances of othering serve as racist legitimations for evictions in Târgu Mureș and Miercurea Ciuc and appear in the voice of local authorities or other residents of the cities. Other reports undermine the legitimacy of the protests against evictions by casting those affected as unqualified for the housing they received, which thus becomes a "benefit" defined as a gift rather than a right. A report on the housing situation of those evacuated in Cluj, for example, contrasts the residents' protesting voices with their previously illegal residence status and the fact that they "did not even qualify to receive housing in Pata Rat," which they "sniff at"—a strong predication employed in the title.[8] This strategy is also used to delegitimize NGO voices arguing for better living conditions: a piece on an

Amnesty International petition submitted to the Miercurea Ciuc local authorities is illustrated with an image of the barracks in question running the caption "Barracks in the outskirts of Miercurea Ciuc. Water and electricity freely provided by the mayors' office."[9]

Whether used to legitimate actions of local governments, to construct an "unworthiness" narrative, or, on the contrary, to point to the discriminatory behaviour of the authorities, othering by ethnical indexing represents the issues involved as pertaining to the interests of a specific community, marginal in terms of the general interest, or extreme in terms of behaviour.

As a primarily local issue, evictions were also far from the concerns of national media, the central government or politicians, and remained an administrative responsibility of the local authorities. This responsibility, when cast as causal, was only included in references to evacuations undertaken by the public authorities, resulting in segregation and discrimination or triggering protests, but never as a responsibility for wider, societal, or policy-level causes that led to the events. Similarly, treatment responsibilities were primarily cast in terms of providing appropriate accommodation to those evacuated, that is, to a particular beneficiary group further particularized by indexing their ethnicity.

Evictions have an impact on the livelihood of those evacuated, with changes in access to employment both in terms of the increased distance, as well as in terms of the new, stigmatized address, which marks them as unemployable. These are grievances of those concerned occasionally cited in the Cluj-Napoca news coverage of evacuation. In a rare piece citing such a grievance, the journalist also casually notes the presence of recyclables and immediately recasts them as litter: recyclables collected appear in the report as contributing to making the living conditions more inhumane, littering the floor of the room already crowded by eight tenants.[10] This referential strategy, which we shall see again, serves as one of the main discursive features denying the status of work to the endeavours of those segregated, and even framing them as inappropriate, worsening their own living conditions. The reference is also occasional: even though the media reports on the concern NGO actors have with evictions making access to work more difficult, there is no systematic interest on the impact of those evacuated on their actual working lives, as we shall also see in the case of reports of everyday life.

Living in the Ghetto

Our second thematic group includes articles on the living conditions in the segregated areas, including human interest stories, pieces on infrastructure or services, accidents, and pollution. The various topics grouped under this theme do not include labour: with our inductive method, the issue of work did not emerge as a topic.

These pieces had the same frequency as those on evictions (83). They came in comparable numbers from Călărași (24), Cluj (22), Ploiești (16), and Târgu-Mureș (17), with a lower frequency in Miercurea Ciuc (4). Thematic pieces, providing more context and in-depth coverage weighed somewhat less (24) than in the case of evictions (33).

The sphere of "life" was much less characterized by strong actors than those of evictions. Local governments, NGOs, residents, police, and public companies figured as actors in similar numbers. It was in this sphere that residents appeared as possessing a strong voice, with 40.4 per cent of the total number of voices coded as belonging to residents, followed by local officials (23.4 per cent). Foreign observers also had a noticeable voice, their weight being similar to that of the police among the voices.

Among stories on living conditions, the news of infrastructure/services and accidents were the more numerous (totalling 24 and 39). However, these were also mostly episodic pieces offering the basic details of events, with only three stories of accidents and seven stories of infrastructure/services offering thematic coverage. News of pollution were even less numerous, with one thematic and three episodic pieces. The tendency for episodic coverage changed only for human interest stories, where most of the coverage was thematic (13 articles of the 16). Thus, human interest stories also made up the largest group of articles on life in the ghetto that offered in-depth coverage.

The importance of this group lies in the fact that these are the materials for which the journalist needed to get close to the world of those living on the spatial and symbolic margins of society. This is because stories coded as focusing on the theme of everyday life were based on fieldwork, as opposed to the other categories, where the predominant sources for themes were either the authorities or the news management practices of various NGOs and local authorities.

Stories of everyday life tended to depict emotions or appeal to emotions. Strong, emotional language is one of the means of creating newsworthiness. In a discursive approach to news values, these are neither properties of the events, nor journalists' selection criteria, but are values created by the news text and attributed to the events depicted. References to emotions can serve to create the news values of negativity, personalization, and superlativeness (Bednarek and Caple 2012, 106).

The value of emotions is particularly clear for creating the newsworthiness of stories on everyday life in the segregated areas. In our corpus, emotions depicted were mostly negative: fear, sense of danger, feelings of helplessness, anger. A story on flooded homes evokes fear: "winter is coming, who knows what might happen?"[11] The environment of the Ploiești ghetto is "depressing," and inhabitants of the Mimiu area in Ploiești are "badly angry" with the mayor. The main positive emotion depicted was hope, which appeared in connection with children who "dream of becoming painters or football players."[12]

Appeals or references to emotion not only serve the function of creating the news values of negativity or personalization, as in the above examples, but also to engage the reader or at least decrease the symbolic distance between the world depicted and that of the audience, as they create an emotional connection between the reader and the people or stories depicted. This is especially the case of stories depicting positive emotions, like hope, particularly if accompanied by images of children and children's drawings. That such stories are meant to decrease rather than increase the distance between the reader and the segregated world is also reflected by the lower weight of ethnical indexing: of the 24 thematic stories, only 10 indexed the residents as Roma.

However, vivid descriptions of extreme poverty can also have the effect of constructing poverty as distant from everyday experience. As a study of representations in the news of poverty in Serbia argued, such approaches contribute to the construction of poverty as extreme and out of the ordinary, and discursively place poverty at the very margin of society (Kleut and Milinkov 2013, 82). The distance from everyday experience is emphasized in our case by the title of a piece on the Ploiești ghetto, referred to as a place where one dies for a piece of bread, and described further on as "a land of poverty where life and death have different rules."[13] The area behind the Ploiești train station, the article reports, "looks like a set from a war movie. Deep trenches run for hundreds of meters, like arteries dug in the flesh of the earth, following a capricious trajectory, and appear senseless at first sight."[14] The movie metaphor again points to the ghetto as an "other" place, different from everyday reality.

Temporal metaphors can also have a similar distancing effect. The title of a piece on the conditions of the streets in a segregated area of Târgu Mureș, giving voice to the strong feelings of the locals about the lack of action on the part of the authorities, emphasizes their point by metaphorically placing them in the distant past: "They live as in the Middle Ages."[15] Journalists writing on segregated housing areas, or the voices they cite, rarely offer actual historical perspectives on the formation of the ghettoes. One of the exceptional pieces in this respect, a piece on the Mimiu area of Ploiești, told the story of the area to make the point that here, "people live in the same conditions as a hundred years ago."[16] Again, the historical perspective serves to describe the area in question as part of another temporal reality: "Mimiu district, from the southern area of Ploiești, has remained throughout the passage of the years, as isolated and pained as in the descriptions of people from the interwar period."[17]

Living conditions in the Pata Rât ghetto from Cluj-Napoca were reported upon several times by British media, and these reports were also covered by the Romanian media, traditionally sensitive to the image of the country abroad. *The Sun*'s report creates an extreme form of otherness by situating those reported on in a far away, "freezing" country and referring to them as "nomads," a term involving an inherent difference in the way of life of the Roma:

> Nomads in Romania and Bulgaria want to head to our shores en masse as soon as the restrictions blocking their migration are lifted. More than a million have already set up camp in wealthy countries in Western Europe, including Britain and Ireland. But even more are expected to flood in when borders open in January next year. The Scottish Sun travelled to freezing Transylvania in the heart of Romania to see first-hand how gypsies are being forced out by authorities who view them as thieves and beggars.[18]

The Independent also ran a piece on segregated areas in Cluj-Napoca and București, cast as part of an effort to diffuse stereotypes perpetuated by the tabloid press, and, rather, to present the origins of the problem in the discrimination the Roma endured:

> The small but steady increase of Roma arrivals in Western Europe has already led to a plethora of scare stories from populist media which portray them as endemically criminal communities thriving on begging networks and illegal settlements.[19]

The piece includes a metaphoric transfer of the meanings of the location of the Cluj-Napoca ghetto, the local garbage dump, and the people inhabiting it, formulated in the voice of an interviewee:

> Back in the rubbish-dump of Pata Rat, Romeo Greta Petra says he has plans to leave the squalor and discrimination behind him. Standing next to a single bathroom which serves 40 people, he declares that his family has simply had enough. "Just look at the filth in which they threw us," he says, sucking deeply on a rolled-up cigarette. "Come summer, we're going to leave. Everyone here just thinks we're garbage. If I could have the possibility, I would go with my whole family."

In the case of these British reports, the newsworthiness of the story is constructed by making reference to the wider issue of migration. *The Sun*'s piece led with the statement "Huge numbers of Roma gypsies are planning to move to Britain after being forced out of their home countries," a claim disputed by *The Independent*'s report entitled "The Truth about Romania's gypsies: Not coming over here, not stealing our jobs." Fear and animosity also figure prominently among the explanations of the latter report:

> Suspicions have been raised in Bucharest and Sofia that what the UK Government really fears "but dares not say publicly" is the mass migration of Roma, Europe's most marginalised and maligned minority. That, in turn, has created further animosity towards the Roma, with other Romanians and Bulgarians blaming those communities for tarnishing their country's image.[20]

We have seen above how the literature of news of poverty asked the question of responsibility in terms of the agent responsible, whether individuals or the government. The stories in our corpus assign little if any agency to the residents of the segregated areas. The most frequently coded actor was local government. Thus, it is recurrently the authorities who are depicted as responsible for the living conditions in segregated areas. A recurrent sub-theme in stories of life in the ghetto is administrative failure or abuse, either cast, as in the above quotation, as the causal responsibility of the authorities, or as a failure to live up to their responsibility in finding solutions for improving living conditions. When referring to solutions, however, articles, as well as the actions covered in them, refer to the particulars of the problem rather than to systemic, society, or policy-level interventions. For example, a piece on a Târgu Mureş family living in council housing, with water infiltrating the apartment walls, contains reproductions of official documents detailing the causes of the failure in the construction and specifies the person responsible who could direct the maintenance company to intervene, but who fails to do so.[21] When the solutions to problems are sought after from other social actors, be they private individuals exercising charity or NGOs, the problems and the solutions are also particular to the issue at hand. Such is the case of an otherwise uncharacteristically nuanced report on a segregated settlement formed on the Cluj-Napoca garbage dump, which was provided with an IT cluster made up of computers without Internet connection. But thankfully, the piece reports, a local student won a grant to solve the issue of the Internet connection as well.[22] Similarly, the BBC reported on the efforts of a Dutch couple to offer education and lunch to children in Pata Rât, a story again taken over by the local media.[23] In general, even though solutions for improving the particular living arrangements of those living in segregated areas are sought, the phenomenon of residential segregation does not appear as a problem in itself that ought to be tackled or the systemic sources of which ought to be investigated.

Stories on life in the segregated areas often cast these locations as dangerous, either for the visitor or for the residents themselves. It is in this context of dangers to one's life that the issue of collecting recyclables appears: as a source of danger, sometimes also framed as originating from illegal behaviour on the part of those affected, who are hit by trucks dumping garbage. Officials of the company involved in the accidents describe the activity of those affected as "collecting waste"[24] or "scavenging in the garbage"[25]—"reclaiming" or "recycling" is not part of the referential strategy. They also cast the victims of such accidents as victims of their own behaviour, as, in their view, it should be illegal for them to scavenge on the dump.

The lack of a conceptual differentiation between recycling and scavenging is one of the main reasons for the activities of those marginalized to not be seen as labour. It is also the discursive equivalent of the policy of developing waste management systems without recognizing as stakeholders those who had been undertaking this work informally. The conceptualization of the reclaiming of various recyclables as scavenging also explains the lack of the companies buying the recyclables in the reports. They only make an appearance as partners of the local authorities in waste management, but never in relation with the work of those doing the actual reclaiming.

This lack of differentiation is a form of epistemic injustice that is not particular to the Romanian context. As Melanie Samson has pointed out,

> The labelling of reclaimers as scavengers is widespread around the world. Rather than valuing reclaimers for the intimate knowledge they possess about the actual workings of the waste management system and the crucial role they play in it, referring to reclaimers as scavengers enables municipal governments and private companies to dismiss them as nuisances who need to be eradicated. (Samson 2015, 825)

The strong stigma attached to scavenging is apparent in the furious reaction to a YouTube post by an American preacher, showing people scavenging in a roadside garbage bin as an illustration of local poverty, which was interpreted by the local media as an attempt at "discrediting Romania and Romanian society."[26] A comment by a journalist interviewed for our project also casts the reclaiming practised by the local poor as scavenging, to be renounced if they should become worthy of the help received from the local authorities:

> In Valea Rece you could say that the Târgu Mureș mayor's office really put an effort into developing the area. Blocks of flats were built, and apartments were given to persons of Roma ethnicity, under the condition that they should have a job and send their children to school. It is untenable that I give you an apartment and you go on with your cart, to look in garbage bins.[27]

As we shall see in the next section, this is also one of the points on which local activists have tried to intervene.

News of Social Interventions

We have grouped under THEME: *social* the coverage of various charity or aid activities, social housing, and social inclusion programmes. In general, these are the pieces where the most systemic, policy, or society-level interventions ought to be expected. Indeed, with one exception, all thematic stories in this group focused on treatments rather than causes, local government and NGOs were the main actors and voices, and this was the only group where a positive evaluative tone dominated. There were few such stories from cities other than Cluj-Napoca: of the 21 thematic pieces, 16 reported on programmes related to Pata Rât, and 5 came from Târgu-Mureș. No such thematic reports came from Miercurea Ciuc, Călărași, or Ploiești. This group also contained emphatic ethnical indexing, as most interventions or projects covered were framed by the actors themselves as an issue of Roma integration. In fact, most stories in this group originated from the actors themselves. Thematic stories in this case differed from the episodic ones—largely consisting of announcements of various project launches—in that they chose to include some of the background materials provided by those initiating the projects but were less likely to be based on reporting from the segregated areas than the stories of living conditions discussed above.

The areas of life in which the programmes covered aimed to intervene included education, health, Internet access, jobs, housing, and cultural stereotypes. In the introduction, we saw how local economic development agencies do not consider problems of segregated areas as parts of their concerns, and, indeed, such agents did not figure in the news. There were, however, several articles reporting on social integration in terms of job creation, mostly generated by an international actor, the United Nations Development Programme (UNDP).

In this group of news, international actors other than the UNDP also had a presence. These included representatives of foreign governments like the French minister of domestic affairs and officials of the EU, with their presence again increasing newsworthiness. A national news agency, Mediafax, made a rare appearance among the sources of news reporting on a project developed with the help of UNDP, aimed at "making the most of EU Fund for Sustainable Housing and Inclusion of disadvantaged Roma." A subheading of the report highlights a point made by the mayor of Cluj-Napoca: "The Roma problem is not only a problem of Romania," framing the issue as a European one and explicitly claiming that responsibility for the issue does not reside on the local level:

> We are doing everything in our power not to ignore the European dimension of the problem of the Roma, because it is not only a Romanian problem, but a problem of the European Union as well, and to the extent that we will have the financial support of the EU, we will have better chances of integrating the Roma community. If the issue will be passed on to the local level, chances to do so will be minimal.[28]

Framing the issue as a European one, either to legitimate the lack of attention to the social dimension of the waste management system or to argue for the need of EU financing for a social intervention programme in the discourse of local authorities, has a clear distancing function: passing responsibility to levels other than the local ones.

The Cluj media also documented an attempt by local activists to contest the invisibility or stigmatization of the work of reclaimers at the dump. Local NGOs staged a protest in front of the county council, demanding that the local authorities recognized the importance and dignity of the work of residents of Pata Rât. These residents made a living by collecting and selecting recyclable waste, and their livelihood was threatened by the planned new waste management system, which involved closing down the Pata Rât dump. In order to make their point, protesters dumped such waste at the doorsteps of the county authorities. As the "performance," as the organizers described it, was addressed to the local authorities, not to the economic agents that had been contracted, the voices cited, apart from representatives of the organizers and residents, only included that of the spokesperson of the county council. Just like the interviewees from the chamber of commerce took care to differentiate their sphere of action from problems of poverty and segregation, defined as "social," the spokesperson cited explained the lack of attention to the issue of the livelihood of those living on the garbage dump by offering a demarcation between the "social" sphere and the EU programme financing the new waste management system:

> This program run by the Cluj county council had European funding, and it is known that European financing does not have a social component. The garbage dump will be closed down anyway as an effect of EU directives… If we do not close it, we will receive huge fines.[29]

The contestation of the policy, as well as discursive logic denying reclaimers the status of workers, is thus countered by a demarcation strategy separating the issue from the domain of the economy. In striving for balanced reporting, journalists of the Cluj-Napoca local media do cite the authorities as well as the protesters. However, the overall lack of the economic actors and their voices, in general characteristic of our corpus, contributes to framing the issue as one distant from the economic sphere. This demarcation is one of the main discursive means of making invisible the connections between the labour of the marginalized and the functioning of the economy.

Local agents working in the segregated areas that featured in the news were charitable individuals offering food or medical services to the poor. In a report on a Târgu Mureș programme, one such local individual who had economic and political roles in the local community as well asked to remain anonymous, a discursive move cast by the journalist in a moral frame as a laudable exercise in humility. However, such moves are also exercises in distancing acts of charity from the economic and political spheres:

> I met Daan De Groot, the initiator and leader of the Association absolutely by chance … Having also learned of them by chance, the owner of a Târgu Mureș restaurant offered them a few hundreds of dumplings and asked me to accompany them. To the great honour of the businessman, who is also a

known politician, he stressed that he was there in his capacity as a Human and his official capacities had no relevance.[30]

The discursive aspect of the issue of segregation is clearly sensed by several Cluj-Napoca NGOs campaigning for integrating Pata Rât into the city, who set up a Facebook group with a name that undertakes a discursive integration by mixing up the place names: "Pata Cluj—Napoca Rât" and argue for "creating relationships of micro-solidarity that bring the two communities closer to each other and thus end the segregation of the residents of Pata Rât."[31] However, this effort is also cast with reference to the external gaze of foreign actors: the founder of the group is presented as a member of the committee preparing the city's application for the title of European Capital of Culture, who, in this quality, takes foreign consultants visiting the city to visit Pata Rât as well. Similarly, the press release of a group of local NGOs trying to engage the local authorities into a dialogue on the situation makes reference to the image of the city abroad and the European scale of the problem as an argument for the dialogue:

> We remind that Pata Rât is the site of the largest ghetto around a waste dump in the European space, a reality that denies the pretensions of Cluj to become a multi-cultural European capital in 2020.[32]

Thus, by situating the issue either at a European level, as a question of relevant EU directives, funding, or aspirations, or at a level of individual charity, a sphere of individual morality, news of social interventions distance the issue from the local levels or from the sphere of economy and politics in general. "Social integration" appears as devoid of any relevance for the shared concerns of the wider community, except when threatening their—unrelated—aspirations.

Conclusions: Discursive Segregation in the News

Romanian news media coverage of segregated housing areas manifest several features that are common to the news media's coverage of poverty and marginalized groups in general, and some of these can even be regarded as inherent features of news discourse. Thus, local officials and NGOs both outnumbered residents as actors in our corpus, a finding that is in line with the general preference of news discourse for official agents as voices, as well as to "Knowns" as opposed to the "Unknowns" (Gans 1979, 8). What is particular to the Romanian news media coverage of segregated areas, and its definition of the problem of segregation, is that the most prominent actors and voices are local. Similarly, news of the segregated worlds made it very rarely into the national news media, and in these cases it was the presence of a newsworthy foreign actor or voice that accounted for the coverage. Central government actors and politicians' voices barely registered (the weight of both was under 0.1 per cent), and there were no economic actors or voices present. What is also particular to our corpus is the relatively low weight of expert voices, at 13 per cent of all voices, the same as the voice of other locals. In general, the issues involved appeared either as an administrative concern for local authorities, like providing appropriate housing to those evacuated, or as an issue of individual morality, like helping those in need and thus exercising the virtue of charity. In both cases, the problems depicted appear as particular to a beneficiary group, requiring particular, rather than systemic, solutions.

Apart from the lack of economic and political agents and voices, journalistic discourse and voices cited undertook several explicit demarcations that further distanced the issues involved from the spheres of economy and politics. In our larger corpus, problems of infrastructure or development tended to be discussed without reference to the inhabitants of the locations in question, a feature that appears not so much as a strategic move on the part of journalists but characteristic of the wider discursive field, as it has been noted by other researchers as well. The explicit request of a person with both political and economic roles, not to mention the latter aspects of his endeavours, also shows that this discursive move is part of a wider language spoken by other social actors, too: he was offering his help out of charity, as "a human being." Interventions cast as charity are thus presented as questions of individual morality, presented in positive evaluative terms, but distinct from the spheres of economic or political responsibility. In general, these demarcations serve to frame the issue of segregation as distant from shared, society-level concerns. The general lack of economic actors and voices and the demarcations between the issues of poverty and the sphere of the economy, undertaken by official as well as private voices, are the main means by which the connections between the labour of the poor and the functioning of the economy remain hidden.

The problem of residential segregation does not have a common label in the news; it does not register as a problem as such. Terms like poverty, segregation, marginalization, ghettos, and slums are not customarily used. Our corpus compiled by using a search for place names is not based on any categorization employed by the news discourse itself. This feature is again in line with the general tendency of news media to avoid covering social processes. However, there is one common referential strategy recurring throughout the corpus: indexing the ethnicity of the inhabitants. "Roma" is the go-to label when reporting from these areas. This shared discursive feature is also the main discursive strategy of marginalization, as it represents the problem as pertaining to the interests of a specific community. The distancing use of ethnical indexing in news discourse is shown by the fact that when reports explicitly aim to bring the reality depicted closer to that of the readers, at least in emotional terms, as in the case of the human interest stories, the weight of ethnical indexing decreases.

One of the strongest means of discursive segregation is the stigmatization of scavenging. The strong stigma attached to all forms of reclaiming waste is coupled with a lack of conceptual differentiation between the various forms of reclaiming waste, between, for example, looking for food in the roadside garbage bin or digging up metals to recycle from the ground or collecting recyclable waste from landfills. All such activities are cast as inappropriate, illegal, or outright immoral, with those undertaking it cast as either unworthy of "benefits" they receive, or guilty of tarnishing the image of the country and of local society. Even though there is some coverage of local activists contesting this form of epistemic injustice, media discourse in general has not yet been sensitized to the issue. In failing to engage in this conceptual differentiation, the media perpetuates a discourse that underpins local policies of waste management carried out without treating those undertaking recycling work as legitimate stakeholders.

The news media coverage of segregated housing areas is predominantly the result of the newsmaking practices of officials and NGOs. The less frequent pieces that are based on on-site reporting frame the issue of segregation as distant from everyday experience by highlighting the physical distance between the everyday world of the journalist and the reader, and the world into which we are offered a glimpse from the outside. Vivid descriptions of extreme poverty offered by human interest stories, with their language stressing the other-worldly, non-real nature of the world depicted, contributes to portraying these locations and their residents as extreme forms of otherness. Temporal metaphors situating them in different ages act in the same direction, placing these locations in different realities.

Another move towards distancing the problem is casting the issues as "European." References to EU financing possibilities or environmental directives appear as constraining the possibilities of the actions of local authorities, thus distancing the problem from their sphere of responsibility. Another use of the "European" rhetoric is disputing the European aspirations of the cities by pointing out the "non-European" state of affairs in the segregated areas. However, such rhetoric implicitly assigns a threatening dimension to these areas and their inhabitants, casting them as a threatening "other." This semantic aspect of the "European dimension" is strengthened by reports on the Western media's coverage on these areas, perceived as threatening the image of the country abroad. It is at this point only that the problem of residential segregation appears to intersect with wider social concerns and anxieties.

Notes

1. Edith Vereș, "Coming home, acasă pentru cei fără de casă." *Zi-de-zi Mureș,* December 27, 2013.
2. Lacrima Andreica, "Solidaritate pe gunoaiele orașului." *Adevărul,* March 31, 2013.
3. The locations searched for were: for Călărași, the neighbourhoods of Doi Moldoveni, Livada, Obor, Cinci Călărași, Mircea Vodă, Cărămidari, and the urban landfills (*groapa de gunoi, cimitir de fier vechi*); for Cluj-Napoca, Pata Rât; for Miercurea Ciuc, the Șumuleu/Somlyó, Primăverii/Tavasz, and Suta streets, and the local waterplant (*stația de epurare*); for Ploiești: the neighbourhoods of the Western Train Station, Mimiu,

Segregated Housing Areas and the Discursive Construction... 175

Bereasca, Boldeasca, Teleajen, and areas of the București street (*bariera București, colonia*); for Târgu Mureș: the Valea Rece/Hidegvölgy and Ady neighbourhoods, the Băneasa /Toldi, the Dealului/Hegy or Domb and Rovinari streets.

4. "Activistii Amnesty International au trimis scrisori de protest fata de situatia romilor din Miercurea Ciuc." *Ziare.com/Agerpress,* April 19, 2011.
5. "Cum arată locuințele romilor din Pata Rât, fotografiate de la înălțime." *Citynews.ro,* December 17, 2013.
6. Kertész Melinda, "Folytatódik a kilakoltatás? A kolozsvári Cantonului utca lakóit is elköltöztethetik." *Transindex,* July 6, 2011.
7. Gabriel Horia Nasra, "Pata Rât 2013. Împreună cu Valentin!" *Ziua de Cluj,* December 16, 2013.
8. Mihai Prodan, "Romii strâmbă din nas. Nu le plac locuințele modulare pe care plătesc o chirie simbolică." *Ziua de Cluj,* January 21, 2011.
9. Kozán István, "Újra akcióban az Amnesty International." *Székelyhon.ro,* May 9, 2011.
10. Mihai Prodan, "Romii strâmbă din nas. Nu le plac locuințele modulare pe care plătesc o chirie simbolică." *Ziua de Cluj,* January 21, 2011.
11. Létai Tibor, "Vízben álló barakkok a cigánysoron." *Székelyhon.ro,* August 16, 2011.
12. Dana Mihai, "Colonia de containere a Ploieștiului. Locul în care copiii visează să devină pictori și fotbaliști, iar adulții să cumpere barăcile încinse." *Adevărul.ro,* July 23, 2013.
13. Dana Mihai, "Ghetoul în care se moare pentru o bucată de pâine." *Adevărul,* November 20, 2012.
14. Ibid.
15. Claudia Sas, "Locuiesc ca în Evul Mediu." *Tvmures.ro,* May 26, 2012.
16. "Cartierul Ploieștean Mimiu, acum și acum un secol." *Adevărul,* May 7, 2012.
17. Ibid.
18. Graeme Culliford, "The Untouchables." *The Sun,* February 8, 2013.
19. Jerome Taylor, "The truth about Romania's gypsies: Not coming over here, not stealing our jobs." *The Independent,* February 11, 2013.
20. Ibid.
21. Alex Toth, "Evul mediu din Valea Rece, întreținut de nesimțirea autorităților." *Zi-de-zi Mureș,* October 17, 2013.
22. Kulcsár Árpád, "A cél, hogy integrálódjunk, vagy legalább élhetővé tegyük ezt a környezetet." *Transindex.ro,* October 25, 2013.

23. "Dump closure threatens community." BBC News, August 25, 2009, http://news.bbc.co.uk/2/hi/europe/8219444.stm; Florina Pop, Gropa de gunoi a Clujului, „vedetă"la BBC, *Adevărul,* November 29, 2013.
24. "Bărbat călcat de o maşină de gunoi la Pata Rât." *Adevărul,* February 23, 2012.
25. "O fetita de cinci ani a murit in Pata Rât, dupa ce a fost calcata de o masina de gunoi!" *Cluj Online,* July 8, 2012.
26. "Atitudinea necuviincioasă a unui pastor american." *Ziar 15 minute,* October 28, 2013.
27. Interview by Enikő Vincze and Camelia Moraru with a local journalist from Târgu Mureş, May 2012.
28. "Proiectul pentru integrarea romilor de la Pata Rât, depus spre finanţare anul acesta." *Monitorul de Cluj,* September 13, 2012.
29. "Romii de la Pata Rât au adus gunoaie la Consiliul Judeţean Cluj." *Adevărul,* March 23, 2012.
30. Edith Vereş, "Coming Home, acasă pentru cei fără de casă." *Zi-de-Zi Mureş,* December 27, 2013.
31. *Kulcsár Árpád,* "Patavár és Kolozsrét között." *Transindex, August 26, 2013.*
32. "gLOC îi cere primarului interimar Radu Moisin să se implice în rezolvarea problemei romilor de la Pata Rât." *Buzznews.ro,* January 24, 2012.

References

Allan, Stuart. 2010. *News Culture.* Maidenhead: McGraw Hill/Open University Press.
Bednarek, Monika, and Helen Caple. 2012. Value Added: Language, Image and News Values. *Discourse, Context & Media* 1: 103–113.
Bullock, Heather E., Karen Fraser-Wyche, and Wendy R. Williams. 2001. Media Images of the Poor. *Journal of Social Issues* 57 (2): 229–246.
Devereux, Eoin, Haynes Amanda, and Martin J. Power. 2011. Tarring Everyone with the Same Shorthand? Journalists, Stigmatization and Social Exclusion. *Journalism* 13 (4): 500–517.
Entman, Robert M. 1993. Framing: Toward Clarification of a Fractured Paradigm. *Journal of Communication* 43 (4): 51–58.
Fairclough, Isabela, and Norman Fairclough. 2012. *Political Discourse Analysis. A Method for Advanced Students.* London/New York: Routledge.
Future of News. 2015. London: The BBC. https://newsimg.bbc.co.uk/1/shared/bsp/hi/pdfs/29_01_15future_of_news.pdf. Downloaded on 21.05.2016.

Gans, Herbert J. 1979. *Deciding What's News*. 2004th ed. Evanston: Northwestern University Press.

———. 2010. News and Democracy in the United States: Current Problems, Future Possibilities. In *The Routledge Companion to News and Journalism*, ed. S. Allan, 95–147. London/New York: Routledge.

Green, Maia. 2006. Representing Poverty and Attacking Representations: Perspectives on Poverty from Social Anthropology. *Journal of Development Studies* 42 (7): 1108–1129.

Iyengar, Shanto. 1990. Framing Responsibility for Political Issues: The Case of Poverty. *Political Behaviour* 12 (1): 19–40.

Kendall, Diana. 2011. *Framing Class: Media Representations of Wealth and Poverty in America*. Lanham/Boulder/New York/Toronto/Plymouth: Rowman & Littlefield.

Kim, Sei-Hill, J.P. Carvalho, A.G. Davis, and A. G. 2010. Talking About Poverty: News Framing of Who Is Responsible for Causing and Fixing the Problem. *Journalism & Mass Communication Quarterly* 87 (3/4): 563–581.

Kleut, Jelena, and Smiljana Milinkov. 2013. Co-construction and Deconstruction of Poverty on Serbian News Websites. *Media Research* 19 (2): 75–98.

Krumer-Nevo, Michael, and Orly Benjamin. 2010. Critical Poverty Knowledge: Contesting Othering and Social Distancing. *Current Sociology* 58 (5): 693–714.

Larsen, Christian A., and Thomas E. Dejgaard. 2013. The Institutional Logic of Images of the Poor and Welfare Recipients: A Comparative Study of British, Swedish and Danish Newspapers. *Journal of European Social Policy* 23 (3): 287–299.

Örnebring, Henrik. 2013. *Journalistic Autonomy and Professionalisation*. Pillar 3 Final Report of the "Media and Democracy in Central and Eastern Europe" Project. http://mde.politics.ox.ac.uk/images/Final_reports/stetka_2013_final%20report_posted.pdf. Downloaded on 24.08.2016.

Pan, Zhongdang, and Gerald Kosicki. 1993. Framing Analysis: An Approach to News Discourse. *Political Communication* 10 (1): 55–75.

Preoteasa, Manuela, and A. Schwartz. 2015. *The Man Who Bit the Watchdog*. Report on Media Ownership Patterns in Post-communist Romania – 5 Profiles. http://transparencycentre.org/pdf/report.pdf. Downloaded on 25.08.2015.

Reisigl, Martin, and Ruth Wodak. 2001. *Discourse and Discrimination. Rhetorics of Racism and Antisemitism*. London/New York: Routledge.

Richards, Barry. 2012. News and the Emotional Public Sphere. In *The Routledge Companion to News and Journalism*, ed. S. Allan, 301–311. London/New York: Routledge.

Richardson, John E. 2007. *Analysing Newspapers. An Approach from Critical Discourse Analysis*. Basingstoke/New York: Palgrave Macmillan.
Samson, Melanie. 2009. Wasted Citizenship? Reclaimers and the Privatised Expansion of the Public Sphere. *Africa Development* 34 (3–4): 1–25.
———. 2015. Accumulation by Dispossession and the Informal Economy – Struggles Over Knowledge, Being and Waste at a Soweto Garbage Dump. *Environment and Planning D: Society and Space* 33 (5): 813–830.
Semetko, Holli A., and Patti M. Valkenburg. 2000. Framing European Politics: A Content Analysis of Press and Television News. *Journal of Communication* 50 (2): 93–109.
Simionca, Anca. 2013. Development, Underdevelopment and Impoverished Roma Communities. A Case Study of High-Level Visions and Agendas of Economic Progress in Urban Romania. *Studia Universitatis Babes-Bolyai Sociologia* 58 (2): 55–76.
Stetka, Vaclav, and Henrik Örnebring. 2013. Investigative Journalism in Central and Eastern Europe: Autonomy, Business Models, and Democratic Roles. *The International Journal of Press/Politics* 18: 413–435.
van Leeuwen, Theo. 1996. The Representation of Social Actors. In *Texts and Practices: Readings in Critical Discourse Analysis*, ed. Carmen R. Caldas-Coulthard and Malcolm Coulthard, 32–70. London: Routledge.
Vasterman, Peter L.M. 2005. Media-Hype: Self-Reinforcing News Waves, Journalistic Standards and the Construction of Social Problems. *European Journal of Communication* 20 (4): 508–530.
Vincze, Enikő. 2014. The War Against Poor (Roma) in Populist Discourses and Practices in Romania. *Studia Universitatis Babes-Bolyai Europaea* 29 (1): 231–242.
Vincze, Enikő, and Cristina Rat. 2013. Spatialization and Racialization of Social Exclusion. The Social and Cultural Formation of *Tsigane Ghettos* in Romania in a European Context. *Studia Universitatis Babes-Bolyai Sociologia* 57 (2): 5–21.

7

How Many Ghettos Can We Count? Identifying Roma Neighbourhoods in Romanian Municipalities

Cătălin Berescu

Impoverished neighbourhoods can be found in many sizes and in many urban and social forms.[1] There is an academic struggle to define and organize them into categories, each discipline pointing at the need for an interdisciplinary approach, while indulging in its own concepts and methods. This effort is methodologically legitimate (a first step in any scientific inquiry is to name and classify) and intellectually valid (we need to know about empirical facts); though, if it would ever reach a successful end, it should also be intellectually legitimate (scientists getting true meaning from their inquiry and finding real solutions to problems) and methodologically valid (the analysis of the areas should give the same results across countries and disciplines). The last point appears to be contentious, and in this chapter we aim to examine the problem of classifying and counting the places where Roma live.

C. Berescu (✉)
Romanian Academy, The Research Institute for Quality of Life, Bucharest, Romania

Usually, this type of inquiry is a morally honest attempt to give a name to the areas, and this is how it is considered throughout this chapter, leaving aside any suspicions about possible hidden agendas of the actors involved in the definition or just in the labelling of extremely impoverished housing areas. Some of the actors, like partisan media for example, are driven by their social role and political position, while some others, like international financial institutions, are acting under the spell of the ideology of development. To what extent they produce or reproduce self-serving or even discriminatory views can only be determined by a case-by-case investigation, but what is of interest in this chapter is a particular type of technical discourse that tries to manage marginality. Within it, typology analysis has a special place, as a critical feature in planning, an unavoidable step in any larger action plan, but one that has its limits and possible misuses. In Romania's case, where neighbourhoods in extreme poverty are predominantly inhabited by Roma, the question is which of them are ghettos, which are slums, and which are just disadvantaged areas with an ethnic touch. I purposefully started this chapter by using "impoverished neighbourhoods" as this is, in my view, the core attribute of the areas we did research in. However, besides a general interest in underdeveloped, ethnically segregated, disadvantaged, discriminated, marginalized areas, a better descriptor of our research areas would be "extremely impoverished Roma neighbourhoods".

As described in Chap. 1, SPAREX project focused on five medium-sized cities in Romania. However, the previous research experience of the members of the team includes many other examples of the same nature. There is a variety of cases that we came across: deprived neighbourhoods with ethnically mixed population, satellite quarters inhabited exclusively by Roma, satellite settlements of Roma that gravitate around the city, central urban areas with semi-formal status or informal settlements, and so on. "Roma neighbourhoods" is a convenient term to name the racialized marginal spaces whose social formation is described by the first three chapters of our volume, while the public policies' failure of responding to the whole set of problems that they accumulate (material deprivation, extremely poor housing conditions, ethnic segregation, etc.) is addressed from a sociolinguistic perspective on the basic vocabulary of planning tools. The challenge is to narrow down the general fact that classifications are politically driven social constructions informed by cultural conceptions to an illustration of the process through which the most affected communities are excluded.

Unlike its Central and Eastern European neighbours, Romania did not have a count and a map of such areas until recently. This speaks volumes about both the lack of real anti-poverty policies of the successive governments that ruled since 1989 and about the intricate web of institutional and casual racism that keeps the problems faced by the Roma in a peculiar position within the public agenda. Counting the ghettos and the slums would first require acknowledging their existence, then understanding their formation and finally fighting the processes that lead to their development and reproduction. There is no doubt that the post-1989 period is one of an extraordinary increase in size and numbers of Roma ghettos in Central and Eastern Europe, a process that was largely ignored by authorities until early 2000, then addressed through measures that mainly targeted insalubrity and lack of urban equipment and infrastructure, but rarely tackling it directly and sometimes preserving or even consolidating segregation (Rughiniş 2004). The failure of public policies is rooted in the policies of visibility. On the one hand, the most deprived areas are rendered invisible; on the other, the very few projects that are done are used as leverage tools that serve various ad hoc political purposes, indefinitely postponing the creation of policies that would address the root causes of the formation of marginal areas and always moving the target from the most stringent problems to more manageable ones. It all starts with a name that is given to that area and it ends with a definition that regulates it.

Who Can Name the Ghetto?

Speaking about really terrible living areas takes different forms in academic literature, public discourse, and common language. It is not merely the description of their variation that will be addressed here but their connection, or lack thereof, with policy documents that pertain to them. A first observation is that policy documents—strategies, national plans, ministerial methodologies—are a genre in itself. Even if they originate in academia, through the simple fact that the authors are generally recruited from there, and use much of the language and tools that can be found in academic papers, the nature of such documents is different. Documents of this sort have very brief theoretical elements, very few definitions, and usually lack references. Moreover, a brief review of the Romanian anti-poverty legislation (Catana et al. 2012) found that around half of the key terms used across the legislation lacked a proper definition. Many reports and studies produced for ministries tend to have a collective author, sometimes an anonymous one. In this respect, the piece of legislation that results at the end of a research effort grows into an almost folkloric product.

We have to believe that it is academia that will give an answer to the problem of classification, but we also must acknowledge the uncertain epistemic status of the terminology that describes impoverished neighbourhoods. Let's take, for example, the tension between architectural typologies and social sciences typologies. One of the first things that is hampering a mutual understanding is that there is a long and well-established tradition of criticism against "formalism". The critique of formalism can be found in a vast number of academic writings. It is commonplace for many introductions to studies to aim for some distance from the previous literature in order to present new findings, and formalism is often mentioned as a plague, a backward status of knowledge. The solution is always an "opposite" concept, a novelty in which "the process" is highlighted, that is, the becoming of the form, the mechanism that can be revealed only through a complex analysis of phenomena that are not to be observed with the naked eye. Because in the realm of housing and urban planning form and process cannot be separated, the above critique is often just a form of rhetorical arrogance. In fact, almost all the authors who must deal with poverty-stricken areas, socio-anthropologists, economists, or urban studies scholars, are involved in an effort to describe an occurrence of a phenomenon and to place it within a general theoretical framework. Anytime we employ a category, even the simplest, the most "formal" (e.g., urban versus rural[2]) we also bring forward some of its underlying explanations and we presume and accept the existence of a process. Besides the presupposition that "processual-ism" is a form of refraining from field work or a simple lack of methodology, there is another, almost funny, theoretical consequence of this artificial conflict:

the impoverished housing area (slum, ghetto, camp, etc.) is a possible victim of the Heisenberg uncertainty principle. If we state that form and process are complementary variables, then the more accurate we describe the form, the less we can describe the process and vice versa.

Another, less obvious, difficulty, but maybe one of the sources of the relative lack of success of academia in establishing a unifying theory of *housing areas affected by discrimination and physical degradation*[3] that are usually described as *slums, ghettos, mahalas, bidonvilles, barrios*, and so on, is that it has to deal with not only a puzzling diversity of formal situations but also a plethora of *forms of judgement* that are present in the public sphere. I am using this term here in a very broad sense, primarily pointing at some ad hoc constructions, which are usually a part of a political or professional metanarrative, but also having in mind their poor relatives, folk theories, and stereotypes. The latest are sometimes the elegant, other times the brutal, part of a reactive discourse employed by key opinion leaders at a given moment in a society that is confronted with a problem or an event that takes place and has a flexible and often unstable form when it comes to reflect the situation of poverty-stricken areas. You can hear terms like *șatră* (tent), *țigănie* (Tsigane-hood), *colonie* (colony), *ghetou* (ghetto), *cartierul lor* (their neighbourhood), "marginalized area", "Roma quarter", or "disadvantaged area" in the same meeting, from different people. These different mindsets are directly governed by education, by the amount and quality of direct experience they have with the area that is under scrutiny *and* with other areas, by their political views, by the format of the meeting, by opportunities and agency, and so on. Nevertheless, it is the variety of expressions, names, and labels that can be observed in meetings, roundtables, conferences, and public talks. Regardless of the level on which they take place there is a continuous back and forth move from *ghetto* to *mahala*, and then in circles around the problem of segregation, using, for example, a strange, but very popular for a while, term like "self-segregation". This idea was used by many Roma leaders to keep communities under control and to gain access to financial resources, by several non-Roma politicians to preserve the status quo and actually reinforce segregation, and by some Roma activists to introduce a utopic idea of a self-governed ethnic quarter that would resemble a kibbutz.

But wording is just the form taken by a process of reflection. It is fair to say that the inconsistency of reflection about impoverished areas in the public sphere and its multiple occurrences and unstable dynamic are an accurate manifestation of the forces that produce the exclusion of the Roma, and that is also keeping various forms of academic and non-academic reflection on poverty lagging behind the current formal developments of impoverished areas. The terms are basically used to move the target. What comes to mind are recurrent episodes of moral panic triggered and used by sensationalist media channels in which a bad neighbourhood is used as a canvas for a tragedy or a crime or any other sort of "incident". This breaks the usual dullness of the image of poverty and resurfaces all the stereotypical and aggressive views about that place. The language is of little importance; an area might be labelled as ZUS (*Zone urbaine sensible*) in the professional French jargon or *carton-city* in an informal discussion in Serbia or any other official or informal denomination that indicates a heterotopic area regime.

Equally treacherous is the long ago established rhetoric of "poverty pockets", as places that concentrate marginal but also rather *negligible* groups. For example, World Bank Romania uses it frequently to introduce the situation of extreme poverty in Romania and, even if it is formally correct in regard with the actual size of the communities, by doing so the gravity and the extent of the phenomenon are diminished. Another particular, yet customary, example of a political construction of a label of that sort is the Italian *campi nomadi*. That phrase names both the internment camps built by various Italian municipalities for ex-Yugoslav Roma war refugees and the informal settlements they built themselves. Another example is *village d'insertion*, expensive correctional facilities created by the French government to give a strong answer to the problem of Romanian Roma informal settlements that mushroomed in all the major cities in France after Romania joined the EU. Each of these instances deserves a lengthy description for which there is not enough space here, but together they constitute powerful examples of the way in which words are used by people in power.

Official documents carefully avoid mentioning any conflict within society, the fact that some people live in improper conditions appears to be a natural and historically inherited condition, and the only problem is that that they are exposed to insalubrious housing conditions. No matter how complex a critical and theoretical apparatus might be, it cannot change, or even standardize, *the name* that is in use to indicate a socially excluding housing area marked by poverty and that has a strong ethno-racial dimension whether we call it a *slum*, a *ghetto*, a *baracopolli*, a *campo nomadi*, or a *mahala*. Whatever term used is a strong indication of the position that the person or institution takes in regard to an area; it is also a reflection of society's view about a particular group. In our case, the Roma's spaces can be called *șatră*, *țigănie*, which are pejorative and reveal an openly racist position, or *colonie*, which is a more neutral term. Once in a while you might find *cartierul gaborilor* (Gabori neighbourhood) used in a fairly appreciative way, as this small Transylvanian Roma sub-group has a particularly high status. "Ghetto" is rare and used only at lower administrative levels. But most of the mentions will just use the name of the place (Pata Rât, Toamnei, Viitorului) and sometimes the nickname ("Dallas", "Columbia", "Doi Moldoveni", "Cambodgia"). From the (auto)ironic nicknames used by the inhabitants and their neighbours to the sophisticated technical language of urban planning—which uses complex arrangements that often end up as acronyms in official papers[4]—and from the daily stereotypes used by the press—which spreads stigma to the dry administrative jargon that aims to hide the problems of impoverished neighbourhoods and areas of exclusion—we are exposed to a vivid variety of nominal strategies that essentially refer to a specific area using different formulas that aim to introduce it into a general category.

A further example, which lies in an intermediate linguistic world that reflects a Romanian reality in a foreign language, comes from a French author who deals with a Romanian reality. He uses: *quartiers tsiganes, taudis* (hovels, slums, messy places), *noyau* (core, nucleus, pit of a fruit, also a technical term used by ethologists to name a territory used by a dominant male), *ghettos, mahala*, and *bidonvilles* (Delepine 2007). These are the words used by Samuel Delepine in his book *Quartieres Tsiganes. L'habitat et le logement des Rroms de Roumanie en question*, one of the first extended reports on Roma neighbourhoods, published as a brief version of his extensive PhD research in several urban and rural places around Romania. The French geographer found himself facing the same problem as any other researcher, he had to describe and compare social and spatial entities using terms from his discipline, and in this case, also from his native language, and we notice that French has a wider vocabulary that points at similar questions. He also had to illustrate a research process that was carried through the local language, one which he understands and speaks very well. It would be natural to assume that he uses French for general concepts and Romanian terms for the local, particular version of slums, like the Serbians use *carton-city* or Northwest Pacific Americans would use *skid row* or Indonesians *kampung*. It is the way we are used to according to most ethnographic narratives, academic or not. But there are no specific terms aside from the widespread regional term *mahala*, a term that has today a pejorative connotation in Romanian. As a result of this lack of choices, the researcher has to stick to a common vocabulary that creates a "weak" typology, one that indicates the ethnic composition, the size, the marginal condition, the segregation status, or the historical nature of the problems a particular place has in a way that makes sense when you read the descriptions of those places, but does not provide the means to classify them in regard to other urbanistic entities. This is a common feature of all papers published on the topic of Roma neighbourhoods—the description is often excellent, but the researcher faces the insurmountable problem of placing his or her findings in a general disciplinary context that operates with different bodies, and from which the concepts that are used to circumscribe the settlements are as marginal as the settlements themselves.

Returning to administrative documents, we can see that Serbian documents related to the "Roma Decade" but also to the OSCE effort to legalize informal settlements use "Roma informal settlements" in their action plans that mention their unhygienic conditions (Roma National Strategy Secretariat 2007), while in a Bulgarian Annual Report we can find only "Roma quarters" (Kolev et al. 2010). In Hungary, there is a strong emphasis on segregation, and the Ministry of Public Administration created a map of segregated communities, which is mentioned in its National Social Inclusion Strategy 2011–2020. Extreme poverty is described and addressed in detail, and the term is used in the subtitles of the sections on "children in poverty" and "the Roma". The words "slum" and "ghetto" are present throughout the document.

An important Croatian document, a synthesis of the Roma situation, underlines the fact that some settlements are built in a "wild" manner, that is, they are substandard and are close to a *favela* (Stambuk 2005). A "para-urban type" is mentioned as a possible category that encompasses observations and statements like: "The Romani group had 'bad luck' that structures were mainly built in this way". "Wild" equals informal, illegal, and substandard; "detached" is used for segregated communities, and some small squalid slums that have a separate section in the typological divide are labelled "black holes". There are a lot of quotation marks used in the document, an indication of the difficulty of the authors to describe the circumstances in a straightforward manner.

The variety of the examples showed above tells us that there are not only many very different social actors interested in naming these particular occurrences of marginal spaces that are the Roma neighbourhoods,[5] but that they are deeply immersed in their own set of values, and moreover, that the theoretical framework differs from one discipline to another (urbanism, sociology, geography, etc.). It is worth mentioning also that the production and use of most of these documents is part of a practice of interventions in a very well-defined social group, one with clear borders and hierarchies. In this respect, the language that is used and subsequently the discourse that is constructed has primarily a parochial function, and is part of a habitus that helps researchers and planners to get commissions.

Hiding the Ghetto

There is another side of this relation between words (and I include here concepts, labels and names) and power, one that is more important, the power to conceal a reality. In other words, I claim that it is the fierce opposition to naming and defining bad neighbourhoods of the cultivated and not so cultivated public and of the politicians, primarily in Romania, generally in Eastern Europe, and, to a lesser extent, in the rest of the EU, that prevents these areas from having a proper place on the public agenda. There is plenty of talk in the public sphere about inequality and poverty, but there are very few reflections about exclusion and extreme poverty. If we cannot have an agreement on a name, or a set of terms, to be more precise, for a social phenomenon, it is because we are not prepared to use consistent definitions of that phenomenon. The process is similar to what happened to terms like *racism* or *genocide* or *Holocaust*, which needed some time to acquire a standard meaning. They still are, to different degrees, under scrutiny, contested sometimes in various contexts, abused in others, yet, they represent a historical success, a come-into-being idea that went through a complete process of intellectual reflection and public use that made them mainstream. This process is maybe only halfway in its historic development for the topic of extremely impoverished areas that are inhabited by a minority of excluded people.

It is hard to *efficiently* conceptualize in scientific terms a social phenomenon that is actively avoided as a subject matter by the public and, consequently, by politicians. Categorizing housing poverty areas, particularly the ones inhabited by people excluded on racial grounds, is not just a result of a research inquiry but of an interplay of actors with very different agencies. This historically long-term social game might end with a convergence or with a null result. My observation is that, in terms of policies and public discourse and in the language of praxis, in most documents that surrounds an intervention or that aim to create a plan or a policy, the general tendency is to have a soft, non-conflictual, vague definition of that kind of area. If the public realm cannot absorb the academic effort to define the terms, then we cannot expect coherent public policies to combat excluded areas. Looking back at successful, or just relatively successful, policies that addressed the problem, we can see that they evolved around the term *slum*, sometimes accompanied by the term *ghetto*; that is, "slum eradication", "slum upgrading", and so on, are used as part of the urban renewal plans or per se. There is a whole body of literature that deals with the topic, mainly in the Anglo-Saxon world where you can find debates and plans from the Victorian era, followed by a now classic literature that accompanies Johnson's "war on poverty" that comes from social scientist like Gans, Wilson and Hunter or from architects like John Turner, Christopher Alexander or Nabeel Hamdi, but very few Romanian publications address the issue.

Who *can* give the name "ghetto" to an actual ghetto? Usually it is some of the inhabitants, some journalists, and almost all the social research and NGO crowd that would naturally use the term. But if we look at policy-makers and major stakeholders, we can easily see that the main political documents and generally the official documents carefully avoid the use of terms like "ghetto" or "internment camp", which would more properly describe the Italian *campo nomadi* or "administratively abandoned areas", a more exact way to label areas in which social exclusion was intensely practised. In the case of Romania, and to an important extent the EU, there is an astounding silence at the upper levels of public discourse in what regards an area of exclusion and extreme poverty. The discourse is dominated in the EU, less in Romania, by the issues of inequality and relative poverty. The only logical response to the question of naming, which otherwise sounds very rhetorical, is that only the government has the power and responsibility to do that. Before further engaging in an epistemic reflection on the relation between academic knowledge, public understanding, and administrative language, we will expose some of the forms that are currently in use in the intermediate realm of *politically driven research*. I will group under this label documents produced by governmental institutions or by academic institutions at the request of the government, by international financial institutions, and by major NGOs.

A Ghetto-Shy Terminology

In the case of Romania, the term "ghetto" was absent during the "transition period" (Botonogu et al. 2012), a fact that weighs in policy terms nearly as much as the entire array of anti-exclusion and anti-poverty measures. One recent example, which is an exception, can illustrate how things actually work: the Government of Romania launched a new Anti-Poverty Package in February 2016, and, during the event, one of the prime minister counsellors presented the situation of Aleea Livezilor, the most well-known no-go poverty area inhabited predominantly by Roma in Bucharest, using the word "ghetto". It was possibly the first time the term could be heard in a public meeting in 25 years. He was soon followed by other speakers, including the vice prime minister, who was also in charge with the Minister of Regional Development at that time, who used the same term without hesitation in his speech. It is worth noting that the latter minister, Vasile Dâncu, is a sociologist by trade, so the term "ghetto" is part of his professional jargon. But counting this episode as an acknowledgement of the presence of slums and ghettoes in Romania and as a possible start for a desegregation policy would be too much. The word did not make the news, and it has disappeared from the public scene since then. The plan was designed as "a package" of programmes in which social housing was mentioned as an important area for development, but the projects were only following the idea of ad hoc slum upgrading. Moreover, the National Housing Strategy mentions *ghetto* with quotation marks and explains in a footnote that it is just a "locally used name" and the authors of the document disagree with the use of the term (MRDPA 2016: 72).

Looking back in the same area, one of the official documents that should have tackled exclusion areas, the National Anti-Poverty Plan from 2002, the first of its kind that was created 12 years after the 1989 Revolution when "transition" from socialism started, does not contain the word "ghetto" or any other formula that would acknowledge the presence of impoverished areas with harsh living conditions or that are inhabited predominantly or exclusively by an ethnic group. Housing is, throughout the document, reduced to houses, and the problems identified are the lack of access to housing for "vulnerable groups" in terms of affordability, which is mainly presented as a financial problem of young families, the other major concern being the general degradation of the existing housing market. The document shows that there are too few, too expensive houses, and this is a prefiguration of a housing crisis. Roma are still listed on top of a list that summarizes the problems as a "segment of population" "traditionally confronted with poverty", alongside single-parent families, long-term unemployed, large families, and "disorganized" families. The term "traditional" is not just a candid slip of the tongue or a clumsy attempt to acknowledge the long history of discrimination against the Roma, but a stereotypical interpretation of poverty as a result of a particular culture of poverty, one in which poverty is endlessly reproduced through bad habits. A second category introduces "groups that are confronted with difficult housing situations, though the situations are not necessarily specific to housing" (Romanian Government 2002, Chap. 10, 68), which is comprised of homeless families, homeless children, and youngsters who leave institutions of residential child care after reaching the legal age of adulthood. The third category is formed by young people. For whatever reason, elderly people are not included in this ad hoc typology, but there are several mentions in the document about their vulnerability. In terms of housing, the Anti-Poverty Plan presented six measures: (1) emergency shelters for the homeless and people who lost their houses, estimated at a maximum of 15,000 people, (2) access to cheap housing, which might be social houses but with a strong emphasis on affordable houses that can be bought, (3) the modernization of the housing market through supporting owners and local authorities to invest in their houses,[6] (4) access to public utilities for everybody, (5) identifying new sources of financing construction programmes [sic], and (6) reducing exposure to hazards. The plan manages to hide in plain sight several problems of housing discrimination by focusing on physical degradation and market failure issues and hindering the social exclusion of the new poor and the impact of racism on the life of historically disadvantaged communities.

It is noticeable that officially we never had ghettos. Since the launch of the National Strategy on Social Inclusion and Poverty Reduction 2014–2020 (M.L.F.S.P.E.S.S.I 2015), we now have marginalized communities, and "ghetto type communities" are mentioned as part of the new typology of disadvantaged areas. What makes things less consistent is that the section dedicated to the integration of marginalized urban communities is followed by a section dedicated to the integration of marginalized Roma communities in which the term "ghetto" can no longer be found. However, the typology can be found again in other documents produced with the help of the World Bank. The National Strategy for the Inclusion of the Roma does not even mention marginalized communities but has within its objectives the legalization of informal settlements and the eradication of insalubrious habitats.

Romania's Ghettos

There is a long history of Roma communities cohabiting with different majority groups in Romania, be they Romanians or regional majority groups like Hungarians or, until fairly recent, Germans, and their spatial relationship from the past is what can give us a clue about their present situation. Not all housing areas inhabited by Roma are ghettos, but many of them have enough features that fit most definitions, from the classic perspective of Louis Wirth to its contemporary form that can be found at Wacquant (1997), that is referring to an area inhabited by an ethno-racial group that is excluded by the majority and that develops institutions that can regulate various aspects of community life or mediate with the outer world. Throughout the book, the marginal spaces that are presented as a result of our research did not develop significant parallel economic institutions disconnected from the outside world, but they are rather well integrated into the global capitalism system. Their raise can be explained by the development of capitalism in Romania. In other words, they are on the path to becoming more like the slums of the world than like classic ghettos.

Nevertheless, parallel institutions and ways of living exist in enough Roma communities and a general law of distribution of characteristics can be uttered: the more wealthy a community is, the more it is like a ghetto; the poorer it is, the more like a slum. Stigma is still the first element that governs the territorial relationship between this minority and the majority, and what is particular to Romania is the size and spatial distribution of the communities. While most traits can be attributed to major historical processes, like the slavery of the Roma and the Holocaust, and to general urban policies, like the forced settlement of the nomads and the impact of general housing policies in communist times, there is also a visible recent dynamic of growth that has to do with the processes of transition from socialism to capitalism, like the two interrelated processes of retrocessions of dwellings nationalized by the communist regime and evictions, and the general regime of housing exclusion in neoliberal regimes.

Many of the Romanian urban ghettos and slum areas have their origin in *țigănii*, the places inhabited by Roma slaves, which were slowly pushed over time towards the outskirts as the cities grew. The establishment of Roma slums that followed their liberation in the mid-nineteenth century was only much later followed by their relative modernization, which was brought by the socialist industrialization in the second half of the twentieth century, and a period of slum eradication and forced settlement of the nomads and of some major displacements that had to do with the development of collective housing. The legacy of communism is that of a relatively successful integration, followed by transitional phenomena like privatization and retrocessions. Forced evictions and administrative abandonment would be the main characteristic of the last 25 years, and this led not only to an unprecedented increase of the number of inhabitants but also to the formation of new settlements.

Though the physical configuration of these places varies a lot, their public image appears to be fairly homogeneous, both in terms of racist stereotypes that abound in everyday language or in those of the apparently neutral and rational academic typologies that are present throughout the scientific literature. Stereotypes and typologies are placed at opposite ends of a discursive spectre that tries to circumscribe a coherent (subjective or objective) set of characters under a name, of wrapping what we see on the ground and what we imagine about that particular place in a label.

Roma settlements in Romania are rather small and inconspicuous, and their territorial distribution is quasi-homogeneous. Most of the settlements are in dire condition. The key features that summarize the situation of predominantly Roma settlements affected by extreme poverty housing and spatial exclusion are:

1. Roma slums and ghettos are part of a large phenomenon with historical roots, and they are distributed relatively homogeneously in the country, present in all urban areas and in many rural localities. Based on 2001 Census Data, the total number of ghetto inhabitants might reach 900,000 (Berescu et al. 2006).
2. The housing situation in most of them is disastrous. Living conditions are among the worst in the world.
3. Many of the settlements are placed in marginal areas; often physically and symbolically separated, they are small, affected by informality or illegality and hardly visible.
4. The Roma groups are culturally diverse, and their various social history, language skills, and customs make them less inclined to find a common political position (Berescu et al. 2008).

The typical size of a settlement varies between 200 and 600 inhabitants, very small in comparison with other examples in history or elsewhere in the world, even in the immediate vicinity. In spatial terms, the general view that can be plucked out of the vast body of literature that deals with slums, ghettoes, and other forms of poverty housing or social or ethno-racial exclusion which also fits the Romanian situation is that of an *archipelago*, with the full range of connotations of the geographical term: exoticism, fragmentation, variety of shapes and sizes, a distant, separated world that is disconnected from the mainland. Due to the nature of access to these places and their very limited role in the economy of space in Romania, the public sphere is predictably inclined to use stereotypical views about ghetto-like neighbourhoods (Botonogu 2006). In addition to various physical barriers, there is also a much thinner social interface between the ghetto and the rest of the society.

Our field research led us to compare the dynamics of urban housing in several communities in the town of Ploiești with the situation in four other medium-sized cities. The challenge was to connect a spatial setting with a community profile[7] and at the same time to relate the spatial practices of various Roma groups with the general political views and values of the actors that belong to a dominant group. The result of the comparison led to the conclusion that the ghetto character of a neighbourhood varies from a pure form of hyperghetto, like Primăverii (Tavasz) Street in Miercurea Ciuc—a row of old minuscule metallic barracks with the official status of "social housing" placed near the wastewater plant of the city, which were housing a community that was evicted from the centre, to a calm ethnic settlement like Livada in Călărași, a traditional "spoitori" community, hierarchical, united, and well self-organized, which was in the process of legalizing their previously informal neighbourhood. Even in the same city, such as Ploiești, the dynamic of discrimination and physical decay ranges from very severe instances, like in the workers' dormitories of Mimiu, a place where water was fetched by children from a tap that was 250 m away from the derelict block of flats, to positive trends of improvement in several areas of Bereasca, an ethnically mixed neighbourhood with virtually no difference in terms of housing standards, public utilities, or appearance. There are also places where you can observe all forms and qualities of living conditions, like in Valea Rece (Hidegvölgy) in Târgu Mureș, or even more complex areas that house several distinct communities with very different histories and interests, like the dramatic and internationally famous garbage pit settlement of Pata Rât, near Cluj-Napoca. Labelling all of them as ghettos would be more of a political act than the result of applying a scientific methodology; however, *not labelling* them as ghettos is also a political act that has the precise role of concealing the severe situation of a very large number of Roma communities in contemporary Romania and to disguise the general and administrative racism as ethnically oriented interventions.

Typologies of Roma Housing Areas

The ethnic enclaves of today are strictly descended from the colonies and ghettos of yesterday, and their mixed and often uncertain status makes it often difficult to categorize them either as pure forms of segregation or ideal forms of aggregation. Both perspectives are at the end of a spectrum that opposes, and sometimes reunites, ad hoc visions that emerge following various debates that take place regularly in the confused arena of European administration, where human rights activists, policymakers, and community representatives sometimes discuss "what has to be done". However popular these ideal types might be amongst different political actors, and therefore widely used in discourses that cover the full range between racist and anti-racist speeches, and no matter how many calls for integration from socially aware individuals or the opposite arguments for separation—which originate not only from the classic advocates of exclusion but also from a more recent and vivid search for autonomy that is practised by many Roma activists—we have to acknowledge that the situation on the ground is frequently contradictory and fluid, and any essentialist view is hampered by a mix of factors, by a sum of features that are perceived as contradictory or, at least, non-unitary.

The places of symbolic exclusion do not overlap with the places of physical exclusion. One can easily notice how stigma usually spreads from the ghetto to the surrounding impoverished neighbourhoods, and how the divisions inside the groups that inhabit excluded areas are frequently underestimated or ignored. It is mainly tragedies and success stories that tend to dominate the regimes of representation and ultimately justify the choice for interventions, which use as key terms the ideas of "emergency", "charity", and "pilot programs". This "acupunctural" philosophy of intervention, which essentially states that you only need to start a process that will further self-replicate or to break the famous circle of poverty, is what hinders mainstream policies, if not stopping them at all. If we are to focus on recent housing policies, we notice the strange convergence between the pro- and anti-Roma positions that appear to lead to the construction of new ghettos using European funding.

In this context, the use of typologies has its specific sociolinguistic setting. What makes it remarkable is its occasional presence in documents that aim to produce change: policy papers, reports, planning documents, methodologies of intervention, documents ideologically charged. What they share is that many of them have a weak or absent theoretical dimension, a fact that we are used to and that appears to be natural for a policy paper, a tacit convention that assumes that the explanatory part of a policy is brief and, in the case of Roma policies, also contemptuous. There is a visible gap between a sociological paper and an international NGO report even when they have the same author. But in a world where these pieces of literature coexist and in which the governmental papers are often produced by authors who usually have also academic engagements, it is hard to draw a line between the kind of knowledge that is produced in an academic context and will be scrutinized by a virtually infinite number of qualified reviewers and papers that are destined to validate various policies at a specific point in time.

The immediate purpose of a typology is to help us identify settlements, count them, and group them in a meaningful and pragmatic way. Whether this reflects a reality or it is just a tool to control and manipulate it is particular to each case, and it raises the question of whether it can have its own performative value. "Roma impoverished neighbourhood", for example, is a term that aims to combine the ideal type of the ghetto with the non-racialized "impoverished neighbourhood". In various contexts, and specifically in Romania, the essentialist idea of a Roma housing area inhabited by a compact community with a strong cultural identity, can take numerous forms. Though mainly used by activists and researchers as a tool to identify a ghetto and to fight exclusion and other forms of housing discrimination, it is sometimes embraced by local actors or activists as a positive feature and used to maintain control over a territory. If we assume that the practices of urban planners reflect the views of the society, then we should not underestimate how the options of the minority group or at least of its most prominent members influence policies. "But it is their choice to live separately!" is what you can hear when you question a housing solution that reinforces physical separation. What can be found is that new forms of exclusion are occasionally disguised as integration and that in urban policies this takes its most obvious forms. The contemporary ghetto nowadays is a process, not a product, surrounded by an ideological context. While characterized by fluidity and determined by soft forms of racism, it is primarily defined by its history and shaped by contemporary practices.

My interest in typologies originated in the first study that my university did for the Romanian Ministry of Development, which aimed to identify types of housing specific to Roma and used the identified features in order to guide architects and planners in their effort to produce what we now call "culturally adequate" houses. The research theme and the title—Types of Housing in Roma Communities—were defined by the ministry, so the hypothesis was already built in. After an enthusiastic tour of the slums and ghettos around the country, and after collecting numerous examples from many other impoverished settlements throughout the world, the first conclusion that we presented to our colleagues from the ministerial commission was that there are no such housing types that are related to ethnicity, but, rather, more like universal strategies of survival in settings of extreme poverty that produce the same very simple shelters throughout history and across various geographical spaces (Berescu et al. 2006). That challenged the dominant perspective about Roma, which was mainly informed by the more visible, picturesque images of the "Tsigane palaces". Roma people do not need colourful houses, and they do not sleep in the kitchen because of their cultural heritage. Their houses will look like Romanian poor houses in the countryside and like South African shelters in the cities.

What differs among such settlements across the world is the adaptation to climate and the use of local materials; however, the organization of space and the dimensional variation is minimal. Very poor people do not have enough resources to express their culture in their shelters; they are constrained so hard by the lack of security, lack of resources, and daily hardships that they are compelled to produce a basic shelter that is, in many respects, a universal, atemporal housing device.

We finally produced a loose, weak typology for the paper from 2004 that aimed to provide minimum guidance for identifying and generally classifying spaces inhabited by communities, not houses or cultures of living. The only aim was to provide a background for a variety of policy interventions, as opposed to the ethnically driven programmes that were and are still in place. There were six types that were introduced, defined, and for which examples were given, three urban and three rural. The first urban type was "the centre communities", small enclaves in historic centres, inhabited by populations with urban background and urban lifestyle, affected by overcrowding and always under threat of eviction. The second was a "block of flats" type that was created by the transformation of former workers' dormitories in urban ghettos, and the third type, the "peri-urban", very much part of the city, was usually an informal development that develops around the recycling industry. For the rural situations, we defined three types. The first was a "para-rural" type, referring to scattered groups of houses within the main tissue of the locality. The second was the "peri-rural", extensions that do not benefit from the same conditions as the rest of the community; though they are officially part of the village, it is often that the road suddenly becomes a dirt path and the electricity network vanishes before reaching the last houses. Many of those places have a history of conflict with the majority. The last type was the so-called autonomous communities, completely separated bodies that, even extant for a long time, can be rarely found on an official plan.

Another example of a typology, and probably the one that stays at the origin of the current Atlas of Marginalized Areas in Romania (Swinkles et al. 2015), comes from a collective volume on extreme poverty in Romania from 2004, coordinated by Manuela Stanculescu and Ionica Berevoiescu (2004), the first dedicated to the subject during the transition period. The chapter that describes housing proposes a classification of seven types of urban areas with "concentrated poverty", three in residential areas and four in blocks of flats as follows: (a) semirural, (b) garbage pits, (c) "Cotorga type"—a combination of the semi-rural settlement and garbage pit with improvised shelters, taking its name from an old neighbourhood in Roșiorii de Vede, (d) historical centre multifamily, formerly nationalised houses, (e) areas popularly named ghettos (*nota bene*, not named by the researcher, just a given name), (f) blocks in dilapidated industrial areas, and (g) blocks of flats with major debts. All of them are detailed in a short paragraph that describes in several words a historical development or process, the physical state of the buildings, and the urban equipment and utilities. We should keep in mind that the book is written to the general public in an attempt to share the findings of two research projects that took place in previous years. The naming has a genuine quality; though it looks almost like a naïve description, it gives you, as a Romanian reader, precisely the clue that you need to identify the area. But why would an experienced researcher[8] use such less technical, ambiguous terminology? What is the function of such a candid epistemic set? The answer lies again not just in the complex nature of the objects but in the need to preserve the ingenuity, the idiomatic quality of representation through language that would conserve and further transmit the shock of the discovery of these poverty-stricken areas. We should also notice that this also takes away the temptation to use strong labels. The power of the expression "Cotorga type", for example, rests in the fact that it postpones the judgement on those areas but keeps your attention attuned to them specifically.

Writing under the constraints of an official document, a team of researchers that also includes Stănculescu created a simpler, but still open to interpretation, set of terms in order to denominate poverty-stricken urban zones. The Atlas of Urban Marginalized Zones of Romania (Swinkels et al. 2015), produced by the World Bank for the Ministry of Regional Development and Public Administration in 2013 and officially launched in 2015, and its counterpart, the Atlas of Rural Marginalized Zones and Human Development (Teșliuc et al. 2016), produced for Ministry of Employment, Family, Social Protection and the Elderly and released in 2016, have both a classification of area types that in fact should form the basis for the national policies in the coming years.

In this classification, urban zones are divided into six types, the first two being the "ghetto" type, defined as a result of the dilapidation of the former workers' dormitories or colonies, the first ones in blocks of flats, the second in smaller derelict, almost dangerous buildings that could only be described by indicating a picture on the same page of the document. The third and the fourth are the "mahala" and "improvised shelter" type, old neighbourhoods with substandard houses inhabited mostly, but not exclusively, by Roma and sometimes affected by informality and, again, the same mahala but with improvised shelters. A fifth type is that of the "modernized social housing units", created through integrated projects. They are characterized by the fact that the inhabitants are not able to pay their basic utilities and, by segregation, as they are usually the result of the relocation of the poor outside the city. The sixth is the "historical centre" type, formerly nationalized houses, used as social housing and now retrocessed, occupied by smaller communities and often in an advanced state of physical degradation.

After listing a large number of urban areas, the Atlas ends with a number of annexes in which the typology is further refined, and the numbers are gathered in several tables. Marginalized areas are now a division of a larger typology of disadvantaged areas with three parts: first is "zones with reduced access to infrastructure", second is "economically disadvantaged zones", and third is "marginalized zones". The idea is that the first one has housing problems, but the employment situation is good and the human capital is variable; the second type has employment issues, but human capital is fine and housing has a variable quality; and the third has problems in every aspect. All of them have a variable ethnic composition. The number of areas can be retrieved in Appendix 5 of the Atlas (Swinkles et al. 2015, 263), which groups the census areas according to this typology (Table 7.1).

Table 7.1 Typology of disadvantaged urban areas in the *Atlas of marginalized urban zones* issued by the World Bank and the Romanian government

Low human capital	Precarious housing	Low level of employment		Total
		No	Yes	
No	No	34,495	4706	
No	Yes	2134	405	
Yes	No	1769	3463	
Yes	Yes	287	1130	
Total		38.685	9713	48,398
Sectors with fewer than 50 inhabitants				1901
Total census sectors in urban areas				50,299

Source: Swinkles et al. (2015, 263)
Non-disadvantaged Area = 34,495
Housing disadvantaged Area = 2134 + 287 = 2421
Employment disadvantaged Area = 4706 + 405 = 5111
Human Capital Disadvantaged Area = 1769 + 3463 = 5232
Marginalized Area = 1130
Other Areas = 1901

There is no physical map to tell how many of the zones are contiguous, but we can safely assume that most of them are distinct. This indicates around 1100 areas that might be urban ghettos and about 400 dilapidated impoverished areas. Another 287 are areas with working, uneducated poor people living in bad housing conditions, and more than 2100 are just substandard and underequipped. It is impossible to say which areas are slums and which are ghettos, not only because 'ghetto' was defined as a dilapidated area, but also because the Roma are reported as just 30.8% of the population of marginalized areas, out of a total urban population of marginalized inhabitants of 342,922 persons.

The most recent study that tells us about marginalized areas using a scale is SocioRoMap (Horvath 2017), a product of a two-year long research done by a collective from the Romanian Institute for Research on National Minorities from Cluj, an institution under the authority of the Romanian government. The project aimed to do a mapping of the Roma communities and to monitor changes in regard to Roma integration at a local level, so the main criterion is the ethnic one.

The total number of "compact Roma communities" found was 2315, living in a number of 1661 localities and consisting of 177,525 households. A further analysis breaks down the numbers using different criteria that were defined by the questionnaire that was applied. We can find that just 35 settlements are "difficult to access". The authors avoid the term segregation because of insufficient data. Around 44 communities appear to be situated at a seriously large distance from public utilities, but a total of 145 are disadvantaged in terms of access to schools and another 557 are at a "significant distance" (15–30 minutes). According to the authors, an indicator of ghettoization was revealed by the social isolation of the community with a question related to stigma. This revealed 344 communities that were considered *no go* areas. As a synthesis, after creating a scale that combined the criteria, 58 communities were classified as marginalized, 356 "relatively peripheral", and 1115 "with minor signs of social and spatial differentiation". "Marginalized" is used here in an exclusively spatial meaning. Moving forward to the quality of housing, we can find that almost half of the communities are affected by severe overcrowding and another third by moderate overcrowding (higher than the national average). A last synthetic indicator follows inadequate housing, split into "pronounced precariousness"—382 communities; "precariousness"—701 communities; and "visible poverty"—390 communities. A total of 1473 communities appear to have serious housing issues, and an extra 200 are reported to have infrastructure problems.

The two studies are a major step forward from the lack of data in recent years; unfortunately, they manage to expose the existence of either "marginality" or "Roma" in a way that makes sense within the limits of their own study. A solution to advanced marginality (Wacquant) cannot be found as long as the object of study is divided into various categories of precariousness—which, of course, trigger the call for development—and circumvent the problem of racial exclusion through the use of split indicators. After all, the "Cotorga type" approach may tell us how many ghettos we can count, which is a political problem, while the marginalized areas methodology is only able to show where less-educated people with no jobs live in bad houses.

Conclusions

If the use of typologies in policy documents has the general purpose of creating a meaningful connection between a particular form of reality and an intervention that aims to deal with it, then the first thing that must come out of it should be *a number*, no matter how low, or how high, or how accurate, but one that would reflect the existence of *extreme poverty ethnic settlements*. All these documents have an analytical part and a proposal for action, sometimes intertwined but easily identifiable within the text. The analytical parts are usually well informed by academic research, but there is an inconsistent and imprecise use of the term "ghetto" and a weak correlation with both its political meaning and the policies that might be developed based on the research.

The actual failure of proper public policies takes different forms. First is the lack of explicit policy; that is, simply there is no public policy to fight residential segregation. Second is the preference for very vague policies that have to do with general development, but combating marginalization by improving infrastructure will never desegregate a ghetto; in fact, it might actually reinforce its character or just replace it with a regular housing area while the actual ghetto is moved in another location. A third one has to do with the ridiculously small volume of the interventions combined with huge delays in the implementation of the development projects.

Whenever money is going to be spent, the language tends to become imprecise. It does so in a process that starts with an academic paper and ends with an administrative one. Any typology serves a political need, and, if it doesn't, it will just stay in academia.

The critique of semi-official and official reports and studies can be summarized as such: lavishly printed on heavy paper and adorned with numerous logos of major institutions, they always have a disclaimer that states the fact that the document does not necessarily represent the position of the institutions that were part of the project; this is the perfect illustration of the way in which ghettos were formed, are concealed, and will be governed.

Notes

1. "Urban form" is a classic term in urbanism, as "social form" is in sociology. This chapter deals less with the meaning of marginal spaces but more with the way the various forms they can take are used in policy documents and in the studies that precede them. The aim is to analyse the interplay of the terms that are used to operationalize interventions seen as a mechanism that is part of the process of formation and management of marginal areas.
2. In particular, the rural/urban administrative dualism creates an intermediate, sometimes residual urban space that is exactly where informal impoverished neighbourhoods flourish.
3. This is the expression used in the title of a ministerial methodology that was commissioned by the Romanian Ministry of Development in 2008 and that aimed at the improvement of Roma slums and ghettos.
4. See, for example, ZUS—*Zone Urbaine Sensible* in the French planning vocabulary or ZUM—*Zona Urbana Marginalizata* in the Romanian Atlas of Marginalized Areas (Swinkles et al. 2015).
5. Here we are, back again, at the challenge to find an acceptable overarching term for an object of research that is best circumscribed by an extensional definition, and sometimes needs to be helped by an ostensible one, which is the reason why most of the papers we analysed have pictures. We use here "Roma neighbourhoods" as a short form for "Central and East European

Roma neighbourhoods that are inhabited predominantly by Roma but sometimes heavily mixed and that can be slums, ghettos and, more rarely, ethnic group settlements". The derogatory term "Țigănii" is also very useful, as it strongly indicates both the existence of discrimination and the process of racialization.
6. Romania has 98% private ownership in housing out of which 96% are owner-occupied. Source: http://ec.europa.eu/eurostat/statistics-explained/index.php/File:Distribution_of_population_by_tenure_status,_2014_(%25_of_population)_YB16.png
7. Community profile is a term in use in many countries around the world in planning activities and it is an obligatory part of any action plan. It refers to a basic collection of data and an opinion survey about issues related to that area.
8. Manuela S. Stănculescu is a top researcher that works for the Romanian Research Institute for Quality of Life, and one of the leading experts that collaborates with World Bank Romania.

References

Berescu, Cătălin, and Maria Celac. 2006. *Housing and Extreme Poverty*. Bucharest: Ion Mincu Architectural Press.
Berescu, Cătălin, Maria Celac, Florin Botonogu, and A. Bălteanu. 2008. *Metodologie de îmbunătățire a calității locuirii în zone afectate de sărăcie și excluziune socială*. Bucharest: Ministry of Regional Development and Public Administration.
Botonogu, Florin, et al. 2012. *Comunități ascunse: Ferentari [Hidden Communities. Ferentari]*. Bucharest: Expert Publishing House.
Catană, A., C. Fălan, and V. Ștefănescu. 2012. *Impactul fondurilor Structural asupra comunităților sărace*. București: RCR Editorial.
Delepine, Samuel. 2007. *Quartiers Tsiganes. L'habitat et le logement des Rroms de Roumanie en question*. Paris: L'Harmattan.
Horváth, István, ed. 2017. *Raport de cercetare SocioRoMap. O cartografiere a comunităților de romi*. Cluj-Napoca: Institutul pentru Studierea Problemelor Minorităților Naționale.
Kolev, Deyan, M. Metodieva, S. Panayotov, G. Bogdanov, and T. Krumova. 2010. Annual Report. In *Roma Integration in Bulgaria 2007–2008*. Plovdiv: ACTAPTA.

Ministry of Labour, Family, Social Protection and Elderly, State Secretariat for Social Inclusion. 2015. *National Strategy on Social Inclusion and Poverty Reduction 2014–2020*. Bucharest: The Romanian Government.

Ministry of Regional Development and Public Administration. 2016. *National Strategy for Housing*. Bucharest: The Romanian Government. http://www.mmediu.ro/app/webroot/uploads/files/2017-01-13_Strategia_Nationala_a_Locuirii_2016-2030.pdf, accessed 01.02.2018.

Romanian Government. 2002. Planul Național Anti-Sărăcie și Promovarea Incluziunii Sociale (National Anti-Poverty and Social Inclusion Plan). Retrieved from http://gov.ro/ro/obiective/strategii-politici-programe/planul-national-anti-saracie-i-promovare-a-incluziunii-sociale&page=2

Romanian Government. 2014. *Strategia Guvernului României de incluziunea a cetățenilor români aparținînd minorității rome 2014–2020 (The National Strategy for the Inclusion of the Roma 2014–2020)*. Bucharest: The Romanian Government.

Roma National Strategy Secretariat. 2007. *Challenges of the Roma Decade*. Belgrade: Agency for Human and Minority Rights.

Rughiniș, Cosima. 2004. *Social Housing and Roma Residents in Romania*. Budapest: Central European University.

Stănculescu, Manuela S., and Ionica Berevoiescu. 2004. *Sărac lipit, caut altă viață*. Bucharest: Nemira.

Stambuk, M. 2005. *How Do Croatian Roma Live?* Zagreb: Ivo Pilar Institute.

Swinkels, R., M.S. Stănculescu, S. Anton, B. Koo, T. Man, and C. Moldovan. 2015. *Atlasul zonelor urbane marginalizate din România (The Atlas of Urban Marginalized Areas and of Local Human Development in Romania)*. Bucharest: Ministry of Regional Development and Public Administration.

Teșliuc, Emil, Vlad Grigoraș, and Manuela Stănculescu. 2016. *The Atlas of Rural Marginalized Areas and of Local Human Development in Romania*. Bucharest: World Bank and the Ministry of Labour, Family, Social Protection, and the Elderly.

Wacquant, Loic. 1997. *Three Pernicious Premises in the Study of the American Ghetto*. Oxford: Blackwell Publishers.

8

Conclusion: (Re)centring Labour, Class, and Race

Giovanni Picker

Introduction

In his critical intervention on Mike Davis' (2004) *Planet of Slums*, Tom Angotti (2006) exposes one of the possible pitfalls of research on the urban margins. Davis' noir-like and apocalyptic language depicting urban decay and climate threats, Angotti maintains, "feeds into longstanding anti-urban fears about working people who live in cities" (2006, 961). The six chapters of *Racialized Labour in Romania* firmly distance themselves from apocalyptic tones and narratives of threat. Instead, they account for a twofold sensitive oscillation, at once in terms of research approach, that is, between empirical embeddedness and theoretical

---

I wish to thank Enikő Vincze and Cristina Raț for their sharp insights into an earlier draft. This project has received funding from the European Union's Horizon 2020 research and innovation programme under the Marie Sklodowska-Curie grant agreement No. 661646

G. Picker (✉)
Department of Social Policy, Sociology and Criminology,
University of Birmingham, Birmingham, UK

distance, and in terms of sociological processes, that is, between global and local social arrangements.

As a matter of fact, and an issue Angotti acknowledges, Davis' analysis remarkably contextualizes the formation of marginalized urban areas within the making of post-1970s global capitalism and connects it to long-lasting colonial legacies. This point reapproaches *Planet of Slums* to *Racialized Labour in Romania*, as both strive to shed a sharp light on some of the impacts of global capitalism on peripheral urban spaces. And yet, indeed, the six chapters of the present volume seem to have a better capacity than *Planet of Slums* not only in avoiding apocalyptic tones, but in simultaneously focusing on the connections between labour organization, class formation, and processes of racial stigmatization.

This has arguably been possible due to both in-depth field-based research and a special attention granted to racializing processes, two gestures largely absent in Davis' otherwise seminal book. As discussed in Chap. 1 to *Racialized Labour in Romania* (hereafter "RLR"), opposite to "feeding into anti-urban fears," the six chapters continue some of the conversations started by critical geographers in the 1980s. In bringing those conversations close to more recent anthropological reflections on global capitalism, labour, and class divisions, the six analyses uncover the ways in which twenty-first-century capitalism does not actually *exclude* (in the literal sense), but rather *includes* (with a productive function), low-skilled and unskilled labour into accumulation processes, primarily by means of racialized and racializing material dispossession and spatial isolation. The six empirical analyses and the preceding Introduction have shown the importance of keeping a relational approach to labour, class, and race conjointly. These three phenomena can be summarized as follows.

1. *Labour organization* at present entails: lack of unionism; de-socializing the social bound deriving from the workplace; the production of a subaltern class of workers primarily employed in cleaning and other low-skill services, such as collection of recyclable waste (plastic, scrap metal, etc.); increased facility of capital to cross borders that brought forth the establishment, especially in the periphery and semiperiphery, of international companies exploiting cheap(er) labour; reduction of a number of jobs due to hyper-financialization; consequent increasing

competition for jobs, low-paid and unpaid contracts, and day labour especially in the agricultural sector. These conditions lie at the core of contemporary labour market restructuring in Central and Eastern Europe and beyond.
2. *Class formation* refers to mechanisms of social reproduction of the structure of opportunity for employment and education; processes of spatial containment, confinement and isolation, largely leading residents of destitute areas to getting stuck at the bottom of the social ladder. These conditions are likely to remain in place so long as employment, education and housing remain scarce resources.
3. *Racial domination* operates as a vehicle for the previous two. Why are Roma overrepresented to an astonishing extent in (a) lower social class positions, (b) low-waged and unwaged labour, and (c) urban segregated territories? As Chap. 2 clearly showed, the twofold legacy of the "capitalist transition"—labour market organization and urban spatial seclusion of Roma—are fundamental. But the question "Why the Roma?" remains. The Introduction explained in a very comprehensive way that the 500 years of Roma slavery in Romania is a fundamental condition for understanding exclusion and exploitation in the twenty-first century. And slavery, as much as serfdom and other forms of subjugation, including unwaged and underpaid jobs, deeply relies on the historically constituted racial conception of moral worth.[1]

Wrapped within an encompassing sociological imagination, specific foci on political economy (Chaps. 2 and 3), labour law and the welfare state (Chaps. 4 and 5), and cultural processes (Chaps. 6 and 7)—all in conversation with each other—compose a multidimensional study, which ultimately strives for rethinking the analysis of global capitalism in the twenty-first century. The precise theoretical reasoning that sustains the empirical work (see Introduction) suggests not just a generic, but a precise rethinking—one which squarely (re)centres class, labour, and race in social research and practice.

Over the last 20 years, the literature on global racial inequalities, while uncovering global relations and comparisons, seems to have largely overlooked the varied and variable intersections of two main issues, namely (a) the role of class formation and labour organization (two processes that seem to often emerge as epiphenomena, rather than structuring forces, of racial hierarchies and racialization processes), and (b) the urban dimension and especially its socio-spatial organization (privileging, instead, national and supranational units of analysis). By contrast, RLR shows the importance of including these two issues—class and labour, and the city—which the six chapters not only foreground, but also connect to each other.

The task of this concluding chapter is to discuss this twofold contribution and to suggest ways forward in the research on intersections of class, labour, and race, especially in urban areas. I will first position RLR within the literature on racial inequalities globally; in the process, I will refer to how each of the six chapters innovatively engages with the class-labour-race complex. I will subsequently zoom out of Romanian localities to identify connections between them and cities across the urban global North and South; in this regard, the five Romanian cities and their marginalized areas will emerge as concretions of both global capital *and* global capitalism, insofar as the formation and maintenance of these urban areas—as the Introduction made clear—is made possible by the combination of socio-economic dispossession (i.e., capital) and local variations of capital accumulation strategies (i.e., capitalism).

This zooming out gesture not only shows the square embeddedness of the Romanian case within global processes of labour organization, class formation, and racial domination, but also underlines the importance of focusing on contingent local dynamics for studying global social processes relationally (Burawoy 2000; Simone 2004). In the final section of the chapter I will propose some key lines of further research, with special regard to relational and global sociologies.[2]

Racial Globalization and Cities

One of the key legacies of the World System framework has been the study of race from global and comparative perspectives. Over the last two decades, numerous scholars have proposed sharp analyses of this kind. Interestingly, their work has largely remained on a national or supranational scale, virtually never systematically approaching the urban dimension, where processes of economic dispossession and dehumanization (i.e., racialization) clash and combine in particularly brutal ways. Relatedly, these studies have remarkably distanced themselves from a systematic analytics of labour exploitation, class formation, land expropriation, and hyper-financialization. At the other end of the spectrum, in this sense, Polanyi's (1944) fundamental contribution in considering labour, money, and land as the core of the capitalist system curiously lacks reference to logics of human hierarchization and wealth distribution such as race.

The study of racial formations globally has provided a pivotal understanding of race across national and supranational polities. In his reflections on multiple racial formations—that is, racial Europeanization, racial Latinamericanization, racial Americanization, and racial Palestinization—Goldberg (2009) has provided insightful analytical declinations of global racial inequalities and different racist exclusionary processes. One logical extension of Goldberg's research agenda, it can be argued, is to think in terms of "racial globalization." Would this, however, be possible without foregrounding the various crystallizations of racist exclusions and their intertwining with global flows of capital, goods, and people in precise local contexts? Elsewhere, the author (Goldberg 1993) has concisely excavated the connections between colonial and postcolonial urban planning and racial hierarchies across Africa, the United States, and Europe. This latter work, therefore, although not foregrounding processes of capitalist accumulation and dispossession, becomes a key reference for considering the urban dimension in research on racialized labour and spaces of marginality globally.

Another fundamental reflection on the global spread of race is Winant's (2001, 2004) comprehensive social history. His work is perhaps more than anyone else's rooted in the projects of colonial expansion to the extent that he identifies in capitalism and nation-building the two main conditions under which race became a major organizing principle and social structure of the world, shaping the North-South socio-economic steep inequalities. Labour, in Winant's analysis, becomes essential: "Between slavery and peonage, and between peonage and 'free labour', there was in practice (and remains today) a continuum, a spectrum, rather than a clear-cut, formal distinction [...] slavery was the linchpin, the core activity, in the creation of modern world economy" (Winant 2001, 25, 27).

This continuum, this spectrum, however, does not only concern forms of labour but extends to temporal connections. There is a logical and ideological connection between the five centuries of white colonial domination and contemporary global flows, and this connection is related to land and labour:

> Today soy cultivation in Brazil, oil extraction in Cabinda and the Ogoni region, and labour practices in Ciudad Juarez, or Calcutta, are matters of concern in corporate headquarters in St. Louis and New York, as well as on Wall Street and at the IMF headquarters in Washington. (2004, 134)

In this regard, the author relates to RLR insofar as, as the Introduction made clear by referring to Subaltern Studies and Decolonial Studies, the five cities are understood within a global and *longue durée* perspective. Echoing Gregory's (2004) global geography of contemporary colonial practices, Winant (2001, 2004) firmly grounds his global history of race onto the making of class formation and labour exploitation. While decisively comprehensive, however, the work overlooks the urban socio-spatial dimension as a chief medium of these political-economic processes.

The socio-spatial dimension is at the core of another global history of racial formations. Nightingale's (2012) pioneering study of racial segregation globally is the first work of this kind. While remarkably surveying the major colonial and postcolonial planning endeavours that resulted in segregated local arrangements, however, the work leaves labour organization and class formation, and more generally political economy, in the background. It would be probably impossible to impute this to a lack of empirical material, as the author provides a significant amount of data. It is, however, outstanding that, while land and urban space occupy the front stage, labour and class remain, though considered, not thoroughly discussed.

Finally, Wolfe's (2016) seminal work on racial structures globally contextualizes different "regimes of difference with which colonizers have sought to manage subject populations" (Wolfe 2016, 3) in a multistate framework—Australia, United States, Central Europe, Brazil and Palestine. In dissecting the ways in which race's versatility paves the way for various types of domination, Wolfe provides a compelling global overview. However, after acknowledging the primacy of labour exploitation and land expropriation as the founding principles of race during the Enlightenment (for example, in John Locke's philosophy), the author soon diverges to a conception of race as an ideology rather independent from processes of labour and class: "Thus race is not a negotiable condition but a destiny, one whose principal outward sign is the body. In systematically harnessing social hierarchies to natural essences and recruiting physical characteristics to underwrite the scheme, race constitutes an ideology in the purest of senses" (Wolfe 2016, 7).

RLR sits originally within these global perspectives on race. Not only because it shows multiple intersections of labour, class, race, urban governance, spatial isolation, and gentrification, but also because it considers these processes within the global circulation of capital, from the perspective of Romania, a semi-peripheral national economy. In addition, RLR discusses a country in a global region—Central and Eastern Europe—which is typically overlooked in global and comparative studies of racial formations (Law 2012).

Hence, Norbert Petrovici's (Chap. 2) socio-historical analysis of the formation of our researched urban areas over the last 25 years shows that most of the inhabitants were actually born in these areas. This means that the most common reason why they are still living there is that they lost their jobs in the 1990s and remained trapped in those areas. Today, far from being useless "pockets of poverty," as these urban areas are often described in the media and in policy documents, they are useful providers of cheap and unregulated labour. Moreover, as Cristina Raț, Enikő Vincze, and Anca Simionca explain, their labour is not only consistently underpaid but also often unrecognized; and in the context of recent and current neoliberalization of the welfare state, these labour-intensive families are left with highly inconsistent and intermittent social support, and the resulting socio-economic precarization leaves them with very little chance to obtain regular job contracts.

Moreover, as Enikő Vincze (Chap. 3) makes clear, the privatization of the public housing fund, the commodification of housing by developers supported by the state, and the pauperization and precarization of the labour force, who are pushed to find cheap housing at the urban margins, become key conditions for ghettoization and spatial seclusion. What the author calls "hidden politics of destitution" is the state's strategic omission of housing reconstruction and maintenance, within the current privatization, marketization, and hyper-financialization of housing and land. This occurs in line with the dominant idea, shared by policymakers and economic elites, that the inhabitants of marginal spaces are somehow "less human than their fellow citizens." Racialization, therefore, emerges as a process of inferiorization of Roma ethnicity, poverty, and precarious spaces, and as the discursive construction of moral (un)worthiness—a point which also Simionca uncovers. And, as Orsolya Vincze discusses in Chap. 5, such a racist discursive construction is also widespread in local media. For example, deploying narratives about "Roma" as different from "citizens" forms a divide that clearly becomes useful for maintaining conditions of segregation and material destitution. This is consistent with the general lack of contextualization in the media discourse on these areas, and within economic and political processes privileging instead the individualizing narratives of urban marginality.

Media representations may also become a source, rather than an analytical object, of academic studies. This is sometimes the case when it comes to the various nouns attached to destituted and segregated urban areas, such as those under scrutiny in this book. Berescu's point about the ambivalence and typical lack of rigour in deploying the nouns "ghetto" and "ghettoization" sheds an important light on how such ambivalence often plays into situated processes of stigmatization and racialization of peripheral urban locations. Finally, the value of approaching processes of dispossession and labour racialization from a joint political-economic and cultural perspective becomes even clearer in Chap. 7, by Simionca, which is devoted to imaginaries of urban development within institutional narratives. In all five cities under scrutiny, the dominant visions of urban development revolve around both the centrality of foreign investments and a very specific idea of a worker. The ideal worker who, according to policy and economic elites, would contribute to the success of the urban economy is the hyper-flexible, hyper-productive, and fully "employable" subject. To this ideal, the imagined Roma stands out as the perfect antithesis—racist idioms relating to a corrupted work ethic become the vehicle for constructing the "unproductive" Roma subject.

In (re)centring labour, class, and race, the six empirical chapters build an integrated analysis, which sits originally within contemporary studies of racial formations globally. Its contribution also rests on a focus on local, rather than national or supranational, contexts.

Conclusion: (Re)centring Labour, Class, and Race   215

Local Concretions of Global Capitalism

So far, I have situated the six empirical analyses within recent studies of race globally. In accounting for the linkages between racialized labour, class reproduction, and spaces of marginality in a number of medium-size and small urban centres, as I showed, RLR stresses the importance of keeping a multidimensional approach to twenty-first-century processes of racialized dispossession and spatial relegation; an approach which, rather than compartmentalized and fragmented, integrates political economy, culture, and law and policy towards analysing the various ways in which class, labour, and race intersect in the making and reproduction of various forms of subjugation and dispossession. These diverse yet tightly connected processes account for situated intersections of global and local socio-economic dynamics. In this regard, RLR does not only provide the case of a country, which, as discussed, sits originally in the landscape of a global analysis of race, but also the case of specific types of urbanism.

The five cities can indeed be viewed as urban formations in connection with key dynamics of twenty-first-century global capitalism, such as massive privatization and decentralization of means of production, de-socialization of labour (i.e., disempowerment of unions), cutbacks in public spending for social care, and financialization of housing (Rolnik 2013; Sassen 2014).[3] Crucially, one of the impacts of these global dynamics is the global increase, from 1990 to 2014, of the size of slum populations by about one-third—from 689 million to 881 million (UN-HABITAT 2016a); related trends are the multiplication of confined dwelling arrangements among the urban poor (ibidem), the highest number of displaced people since World War II, that is, more than 65 million (UNHCR 2017), and steep inequalities in real wage growth between developing and developed countries (ILO 2017). In this global context, it becomes heuristic to outline similarities between dynamics in RLR's five cities and in other urban locations across the globe. This is the task of this section.

A premise, however, feels necessary. As discussed in the Introduction, we consider the case of stigmatized and deprived areas as "peripheral" concretions of global capitalism. While Romania—just as Central and Eastern

Europe more generally—is considered to be in the "semi-periphery" (Wallerstein 1974), we contend, and support with empirical evidence, that these areas constitute "periphery" formations within one "semi-peripheral" national context.

The centre-periphery distinction was first introduced in order to account for the organizing logic of global capitalism in a time of major political and economic transformations, primarily due to decolonization and the making of renewed geopolitical balances. The global perspective that such a distinction provided was a major novelty in the political-economy literature of the 1960s, which typically took the nation state as the only unit of analysis. Considering the post–World War II emergence of global neoliberal doctrines, which were drawing on economic ideas from the 1940s—first implemented nationally in the West by Thatcher and Reagan in the late 1970s and early 1980s, and bearing tough consequences in the twenty-first century (Hall et al. 2015; Hilgers 2012)—Wallerstein's global framework becomes particularly helpful. At the same time, it can be used with a certain degree of adaptability, for instance in considering the concept of periphery as an ideal type, as heuristic for looking at socio-economic arrangements on the urban, in addition to the national, scale.

Hence, the value of building cross-national and cross-urban linkages and comparisons between peripheral forms of urbanism is not merely analytical. By structuring a sharp gaze on marginalized territories, racialized labour, and dispossession processes across the tiers of global capitalism, I maintain, a deeper knowledge of the common features of these phenomena can be gained. Such deeper knowledge will be able, in turn, to engage not only in further research venues and topics—a point I will discuss in the next section—but also in transformative analyses and actions.

One important work which accounts for global capital's connections with labour, class, and spatial confinement is Buckley's (2012) study of Dubai's construction labour force governance. Since the mid-2000s, charities and corporate social responsibility activities provide a private welfare to the massive number of migrant workers in the "autocratic city." By focusing exclusively on workers' bodies in view of maintaining a "body capital," the author contends, these organizations contribute to the persistence of labour exploitation. The chief condition for this situation is the marketization and commodification of the urban space that creates a

Conclusion: (Re)centring Labour, Class, and Race 217

need for cheap and exploitable working bodies, whose "health and hygiene became centrally important to a highly speculative property development market that, by the mid 2000s, lay at the heart of Dubai's economy" (2012, 264). Workers' confinement to labour camps inside construction sites is the main working condition, which once became—in the instance Buckley focuses on—a strategic site for workers' organization and politics.

The labour camps of Dubai's construction sites are highly precarious and unhealthy locations in or nearby cities where thousands of migrant workers, primarily from Southeast Asia, work for months and years (Abdul-Ahad 2008).[4] They are one example of how the transformation of workers' locations and spaces in the city is connected to the changing trajectories of capital accumulation in the form of marketization and commodification of housing and land, especially urban land.

Another refraction of these developments is eviction, which can be described as a specific type of "accumulation by [housing] dispossession" (Harvey 2004; see Chap. 1). Bahn's (2009) account of the multiple evictions of Delhi urban poor shows how "housing dispossession" signals a shift in urban politics. From 1990 to 2007, about 100,000 homes were demolished in Delhi, and about half of these occurred between 2004 and 2007. By looking at court judgements, the author argues that this massive increase was mainly due to three factors: (a) misrecognition of the urban poor and responsibilization of them for their own socio-economic conditions; (b) the rise of neoliberal doctrines of self-government and market participation, which paved the way for a fall in real wages starting in the late 1990s and the concomitant precarization of labour; and (c) the "aestheticization" of poverty, by means of huge investment for refurbishing cities aesthetically at the expense of real housing upgrades or support for the well-being of the urban poor (see also Roy 2005).[5]

Similar neoliberal developments can be found in RLR's five cities—as Enikő Vincze explains in Chap. 3, forced displacement, dislocation, spatial destitution, and selective development of periphery urban areas occurred in some or in all of these cities. The major transformations in urban policy that paved the way for these developments included the commodification of urban spaces and gradual dismantling of the social housing system. The 2010 eviction of 76 families (the vast majority

Roma) from the centre to the far periphery of Cluj-Napoca, close to the regional landfill, shows similarities with urban policy trends in Delhi that Bahn (2009) examines. In particular, the "aestheticization" aspect of Delhi's urban policy resembles almost strikingly the municipality's rhetoric that accompanied the 2010 eviction. The dominant discourse, which featured both in the media and as the public justification to national and international human rights NGOs, was that the 76 Roma families were living in unhealthy and overcrowded conditions and this was considered improper for a "civilized" city. The construction of a large multifunctional building that jointly belongs to the Orthodox Church and to Babeş-Bolyai University, in place of the 76 families' housing, accounts for an urban policy which prioritizes "aesthetic" values over the well-being of urban dwellers.

Evictions are a particularly interesting lens through which to understand key urban processes globally. As Roy (2017, 2) discusses, "Evictions thus provide a window onto the urban land question, specifically who owns land and on what terms, who profits from land and on what terms, and how the ownership, use, and financialization of land is governed and regulated by the state." As such, evictions can be taken as entry points anywhere in the world, to study local concretions of global ideologies of capital accumulation (i.e., capitalism). And yet, Roy (2017, 8) further explains, "in what ways are such forms of urban banishment also racial banishment?... If banishment is enacted to uphold the norms of 'order' and 'civility' then it is necessary to recognize the social meanings associated with these norms." It is at this precise conjuncture that the 2010 eviction in Cluj-Napoca needs to be placed and its racial meanings to be recognized (Picker 2017, 84–106). More generally, Roy's (2017) analysis is a seminal attempt to summarize recent research on material dispossession especially at the urban margins and to connect it with conceptions of humanhood and principles of human hierarchization such as race.

The Clujean landfill (called Pata Rât) as a radically marginalized settlement, as Vincze discusses, is an example of "long dispossession" (Carbonella and Kasmir 2014), meaning its history includes about five decades and multiple generations of hundreds of people, the majority of them Roma. This parallels Bayat's (1997) seminal depiction of the long history of the urbanization of the poor in Iran; the author shows with great details and a masterful narration that rural-urban migration, housing problems, and an increase in street subsistence work have all been key factors for the increase in number of slum dwellers and squatters: "by the eve of the Islamic Revolution [1978] the poor constituted a fairly distinct social group identified chiefly by the place of their residence" (1997, 23). As a result, by 1980, Tehran's slums were home to over one million people; today, their increased number (UN-HABITAT 2016b) suggests a complex combination of market-centred policy and global political economy, including economic sanctions and the more recent embargo.

This brings the discussion to a last example of how dynamics in and around the five cities speak to other contexts worldwide. Not only can similar dynamics be found in the urban global South; in Madrid, for example, the neighbourhood of Cañada Real is home to one of the largest slums in Spain. Gonick (2015) offers an in-depth examination of the ways in which big foreign investment play out in the local governance of the neighbourhood that has increasingly made use of racial tropes for enacting measures aiming at the "improvement" of the area. One of the main justifications used to adopt this governmental approach was Madrid's candidacy for the summer Olympics, every year since 2005, as well as negotiations with Las Vegas Sands Corporation to build "Eurovegas," Europe's largest gaming city, right close to Cañada Real. The racial rationale of neoliberal governance was evident in the 2007 government's campaign to demolish the slum, especially in its most widespread media echo (the state-owned TV channel), underlining the ethnic identity (Roma) of some of the inhabitants, and coupling images of veiled Muslim women with danger and death.

The Class-Labour-Race Complex: Ways Forward

> That dark and vast sea of human labor in China and India, the South Seas and all Africa; in the West Indies and Central America and in the United States—that great majority of mankind, on whose bent and broken backs rest today the founding stones of modern industry—shares a common destiny; it is dispersed and rejected by race and color; paid a wage below the level of decent living; driven, beaten, prisoned, and enslaved in all but

name; spawning the world's raw material and luxury-cotton, wool, coffee, tea, cocoa, palm oil, fibers, spices, rubber silks, lumber, copper, gold, diamonds, leather—how shall we end the list and where?

W.E.B. Du Bois 1975 [1935], quoted in Winant (2004, 27).

Inspired by Du Bois' sharp reflections, the multiple global connections and correspondences I outlined in the previous section suggest new venues of research and a contribution to advance existing ones. (Re)centring labour organization, class formation, and processes of racialization *relationally* in analyses of urban dynamics may take different forms and be carried out from different perspectives. As already briefly noted, Roy (2017) has recently started a global conversation, which attempts to connect urban processes of capital accumulation, home and land restructuring, spatial governance, and racial banishment, with philosophies of dispossession.[6] This attempt can inspire new directions and open new perspectives in research on the urban margins.

In view of proceeding within an intersectional approach, moreover, it is important to introduce an emphasis and a focus on gender and gender relations. Labour and class are always gendered—and, equally, racialization happens through and within sexualization and the making of gender roles, divisions, and hierarchies. One example of this intersectional perspective comes from Melanie Samson's (2010) study of waste management. The author interrogates waste management in Johannesburg from a compellingly intersectional lens, demonstrating how in the process of privatization, gender, race, and class *conjointly* contribute to articulate an assemblage of material and symbolic conditions that produce active yet unrecognized workers. Including gender, Samson's work suggests, allows both empirical and theoretical dissections not only of differential forms of subjugation by the market and the state, but also internally, within the community. This is another aspect of research on the urban margins that seems often overlooked—internal power dynamics in typically marginalized communities.

Venues of further research may also include various forms of religion and religiosity, not only as a possible medium for racialization, but also as a symbolic reference, which may become cultural and even economic capital.

The ways in which religion penetrates in marginalized communities (and, for that matter, in any community) typically bear strict connections to fluxes of capital, economic restructuring, and labour organization. This makes religion a particularly interesting resource, which can be both empowering and, as Gramsci (1971, 668–685) noted, an obstacle for the subaltern classes on the way to education and emancipation.

This point brings another, possible venue for further research on labour, class, and race at the intersection of spatial segregation. The making of hierarchical spatial divisions between deemed unworthiness, and (self-)deemed worthiness in cities has its origins in the very first colonized territories of the "New World" (Goldberg 1993; Nightingale 2012). In other words, one of the reasons why today spatial segregation, isolation, seclusion, and confinement largely appear self-evident phenomena in cities worldwide is because this kind of spatial arrangement is rooted in more than 500 years of overseas capitalist exploitation of primarily labour and land. As colonial histories are embroidered with labour exploitation, slavery, land expropriation and financialization, and segregation, they may also be part of contemporary forms of housing banishment, territorial stigmatization, and ghettoization. These multiple histories, from US plantations to reservations for indigenous peoples in the United States, Canada, and Australia, are connected via capitalist accumulation, class formation, and land expropriation. The racial connotation of these processes is variously configured, and, yet, analyses of them are typically limited to the Western world, largely leaving global regions like Eastern Europe out of the picture.

What lines of interrelations exist between contemporary Central and Eastern European (and Russia and the former Soviet Republics contexts) and the legacies of colonial experimentation of racial divisions, slavery (especially second slavery), and spatial segregation? In the Introduction, a hint has been made to Subaltern Studies and Decolonial Studies. To date, however, these disciplines have not been interrogated as sites of analytical efforts towards better understanding processes of labour organization, class formation, and racial domination in contemporary Central and Eastern Europe. More generally, this global region is often left undiscussed in studies on "racial capitalism" (Robinson 1983); an even less discussed issue is the spatial dimensions of capitalism, that is, how the organization of labour, structured through a capitalist logic, contributes to perpetuate racialized hierarchies via the use of (urban) space in Central and Eastern Europe; and how in turn, then, spatial divisions function in the perpetuation of racialized labour relations, keeping socio-symbolic hierarchies in place.

Shifting the key analytical focus from nation-states to cities and urban social arrangements is one of the possible answers. In view of this proposal, it is particularly helpful to consider colonialism as a set of experiments in technologies of governance and, more generally, in organizing the social, including class and labour and race. As Cooper and Stoler (1997) have showed, between the colony and the metropole there have always been numerous circulations and borrowings not only of natural resources, goods, and products, but also of doctrines and theories, of forms of knowledge and governance attitudes towards "native" populations and governance.

From here, and without excessively simplifying the complexity of these processes, a point of departure are the various processes of post-1989 Central and Eastern European governments' borrowing from Western countries policy framings on privatization and entrepreneurialism. So, if the latter have largely built their wealth and statecraft on colonial expansion and domination (Steinmetz 2008), a line could be traced between colonialism, Western Europe, and post-1990s Eastern Europe. And it is precisely in the domains of labour organization and class formation, embedded in processes of spatial segregation, that this triangular connection might appear in the brightest light.

The study of the complex and long history of colony-metropole circulations of goods, capital, ideas, and people remains limited to only those geopolitical contexts that were directly involved in the flows and connections—former colonized countries and Western Europe. By contrast, RLR shows that Central and Eastern European provinces are affected by European imperial and colonial dynamics more than it is usually thought—the twenty-first-century racialization of marginalized labour is one example. This suggests that more research on this issue should be carried out, and we hope our contribution will encourage further work in this direction.

Ultimately, *Racialized Labour in Romania* demonstrates the necessity for thinking relationally about the complex making of sites of social marginality at the periphery of global capitalism, and strives to inform and inspire global and critical perspectives.

Notes

1. This moral subtext of normative understanding of human worth, and lack thereof, remains the core of race as a modern regulatory mechanism of social arrangements (Goldberg 2002). Being predicated upon a continuous oscillation between the biological (i.e., physical appearance) and the cultural (i.e., behaviour), race regulates the interplay of labour organization and class (and gender) formation within the framework of historically embedded processes of labour exploitation and spatial segregation.
2. One last note concerns positionality. In designing lines and trajectories of commonalities between cities at the periphery of the world system, I may get exposed to one of Angotti's (2006) criticisms of *Planet of Slums*, which he deems "a survey of cities in the South by a stranger from the North" (962). As a stranger to Romania, raised and formed in the European West, having only done recent research in Romania (Picker 2017, Chap. 3), I will, to the best of my capacity, adopt a "pragmatic reflexivity" (Herzfeld 2001).
3. Moreover, from 1988 to 2000 inequality between countries has decreased, but within countries it has increased (Sassen 2014, 31). This accounts for the necessity of looking at specific local and regional territories and societies within countries and dissecting common trends and configurations.
4. https://www.theguardian.com/global/gallery/2008/oct/08/1
5. On this point, Bahn (2009) echoes Angotti's (2006) criticism of Davis (2006) that I have mentioned at the start of the chapter. Discursively assimilating the urban poor to slum dwellers, as Davis (2006) does, according to Bahn (2009), contributes to flatten the dominant view on the poor and prevents a detailed understanding of their various material and symbolic living conditions.
6. On philosophies of dispossession and their various declinations, see Butler and Athanasiou (2013) and Bhandar and Bhandar (2016).

References

Abdul-Ahad, Ghathi. 2008. Inside Dubai's Labour Camps. *The Guardian*, October 8.

Angotti, Tom. 2006. Apocalyptic Anti-urbanism: Mike Davis and His Planet of Slums. *International Journal of Urban and Regional Research* 30 (4): 961–967.

Bayat, Asef. 1997. *Street Politics: Poor People's Movements in Iran*. New York: Columbia University Press.

Bhan, Gautam. 2009. 'This Is No Longer the City I Once Knew.' Evictions, the Urban Poor and the Right to the City in Millennial Delhi. *Environment and Urbanization* 21 (1): 127–142.

Bhandar, Brenna, and Davina Bhandar, eds. 2016. *Reflections on Dispossession: Critical Feminisms*. London: Darkmatter Journal, 14.

Buckley, Michelle. 2012. Locating Neoliberalism in Dubai: Migrant Workers and Class Struggle in the Autocratic City. *Antipode* 45 (2): 256–274.

Burawoy, Michael. 2000. Introduction: Reaching for the Global. In *Global Ethnography Forces, Connections, and Imaginations in a Postmodern World*, ed. Michael Burawoy, Joseph A. Blum, Sheba George, Zsuzsa Gille, and Millie Thayer, 1–4. Berkeley: University of California Press.

Butler, Judith, and Athena Athanasiou. 2013. *Dispossession: The Performative in the Political*. Oxford: Wiley.

Carbonella, August, and Sharryn Kasmir, eds. 2014. *Blood and Fire. Toward a Global Anthropology of Labor*. New York/Oxford: Berghahn Books.

Cooper, Frederick, and Ann Laura Stoler, eds. 1997. *Tensions of Empire. Colonial Cultures in a Bourgeois World*. Berkeley: University of California Press.

Davis, Mike. 2006. *Planet of Slums*. London: Verso.

Du Bois, W.E.B. 1975. *Black Reconstruction in America: An Essay Toward a History of the Part Which Black Folk Played in the Attempt to Reconstruct Democracy in America*. New York: Atheneum.

Goldberg, David Theo. 1993. Polluting the Body Politics. In *Racist Culture: Philosophy and the Politics of Meaning*. Oxford: Wiley-Blackwell.

———. 2002. *The Racial State*. Oxford: Wiley.

———. 2009. *The Threat of Race. On Racial Neoliberalism*. Oxford: Wiley.

Gonick, Sophie. 2015. Interrogating Madrid's 'Slum of Shame': Urban Expansion, Race and Place-Based Activism in the Cañada Real Galiana. *Antipode* 47 (5): 1224–1242.

Gramsci, Antonio. 1971. *Selections from the Prison Notebooks*. Ed. and Ttrans. Quentin Hoare and Geoffrey Nowell Smith. London: Lawrence & Wishart.

Gregory, Derek. 2004. *The Colonial Present*. Malden: Blackwell.
Hall, Stuart, M. Rustin, and D. Massey, eds. 2015. *After Neoliberalism? The Kilburn Manifesto*. London: Lawrence and Wishart.
Harvey, David. 2004. Le «Nouvel Impérialisme»: accumulation par expropriation. *Actuel Marx* 35 (1): 71–90.
Herzfeld, Michael. 2001. Epistemologies. In *Anthropology: Theoretical Practice in Culture and Society*. Oxford: Blackwell.
Hilgers, Mathieu. 2012. The Historicity of the Neoliberal State. *Social Anthropology* 20 (1): 80–94.
ILO (International Labor Organization). (2017). *Global Wage Report 2016/2017*. http://www.ilo.org/global/research/global-reports/global-wage-report/2016/lang--en/index.htm. Accessed 2 June 2017.
Law, Ian. 2012. *Red Racisms: Racism in Communist and Post-Communist Contexts*. Basingstoke: Palgrave.
Nightingale, Carl H. 2012. *Segregation. A Global History of Divided Cities*. Chicago: University of Chicago Press.
Picker, Giovanni. 2017. *Racial Cities: Governance and the Segregation of Romani People in Urban Europe*. Abingdon/New York: Routledge.
Polanyi, Karl. 1944. *The Great Transformation: The Political and Economic Origins of Our Time*. Farrar & Rinehart.
Robinson, Cedric. 1983. *Black Marxism: The Making of the Black Radical Tradition*. Chapel Hill: University of North Carolina Press.
Rolnik, Raquel. 2013. Late Neoliberalism: The Financialization of Homeownership and Housing Rights. *International Journal of Urban and Regional Research* 37 (3): 1058–1066.
Roy, Ananya. 2005. Urban Informality: Toward an Epistemology of Planning. *Journal of the American Planning Association* 71 (2): 147–158.
———. 2017. Dis/possessive Collectivism: Property and Personhood at City's End. *Geoforum*, Online First.
Samson, Melanie. 2010. Producing Privatization: Re-articulating Race, Gender, Class and Space. *Antipode* 42 (2): 404–432.
Sassen, Saskia. 2014. *Expulsions. Brutality and Complexity in the Global Economy*. Cambridge, MA: Harvard University Press.
Simone, AbdouMaliq. 2004. *For the City yet to Come: Changing African Life in Four Cities*. Durham: Duke University Press.
Steinmetz, George. 2008. The Colonial State as a Social Field: Ethnographic Capital and Native Policy in the German Overseas Empire Before 1914. *American Sociological Review* 73 (4): 589–612.

UN-HABITAT. 2016a. *World Cities Report.* http://wcr.unhabitat.org/. Accessed 23 May 2017.

———. 2016b. *Sanandaj Declaration Calling for Action in Informal Settlements in Iran.* https://unhabitat.org/sanandaj-declaration-calling-for-action-in-informal-settlements-in-iran. Accessed 23 May 2017.

UNHCR. 2017. *Global Trends Report.* http://www.unhcr.org/globaltrends2016/. Accessed 23 May 2017.

Wallerstein, Immanuel. 1974. The Rise and Future Demise of the World Capitalist System: Concepts for Comparative Analysis. *Comparative Studies in Society and History* 16 (4): 387–415.

Winant, Howard. 2001. *The World Is a Ghetto: Race and Democracy since WWII.* New York: Basic Books.

———. 2004. *The New Politics of Race: Globalism, Difference, Justice.* Minneapolis: University of Minnesota Press.

Wolfe, Patrick. 2016. *Traces of History: Elementary Structures of Race.* London: Verso.

Index[1]

A

Accumulation by dispossession, 6, 14, 25, 65, 75, 85
Activism, 158, 168, 169, 173, 183, 195–196
Adverse inclusion, 26, 98, 105–108
Adverse incorporation, 78
Anthropology of labour, 9

B

Ban, Cornel, 17, 41, 44, 45, 50, 128
Banishment, 218, 220, 221
Benefits, 19, 20, 26, 45, 53, 57, 58n2, 79, 80, 98, 100–105, 107–110, 112–115, 116n8, 116n9, 132–134, 155, 160, 173, 198
Brazil, 212
Bureaucracy/bureaucratic, 98, 105–108, 113–115

C

Călăraşi, 21, 22, 24, 29n1, 41, 43, 44, 47, 48, 50–52, 55, 56, 57n1, 58n3, 65, 66, 69–74, 82, 83, 87, 92, 126, 127, 137, 146, 153, 154, 156, 157, 159, 162, 168, 174n3, 194
Cañada Real, 219
Capitalism, 1–30, 64, 65, 75, 84, 86, 94n13, 97, 111, 129, 148, 192, 208–211, 215–219, 221, 223
Carbonella, August, 2, 6, 14, 77, 86, 92n1, 111, 218

---

[1] Note: Page numbers followed by 'n' refer to notes.

Charitable frame, 170
Children/families with children, 7, 19, 39, 53, 54, 69, 72, 79, 81, 98, 102–105, 107, 108, 113, 115, 116n3, 116n9, 116n10, 117n18, 146, 149, 160, 163, 166, 168, 190, 194
Citizenship/social citizenship, 16, 19, 76, 97–117
Class formation, 5, 6, 208–212, 220–222
Cluj/Cluj-Napoca, 21, 22, 24, 29n1, 41, 43, 44, 46–52, 55–57, 58n4, 64–72, 77–80, 88, 92, 111, 126, 127, 129, 139, 142n2, 146, 153, 154, 156–162, 164–166, 168–171, 174n3, 194, 201, 218
Colonial legacies, 208
Commodification, 17, 75, 84, 98–105, 115, 123, 213, 216, 217
Crime, 137, 138, 148, 151, 155–157, 184

D

Decolonial studies, 3, 25
Decommodification, 101
Deindustrialization, 21, 44, 57
Demography/demographic, 105, 108
Dependence, 4–6, 25, 103
Deprivation/deprived, 2–4, 10, 13, 14, 16, 20, 21, 24, 29n1, 30n7, 39–58, 65, 67, 69, 78–79, 83–85, 98–100, 104, 106, 113–115, 131, 141, 147–149, 153, 155, 156, 180, 181, 215

Destitution, 27, 64, 67–74, 78, 80, 214, 217
Development, 2, 7, 10, 16–18, 21, 25, 27, 42, 45, 64, 71, 72, 74, 78, 83, 85, 98, 123–130, 135, 138–142, 142n2, 148, 151, 153, 154, 168, 180, 181, 184, 188, 190, 192, 198, 202, 203, 214, 217
Disciplination, 86
Disconnection, 64
Discourse/discourse analysis/policy discourse/public discourse, 9, 11, 16, 19, 25, 53, 100, 109, 111, 124, 126, 131, 133, 135, 138–140, 142, 143n1, 146–152, 154, 155, 158, 169, 172, 173, 180, 181, 183, 187–189, 195, 214, 218
Discrimination/ethnic discrimination, 12, 104, 105, 116n5, 134, 138, 151, 159–161, 165, 183, 190, 191, 194, 196, 204n5
Dislocation, 69, 75, 76, 80, 86, 92n1, 217
Displacement, 64, 67–74, 76, 85, 93n3, 192, 217
Dispossession, 2, 3, 6, 12, 13, 15, 25, 78, 84–86, 111, 151, 208, 210, 211, 214–216, 218, 220
Dubai, 216, 217

E

Eastern Europe, 3, 4, 8–13, 16, 17, 19, 26, 40, 98, 152, 181, 187, 209, 213, 221, 222

Employment/employability/
employable, 15, 17, 20, 26, 27,
40–42, 48, 51, 53, 65, 84, 98,
99, 101, 106, 108, 110, 115,
125, 126, 129–131, 133,
137, 138, 141, 142, 161,
200, 209, 214
Epistemic injustice, 124, 140, 141,
167, 173
Ethnical indexing, 156, 157, 159,
161, 163, 168, 173
Ethnography/ethnographic, v, 2, 14,
20–26, 52, 57n1, 133, 186
European Union/European
Commission, 12, 100,
115n1, 169
Evacuation, 157, 158, 161
Eviction, 13, 14, 18, 24, 68, 70,
77, 78, 155–162, 192, 198,
217, 218
Exclusion, 13, 15, 16, 18–20, 24,
28n1, 76, 99, 105, 107,
116n3, 123–143, 184, 185,
187, 189–197, 202, 209, 211
Exploitation/exploitable/exploited,
vi, 3, 19, 48, 67, 79, 84, 86,
124, 132, 151, 209, 211, 212,
216, 217, 221, 223n1
Expropriation/expropriable/
expropriated, 79, 84, 86, 211,
213, 221
Extreme poverty, 163, 174, 180,
184, 186, 187, 189, 193, 197,
198, 202

F

Financialization of housing, 77, 215
Flexibility, 129

G

Garbage dump/waste dump/landfill,
15, 24, 26, 56, 64, 70–72, 77,
79, 82, 83, 88, 89, 93n7, 110,
111, 139, 140, 151, 165, 166,
170, 171, 173, 174n3, 218
Gentrification, 2, 14, 18, 69, 75, 77,
84, 213
Ghetto, 13, 19, 20, 28, 29n1,
30n6, 162–168, 171, 173,
179–204, 214
Ghettoization, 19, 20, 24, 27,
63–94, 201, 213, 214, 221
Global racial inequalities, 209, 211

H

Harvey, David, 2, 6, 14, 15, 18, 65,
97, 101, 104, 112, 217
Homeless/homelessness, 18, 19, 24,
72, 76, 78, 145, 190, 191
Housing, 13, 19–21, 24, 25, 27,
29n1, 39, 40, 63–94, 112,
117n22, 123, 145–176, 180,
182, 183, 185, 188, 190–202,
204n6, 209, 213, 214,
217–219, 221
Human interest frame, 150

I

Impoverishment/impoverished, 11,
13, 21, 28n1, 65, 68, 75, 76,
80, 97, 98, 107, 108, 115,
125, 131, 133–138, 140, 179,
180, 182–185, 188, 190,
195–197, 201, 203n2
Industrialization, 3, 94n12, 192
Informal housing, 78

Informal labour, 84, 86, 110, 147
Investment, 18, 19, 40–58, 100, 124, 127–129, 153, 214, 217, 219
Invisible work, 13, 151
Islamic Revolution, 219

J

Johannesburg, 220

K

Kalb, Don, 2, 6
Kasmir, Sharryn, 2, 6, 14, 77, 86, 92n1, 111, 218
Keynes/Keynesian, 100

L

Labour, 1–30, 40, 63–94, 97, 124, 147, 207–223
Labour organization, 208, 210, 212, 220–222, 223n1
Landfill/garbage dump/waste dump, 15, 24, 26, 56, 64, 70–72, 77, 79, 82, 83, 88, 89, 93n7, 110, 111, 139, 140, 151, 165, 166, 170, 171, 173, 174n3, 218
Lisbon agenda, 98
Locke, John, 213

M

Madrid, 219
Marginalization/marginal/marginalized, v, 2, 3, 12–14, 20–21, 24–28, 30n7, 63–94, 98–100, 104, 106–109, 112, 113, 123–125, 131–133, 141, 145, 147–153, 156, 161, 167, 170, 171, 173, 180, 181, 183, 186, 187, 191–193, 198, 200–202, 203n1, 208, 210, 214, 216, 218, 220–222
Marx/Marxist, 2, 4
Media representation, 24, 151, 214
Miercurea-Ciuc, 21, 72, 89, 127, 137, 146, 153
Minimum income guarantee, 16

N

Neoliberalism/neoliberal, 5, 11–16, 19, 20, 27, 28, 28n1, 45, 67, 75, 84, 94n13, 98, 100, 106, 109, 112, 123, 124, 139, 141, 192, 216, 217, 219
New Delhi, 217, 218
News frame, 155
News/newsworthiness, 145–176, 190

O

Othering, 151, 160, 161

P

Pata Rât, 22, 29n1, 58n4, 64, 70, 72, 77, 79, 80, 93n7, 106, 111, 139, 140, 146, 154, 155, 157, 158, 160, 164–166, 168, 169, 171, 174n3, 185, 194, 218
Pauperization, 64, 65, 77, 84, 213
Peonage, 4, 5, 211
Planet of Slums, 207, 208, 223n2

Ploieşti, 21, 22, 24, 43, 44, 46–52, 55–57, 65–67, 69, 71, 72, 90, 93n4, 109, 112, 114, 126, 127, 131, 146, 153, 154, 156, 157, 162–164, 168, 174n3, 194
Polanyi, Karl, 104, 211
Policy, 2, 12, 14, 16, 19, 20, 24, 27, 29n4, 42, 45, 64, 69, 70, 74, 80, 85, 98–101, 105, 106, 108, 123, 137, 138, 141, 146–148, 151, 157, 158, 161, 167, 168, 170, 173, 180, 181, 188–190, 195–196, 198, 199, 202, 203n1, 213–215, 222
Political economy of housing, 65, 74–78
Politics of housing, 75, 86
Poverty, 11, 15, 20, 24, 64, 78, 83, 85, 98–100, 103–105, 107, 108, 114, 124, 135, 141, 142, 145–152, 154, 156, 163, 166, 167, 170, 171, 173, 184, 185, 187–190, 193, 196, 214, 217
Precarization/precariat/precarious, 1–3, 5, 8, 12–14, 16, 19–21, 25–28, 53, 64, 67, 69, 76, 78, 84–86, 98, 99, 101, 104, 106–108, 111, 112, 114, 115, 135, 141, 159, 200, 213, 214, 217
Privatization, 8, 13, 14, 17, 45, 75, 77, 84, 94n13, 139, 192, 213, 215, 220, 222
Productivity, 17, 19, 55, 97, 106, 127, 140
Public opinion, 155, 157

R
Racial domination, 209, 210, 221
Racialization/racialized/racializing, 1–30, 63–94, v, 65, 76, 84–86, 97–99, 111, 115, 123–143, 151, 180, 196, 204n5, 208, 210–211, 214–216, 220, 222
Racism, 4, 11, 65, 76, 77, 124, 130, 136–138, 141, 159, 160, 181, 188, 191, 195, 197
Reagan, Ronald, 216
Real estate, 71, 72, 75, 76, 78, 84
Recycling, 7, 15, 55–57, 80, 138–140, 151, 167, 173, 198
Redundant, 15, 18, 48, 76, 79, 84, 123, 124, 139
Reproductive work, 139
Restitution, 75
Roma, v, 2, 39, 64, 98, 124, 146, 179–204, 209,
Roma settlements, 21, 193
Roma slavery, 209
Rural hinterlands, 43, 45, 49, 58n2
Russia, 221

S
Samson, M., 14, 15, 56, 124, 139, 140, 151, 167, 220
Segregation/segregated, 3, 12, 13, 15, 20, 24, 25, 27, 28, 29n1, 40, 67, 85, 104, 115, 123, 124, 133–135, 137, 138, 140, 141, 145–176, 180, 181, 183, 186, 187, 195, 200–202, 209, 212, 214, 221, 222, 223n1

Service economy, 48
Slum, 123, 173, 180, 181, 183, 185–188, 190, 192, 193, 197, 201, 203n3, 204n5, 215, 219, 223n5
Slum cleansing/slum clearance, 76
Smith, Neil, 17, 18, 65
Social housing, 16, 69, 75, 78, 91, 112, 155, 168, 190, 194, 199, 200, 217
Socialism, 2, 8, 9, 12, 26, 42–44, 53, 94n12, 127–130, 190, 192
Social policy, 16, 20, 25, 97–106, 108
Social services, 42, 58n2, 101, 154
Social work/social workers, 21, 26, 68, 98, 109–114, 125, 132, 135, 157, 158
Spatial technologies, 64, 67–74, 93n3
Standing, Guy, 16, 97, 101
Stereotypes, 11, 147, 165, 168, 183, 185, 193
Stigma/stigmatization, vi, 2, 16, 24, 30n6, 64, 67, 70, 79, 105, 167, 169, 173, 185, 192, 195, 201, 208, 214, 221
Subaltern studies, 5, 212, 221

T

Târgu-Mureş, 21, 23, 47, 51, 91, 145, 146, 153, 162, 168
Tehran, 219
Territorial stigmatization, 221
Thatcher, Margaret, 216

Tsigane/Tsiganes, 7–9, 12, 13, 20, 21, 26, 27, 29n2, 29n4, 63, 70, 97, 105, 106, 108, 111, 115, 130–134
Typology, 28, 180, 182, 186, 191, 193, 195–203

U

Underdevelopment, 28n1, 72, 85, 125, 134–135
Unemployable, 124, 130, 132, 161
Unemployment, 15, 103, 127, 132, 135, 137
Uneven development, v, 2, 65, 75, 84, 85
Unionism, 104, 208
Urbanization, v, 8, 21, 45, 94n12, 218
Urban planning, 74, 182, 185, 211
Urban policy, 192, 197, 217, 218
Urban spatial seclusion, 209
Urban zones, 42, 44–50, 56, 58n2, 199, 200

V

Valuable work, 56

W

Wallerstein, Immanuel, 4, 17, 216
Wall Street, 212
Waste dump/garbage dump/landfill, 15, 24, 26, 56, 64, 70–72, 77, 79, 82, 83, 88, 89, 93n7, 110, 111, 139, 140, 151, 165, 166, 170, 171, 173, 174n3, 218

Wealth, 21, 81, 124, 148, 211, 222
Welfare state, 15, 16, 27, 97, 100–102, 108–115, 209, 213
Work contracts, 213
Workers, vi, 3, 5, 7–9, 13, 15, 17, 26–28, 39, 40, 42–57, 63, 71, 72, 77–79, 83, 97–99, 101, 103, 104, 106–108, 111, 112, 114, 115, 127–130, 132–136, 140, 141, 170, 194, 198, 199, 208, 214, 220
Working class, 2, 12, 15, 21, 39, 40, 50, 64, 65, 70, 71, 75–77, 84, 86, 92n1, 103
World System, 4, 6, 17, 210, 223n2
Worthiness, 124, 125, 142, 214, 221

PGMO 06/08/2018